ACKNOWLEDG

A CULTURAL MEMOIR AN

D0940612

BY BARBARA KAY

WITH A FOREWORD BY REX MURPHY

ACKNOWLEDGEMENTS: A Cultural Memoir and Other Essays is a collection of previously unpublished writing by *National Post* columnist Barbara Kay. This wide-ranging selection includes original essays – notably the title essay, a mini-memoir of the cultural and intellectual influences that shaped Kay's worldview – as well as a discursive ramble through the bizarre sub-culture of the pit bull advocacy movement.

In between, readers familiar with Kay's weekly columns over the last ten years will find elaborated commentaries on her niche subjects: the negative impact of feminism on our public institutions and families, the erosion of academic integrity in the universities and our politically correct "rights" culture's subversion of social and civic reciprocity in Canadian communities.

Ms. Kay is a weekly columnist for the *National Post* newspaper and a frequent contributor to the *Post*'s opinion blog, *Full Comment*. Her writings have also appeared in conservative U.S. online opinion sites *Front Page Magazine* and *Pajamas Media*, and in print magazines such as *Canadian Observer, Dorchester Review* and *Cité libre*.

In 2009 Barbara was the National Association of Men's recipient of its award of excellence "for promoting gender fairness in the media." She is also a Woodrow Wilson Fellow. In 2012 Barbara received the Diamond Jubilee Medal for "excellence in journalism."

Barbara is a regular guest on many Canadian radio talk shows, from the Maritimes to B.C., as well as more recently on *Sunmedia TV.*

Barbara is the co-author, with Aruna Papp, of *Unworthy Creature: A Punjabi Daughter's Memoir of Honour, Shame and Love.* (2012)

Barbara lives in Montreal with her husband Ronny. She has two children and five grandchildren.

Barbara's collected columns are available in the archive section at her website: www.barbarakay.ca. Her Twitter handle is: @BarbaraRKay.

"Barbara Kay's essay on pitbull politics is the last word on the subject: she's nailed it, and nailed her opponents over the head with more research and more relentless logic than I thought possible."
Michael Bryant, former Attorney-General of Ontario

"There's one group, the best of a bad lot, columnists I call the cream of the crap... Then there are a few like Barbara Kay, who is good when compared to good writers, not bad ones. She started punditry at an age when some people retire from it. Perhaps that's why she isn't one of those writers about whom you feel they've written more books than they've read. She is a chippy polemicist, but only tells readers who may disagree with her that they're wrong, not that they're small and stupid. Most writers know how to assert; some know how to demonstrate; but only the Barbara Kays of columnists have the capacity to persuade..."
George Jonas, columnist, *National Post*

"Barbara Kay's writing contains her personality: direct, precise, intelligent, informed, counter-intuitive. She constantly challenges our era's nouveau "smelly little orthodoxies" in George Orwell's wonderful phrase. She does not write from nostalgia for a lost order but rather to recall us to the permanent order that democratic societies must live within if they are to persist."
Peter Stockland, Publisher, *Convivium Magazine*

ACKNOWLEDGEMENTS: A Cultural Memoir and Other Essays

Copyright ©2015
Published by
Barbara Kay

320 Kensington Ave
Westmount QC
Canada
H3Z 2H3

Printed in the USA

ISBN: 978-0-9947632-0-4

In memory of my parents, Teddy and Florence Richmond

Contents

Author's acknowledgements

Thanks to my son (and Comment section editor of the *National Post*) Jonathan Kay for his editorial assistance on this book.

For guidance in framing my memoir essay, thanks to Concordia associate professor and former creative writing teacher Terence Byrnes.

Thanks to frequent *Post* contributor, Wayne K. Spear, who read, and offered helpful suggestions for improvement to my memoir essay.

I am greatly indebted to dog behaviourist Alexandra Semyonova and *Animal People News* editor Merritt Clifton for their unflagging patience and pedagogical thoroughness in furthering my education on pit bulls.

And not least, thanks to my husband Ronny for his enthusiasm and support for this project.

Foreword

Barbara Kay's writing is brisk and clear. She thinks for herself.

She bravely resists the turn of the moment, and the preoccupations of the politically correct. Ms. Kay is not a provocateur. That is to say she does not harass or vex for the sake of vexation and harassment. Indeed, one notable feature of her writing is her tactfulness.

There's very much shock-writing out there, very much being offensive for effect. Bad manners and worse prose are a job qualification in some parts of the media. Ms. Kay is forceful, but she retains a sense of dignity.

She bravely takes up hard issues – issues that (we are told) have been "settled" by all right-thinking people. Ms. Kay is heedless of these cautions.

The language laws of Quebec, the right of Israel to protect its citizens, hyper-sexualization, feminism – there is scarcely an issue-minefield into which she will not charge. In doing so, she has no tolerance for the weasely euphemisms or the clotted jargon of the pseudo-academics whose very style represents an evasion of original thought.

As I read her, there seems to be implicit, even in her most pugnaciously argued opinions, a genuine invitation freely to disagree – a signal that she will not take disagreement, honest and courteous if ever so strong, as a personal attack. That is because she does not see opinion as a flag of *identity*.

With all her seriousness – on some subjects how can one *not* be serious? – there is an element of fun, too. Sometimes, I suspect a muffled joy behind the lines, under the words, a smile that comes from anticipating the reactions – puzzled, pained or astonished – her views and manner of stating them will evoke.

It can be funny when people respond too predictably, or take a wicked exception to what a person writes. I think of Malcom Muggeridge in this vein, surely the best writer/columnist of the last 60 years. Whatever else Muggeridge offered, he always – from his early days as a reporter with a lance-sharp pen and a gift of sarcasm, even to the solemnity of his later Christian years – spiced his writings with a sense of mischief, and could place a wisp of humour over even the most serious of things. That's because he knew that both his opinions and what he was writing about were threaded with fallibility.

It's nice to have that self-awareness and maturity about this odd world of sounding opinion as a trade. Ms. Kay has it. She fights, but is not fanatic. Holds strong opinions but is not (mostly) dogmatic (some subjects do demand dogma). That's a fair list of virtues for a columnist who came late to the game (as she explains in this book's opening essay), but who has substantially improved it.

Ms. Kay is the least Oprahfied person one could hope to find, and sees no virtues in the self-indulgent, obsessively self-regarding modes of talk and thought that dominate this therapeutic age. Pushing the self from the centre, refusing to turn a column into a diary of the ego, is what distinguishes her writing from the me-saturated scribbles of other pundits. For this sentence alone, we should celebrate her: "I have no inclination to share."

She writes:

> I'm not apologizing for my good fortune, just warning that any reader hoping for a gripping tale of grace and courage under fire, personal demons vanquished, or a suspenseful narrative of adversity triumphantly surmounted will be disappointed. The received blessings of my life would make for a dull plot. And the intimate details – not that they are unusual in any case – I have no inclination to share.

There is a telling sentence in a column (rightly) deploring the hyper-sexualization of modern times, and its attendant vulgarities: "We have the freedom of speech to say we are appalled by [such] indecencies ... but fearing ridicule from those who have seized the cultural heights, we have lost our confidence to use it."

Fearing ridicule from putative betters has kept many a mouth closed, many a talk not given and many a column unwritten. We pride ourselves on being so liberated, so free from the shackles and pruderies of the past. Not Ms. Kay. She'll take the "shame" of alarming the progressives in easy preference over hiding her opinions, or moderating them in (the almost always futile) gesture of trying to gain a wider acceptance for them.

She may not "share," but she gives a lot to those willing to engage with her opinions. She gives all, in fact, that can be asked from a columnist: an independent mind, clear prose and an honest point of view.

– Rex Murphy, November 2012.

A Cultural Memoir

My life has been extraordinarily privileged, and already longish by any but recent measures. If something dreadful happened to me tomorrow, I might complain, but I'd have no right to. Life's lottery wins – uninterrupted peace in a five-star democracy, stable family, health, material security, superior education – were amassed and banked in my name, from which I draw nourishment to this day.

I'm not apologizing for my good fortune, just warning that any reader hoping for a gripping tale of grace and courage under fire, personal demons vanquished, or a suspenseful narrative of adversity triumphantly surmounted will be disappointed. The blessings of my life would make for a dull plot. And the intimate details – not that they are unusual in any case – I have no inclination to share.

What follows, then, is a mini-memoir, with selected recollections and reflections – domestic, historical and cultural – that explains my general friendliness to the world, and throws light on the influences that shaped my life decisions, as well as the opinions I have been declaiming and defending over the last decade in my public writing and talks.

*

Two factors above all have made me who I am, and would have dominated my life, even if I had grown up in wartime, poor, disabled and unlettered. I am female and I am a Jew. Ironically, given that history has not been especially kind to women or Jews, I happened to win the lottery there too. I attribute my confidence in both identities to my epoch. Jews and women of my cohort in North America have enjoyed a golden age unlike any before in history.

1

I was born in 1942. My earliest memories are Jewishly buoyant. I vividly remember my parents' and my community's excitement in 1948 when Israel achieved statehood. Because of the unprecedented wave of post-Holocaust sympathy for Jews, my generation – not all of us, but most of us raised in liberal urban centres – has been the first (and possibly the last) in our history to reach adulthood without encountering overt anti-Semitism. Furthermore we were the first to spend the better part of a lifetime under the empowering illusion that anti-Semitism was once and for all a spent force in a chastened and enlightened world.

I was to discover that covert, genteel anti-Semitism still flourished socially and institutionally, but none of that impinged on my life growing up. I was aware that Jews were still social outsiders, but I don't remember resenting that fact. I had no sense that I was wistfully peering through the glass at a higher caste's festivities in which I could not participate.

I ascribe my complacency to my parents' cheerful acceptance of the social divide. To my parents' generation, anti-Semitism was an eternal fact of life, virtually encoded in the DNA of non-Jews. Both my maternal and paternal grandparents had fled their countries of birth – Rumania and Poland – explicitly to escape growing anti-Semitism of a virulence no Canadian Jew of my generation has ever witnessed or experienced. My parents were grateful that Canadian anti-Semitism was relatively benign and never expressed bitterness when they saw casual proofs of it.

My parents' superficial relations with non-Jews were therefore entirely cordial, but always a bit wary. They would often say, without evident rancour, that if you drilled deep enough below the polite surface of any gentile, you would eventually hit an anti-Semitic seam.

They would also often allude, as well without rancour, but in somewhat righteous tones, to the superiority of Jewish family life and social customs, making disparaging remarks, for example, about gentiles' weakness for alcohol or their affinity for blood sport. They weren't wrong on the evidence; as a rule, Jews are moderate in their drinking habits and loathe blood sport.

But they never gave middle-class gentiles credit for social virtues we *nouveaux riches* lacked and that I came to admire: their preference for aesthetic understatement in their homes and self-adornment; their unspoiled children; their respect for all honest work, not just the kind you get with high marks in school; their love of pristine nature enjoyed in Spartan habitats; and their moderation in eating.

All these traits bespoke what my parents would consider a lack of drive or gusto, but what I considered an enviable instinct for separating life's material chaff from its existential wheat. We Jews were so *excessive* by comparison. I think my parents didn't struggle to be fair to gentiles, because of their history of anti-Semitism. They didn't hate gentiles, but they did feel morally superior to them.

So unless external circumstances brought them into close association with gentiles, their social lives were spent in the trustworthy fellowship of other Jews. Consequently, my social life unfolded within the affectionate embrace of well-endowed all-Jewish summer camps and clubs that had been founded as a practical response to exclusion from gentile establishments. Inside their pleasant clubhouses and expansive grounds were the tribal comforts of utter familiarity and unconditional acceptance.

The more important reality was that even social anti-Semitism was diminishing, not rising, as I grew up. And therefore no educational or career door was ever closed to me on anti-Semitic grounds. Nor can I think of a single friend of my youth who failed to realize his or her potential because of anti-Semitism. In educated circles, in fact, it became quite chic for Jews to acknowledge their Jewishness in playfully confident ways (see under Woody Allen and later Jerry Seinfeld and so many other Jewish comedians) and for educated gentiles to actively seek out socializing opportunities with Jews.

As for being female, I needn't expand here on the explosive turnabout of women's fortunes in the past century. I came to adulthood on the cusp of the feminist revolution, soon enough to benefit from its early reformist agenda, happily too late to be caught up in its more radical toils.

I have observed massive shifts in the cultural zeitgeist. When I was growing up, the West was friendly to Jews and (heterosexual) men. Today the whole world, except for North America, is unfriendly to Jews. All of the West's cultural elites are very friendly to women, gays and people of colour (and cover), but hostile to Christians and, another first in history, rather hostile to heterosexual men.

At the bottom of all these shifts into and out of favour are ideas propounded by university-based intellectuals, today's self-anointed priestly caste that has replaced the moral authorities of my youth. These are some of the changes I have witnessed, and they became the themes I was to write about.

*

I realized what it was I wanted to be when I grew up – a newspaper opinion columnist – at the age of 60. Up until then, I had assumed one needed some special credentials or experience for the job. But it turned out all you need is curiosity, a modicum of writing ability, strong views on what ails the world and, coursing through your veins, a fat combative streak. Thick skin to cover

3

it is a must as well. I'd have put thick skin first on the list, but a high tolerance for humiliation can be acquired on the job, while the others can't.

I don't fault myself for my ignorance, because I did not come to the profession honestly. By which I mean that I had no journalism models to look to. Nobody amongst my forebears or family or friends was a journalist, or ever wrote for a living. In my youth, "reporter" or "columnist" conjured up the image of cynical, hard-drinking, hard-smoking men – occasionally a tough-as-nails woman – of high mental acumen, but low emotional intelligence, with intensely physical and somewhat disreputable "school of life" adventures lurking in their pasts. Small wonder that my parents never even paused to wonder aloud if journalism was a nice sort of job for a Jewish boy, let alone any of their three sheltered daughters (I am the middle one).

Aside from any other consideration, ink-stained wretches didn't make much money or enjoy job security. (That hasn't changed, actually.) Upwardly striving Jews from poor immigrant homes, with an eye on the main chance for their children's future success, could easily see that journalism was a pretty dim bulb beside the bright torches of social and financial capital represented by academia and the "real" professions of medicine, dentistry, law and accountancy (for men; teaching for women).

My parents' indifference to journalism as a profession for their children didn't translate into disdain for journalism's fruits. On the contrary. Newspapers as purveyors of news and opinion and gossip were an integral part of our lives. It was a minor calamity – rare to be sure – if either the morning or afternoon papers failed to land with that reassuring soft plop on our doorstep.

In retrospect, the first slow-germinating seed of my late-life career was planted by a daily newspaper column I glommed onto in my teen years. I'm a bit embarrassed to reveal this columnist's name. She was in fact one of the few well-known Jews in the profession. I'd like to say it was some heavyweight political analyst. But the truth is that I rarely read serious editorial writing in my formative years, because I wasn't engaged by politics or ideology until much later.

At the time of my discovery of this columnist, I had just slipped into the turbulent, hormone-charged waters of adolescence. But even then I took the conservative view of life. I had always assumed certain characteristics of human nature were immutable (still do), and was therefore open to learning life lessons from my elders.

I knew I needed a code of social conduct – a life jacket – to get me through the coming maelstrom without being sucked under, by which I mean engaging in behaviour that would bring shame to my parents and possibly ruin my life, as shaming behaviour could in those days. I had been raised on the socially conformist dogmas of my era, which gave licence to boys and men to engage in sexual experimentation before marriage, but not to girls. Or not to *good* girls.

I believed that girls should "save themselves" for marriage. I also believed that losing her reputation for virtue was the worst disaster that could befall a girl. So I hoped I would fall in love and marry very young; that way I would not be betrayed by my hormones into a fall from social grace from which I would never recover. I was therefore open to external reinforcement and case studies for strengthening my resolve by "experts."

And so it was that my first specifically journalistic influence in the domain of human relations was Ann Landers' daily advice column. It appeared in 1955, when I was 13. In the unriven cultural environment of the 1950s, Ann was a popular moral priestess. Later of course she became a target for ridicule to cultural elites. In spite of her alleged superannuation, though, her column ran in syndication for 56 years. The social theorists had no use for her, but ordinary people always did.

The counter-culture wasn't even a glimmer on my youthful horizon then. Culturally speaking, I was not primed for inter-generational antagonism. Mine was a receptive and biddable mind for authorities I trusted. Though something of a tomboy and rebellious in trivial ways – feigning indifference to disapproving stares, I wore jeans on the subway! – I was immutably bourgeois at heart, so Ann and I were on the same cultural page.

I liked Ann's crisp, dryly humorous "voice" that radiated moral clarity and common sense in equal measure. Ann didn't trade in the passing parade of the news cycle, but in what I considered the far more fascinating domain of real people's personal problems.

The people who wrote to Ann were generally stuck in some intractable conflict with others – parents, wives, in-laws, children, lovers, friends – wielding some emotional or psychological or financial hold over them they were obliged to come to ethical terms with. Stuck too with their human shortcomings, yearnings, resentments, loyalties and dreams, inarticulately struggling amidst myriad obligations and limited options in staking out their modest claims for personal happiness. And they were so desperate for a solution they were appealing to a *newspaper columnist* to decide their fate. What power columnists had!

I was particularly bemused by Ann's suppliants' lack of personal and social insight into how they had gotten themselves into their messes. I was fascinated as well as by their timorousness in confronting those who were making them miserable, even when justice was on their side. So many woeful hearts poured out tales of long-endured abuse, borne in silence to preserve family or social-circle peace.

5

Quite a contrast to the situation in our home, where suppression of any deeply-felt emotion or slight to our amour-propre was anathema. My mother was deeply committed to the spontaneous, therapeutic school of communication, believing it was unhealthy for the ego to bottle up any feelings whatsoever. My parents loved each other, but their relationship was often unapologetically volatile, and we accepted intramural verbal pyrotechnics as the norm in family dynamics.

(Considering the frequent emotional bruising this uninhibited model produced, we could have used a little more diffidence and a little less insight. Visiting the homes of my few WASP friends, I found the air of emotional restraint I observed between parents, and between parents and children, wondrously exotic. It became my habit to seek out relationships with non-Jews – friendships and even occasional illicit summer romances with the vanishingly few gentiles on camp staff, most memorably a sweetly laidback small-town riding instructor – because I found the lowered setting of their temperamental thermostats psychologically restful.)

I didn't make the connection at the time, but Ann Landers was in many ways a journalistic avatar of my mother: Both of them were Jewish-American, direct and judgmental, with no patience for the emotional diffidence my mother used to complain of as a typically Canadian trait.

My mother was the youngest of four children and the only girl, on account of which she was, everyone agreed, terribly spoiled by her parents and brothers alike. This was undoubtedly the source of her supreme self-approval. "Life," my mother would often say, contentedly exhaling a fragrant stream of smoke from her Rothman cigarette, "can be beautiful." Implied was a stricture against Canadian-style self-effacement; one had to take a bullish approach in life in asserting one's wishes and needs. She wasn't advocating impoliteness or overt pushiness. She simply meant one had to be mentally tuned into one's self-worth and strive to realize one's potential *without guilt*.

I was conflicted. My mother's unwavering confidence in herself and her views was persuasive, but our highly anglo-centric public schooling nudged us along the mainstream Canadian path of decorum, of emotional and rhetorical self-restraint. I think I gave a great deal of weight to my school experience, because it was backed up by the King of England (until I was 11 and then by the Queen) and almost two thousand years of British history, while my mother only represented herself.

By which I mean that my mother, and my father for that matter, didn't seem to be at all connected to their own histories. Both my grandmothers had died before I was born. Both grandfathers had remarried, but they were not love

6

matches. Their second wives were more housekeepers than mates, so they were not interested in us, nor we in them.

I didn't see very much of my maternal grandfather, as he never came to Toronto and we didn't stay with him when we visited our American family. On our frequent trips to Detroit, I was far more tuned in to my cousins than to the large, somewhat dour and dignified man who presided over what were for children seemingly endless Passover seders. My sisters and I were just three amongst many other grandchildren. I had no personal relationship with him whatsoever.

My paternal grandfather in Toronto lived downtown, near the future sites of the big hospitals below the Ontario Legislature. Most Sundays my father would take us down to visit him. "Zaidie," a stooped, bushily bearded man would usher us into his little house with unintelligible mousy cries of welcome and sit us down in the living room. He would give us each a certain kind of candy I only associate with him, a hardshelled amber bullet with a soft fruity centre, wrapped in a twist of pale yellow paper.

We would sit in the tiny, dark living room for an hour with nothing to do, while Zaidie and our father went into the kitchen to talk in rapid Yiddish over sweet milkless tea. Since we didn't know a word of Yiddish, and Zaidie didn't know a word of English, we could not enter each other's worlds.

Nevertheless, I have fond memories of the High Holidays, when we would attend the beautiful "Peylische shul" (Polish synagogue) down the street from where Zaidie lived. The women all sat upstairs in the balcony, but because of our youth, we were allowed to join our father and Zaidie in the men's section near the "bimah," the raised platform from which the service was conducted.

Even on *Yom Kippur*, Zaidie would surreptitiously slip us some of those strange candies, the only way he could express his affection for us. But mostly we played on the front steps with all the other modern grandchildren of ancient men, whose histories were of no interest to us, because apart from filial dutifulness, it didn't seem to be of any special interest to our parents.

My mother looked down on the world from the same moral heights occupied by Ann Landers, but while Ann urged a variety of intermediaries on the healing path – social workers, clergy, educators – my mother took a more unitary corrective view. From her enthusiastic reading of best-selling post-Freudians, and proving the poet's caution that "a little learning is a dangerous thing," she concluded that the root of all unhappiness was neurosis, and that the eradication of neurosis would rid the world of evil.

Her favourite writer was a psychoanalyst called Karen Horney. My mother pressed several of her books on her three daughters, but I believe I was the

7

only one actually to read them. My only memory of these books is that one should not allow oneself to be enslaved by life's "shoulds." That was the basis of all neurosis.

My mother believed that if political leaders all submitted to psychiatric therapy before assuming office, swords would turn into ploughshares and lions lie down with lambs. She wasn't alone. An entire cohort of second-generation middleclass Jews had shrugged off the strict observance and unquestioning faith of their fathers, but they still adhered nostalgically to rituals they enjoyed, modified by convenience-oriented amendments. Since my parents' generation was making up modern Judaism as they went along, their need for a secular god was pressing.

(And so we kept kosher at home, but we ate non-kosher in restaurants. We sat down unfailingly to beautiful Sabbath dinners, but we drove cars and used electricity on the Sabbath. Synagogue attendance was mandatory on Jewish holidays, but not on Sabbath. We were welcome to engage in friendships with any girls we liked, but dating non-Jewish boys was strictly forbidden.)

There were many roads to secularism for Jews. Blind faith in psychiatry as a panacea became a kind of mania in the 1950s for those Jews who were too bourgeois and socially conformist to find appeal in political radicalism. But poor Jews to whom the capitalist paradigm had not been kind – that is, Jews who began poor like my father, but couldn't make the upstream leap to middle class rewards – were more likely to turn to socialism and even communism as their new god. I didn't know any poor Jews, though, and the astonishing disproportion of Cold War fellow-travelling Jews in the West was a revelation I was only exposed to in adulthood.

Communism and the therapeutic worldview were alike in that both were a snare and a delusion. Communism was naturally by far the worse of the two evils, but therapeutic culture has not been a great success either.

My mother was intellectually naïve, but in fairness, I think that, optimistic by temperament, she couldn't deal with the fact that six million Jews had just been murdered for no reason at all – or no reason any reasonable person could understand. She could not accept the pure evil of the Nazis. It had to be a mental disease that science could cure.

None of my teachers in high school or university was Jewish – although there would be a disproportionate number of Jewish teachers today – but most psychiatrists I've ever known were and are Jews. Even though I never presented any signs of abnormality, I spent a desultory few months in therapy as a matter of precautionary course and so did many of my peers.

I was assigned to a phlegmatic, inscrutable psychiatrist who seemed bored by the commonplace grievances I summoned up and who didn't seem to think the dreams I assiduously recorded offered much scope for interpretation. I think we both wondered what I was doing there, but what could he do? It was embarrassing to share the sort of intimate thoughts he felt obliged to probe, but I didn't question the value of doing so at the time.

(Strangely, I was somehow able to square this faith of my mother's with a compelling attraction to Orthodox Judaism, taken up partially in good faith and partially as an homage to an Orthodox boy I was besotted by, which I struggled to practice for a few years amidst family tolerance, but no supportive enthusiasm.)

In retrospect, I realize that no secular faith could have been more calculated to encourage narcissism, moral relativism, blame-shifting and arrested development than therapy culture. If you've read J.D. Salinger's *Catcher in the Rye* or *Franny and Zooey*, you know what I mean. Neurosis was supposedly a tragic psychological deficit, but amongst highly self-regarding Jews, it inevitably came to be equated with superior intelligence and complexity. We all wanted to be considered neurotic, just like Salinger's glamourously brainy Glass family.

Later, in the common room at University College, where the student body was disproportionately Jewish, we would sit around in our black turtleneck sweaters – no one to more elegant advantage than the impossibly slender and beautiful Barbara Amiel, now Lady Black, one year ahead of me – drinking endless cups of bitter coffee, smoking the room blue and vying anecdotally for the title of Most Misunderstood-by-Parents Jew on campus.

* * *

It wasn't the usual thing in the 1950s for Canadian women to go on to university – or even for men. But I didn't know that at the time, because it *was* the usual thing in my arriviste enclave of Toronto's Forest Hill Village, peopled by workaholic Jews like my father, their assiduously self-improving and socially confident wives, and their materially spoiled, but achievement-funnelled children.

The high school I attended, Forest Hill Collegiate Institute, served a generally affluent district in which Jews were a minority, yet its school population was about 90% Jewish, or so it appeared to me. It seems that most Forest Hill gentiles discretely whipped their kids into private schools rather than have them mix it up with Jews single-mindedly on the make, just as studiously focused Asian students today tend to drive out university students looking for a more relaxed social environment. We were such an anomaly in the public school system that several sociologists wrote a book about us called *Crestwood Heights*.

9

Forest Hill espoused an unabashedly hierarchical streaming system. If your marks in Junior High weren't very good, or if you wanted to be a secretary as many girls did to tide them over until they married, you were diverted into "vocational" classes, where you didn't take Latin or some of the sciences, but took "shop," typing and bookkeeping. If your marks were decent, you took regular classes.

But if they were very good, you were invited to join the "R" class – I forget what it stood for – where you studied German in addition to the obligatory French and Latin. (The irony of Jews learning German so soon after the Holocaust was not lost on us. But I – guiltily to be sure – enjoyed learning the language, because it reminded me of Yiddish, which I had always heard but not understood, and knowing German meant my parents could no longer use Yiddish as their "secret" language for gossip they didn't want us to understand.) We were assigned the best teachers too, which meant the *crème* at the top of already-rich *crème*. It was a great honour to be an R student, and we all worked very hard to live up to our image as "brains."

We were model students. We were intensely focused, voluble – no prodding necessary – and competitive. I can't remember a single "discipline" episode. More than half our teachers were men, and some of them had graduate degrees. Much was expected of us, and much was given to us, especially in writing competence. When the first essay I wrote in university was returned to me, my professor asked me where I had gone to high school. When I told him Forest Hill, he smiled and said, "I thought so."

Revisiting what I chose to call us – "dream students" – well, that is my perspective, simply because we never made trouble in class. We soaked up information with enthusiasm, perhaps a bit of impatience and more than a touch of showboatism. But I wonder if it was that uncomplicated for our gentile teachers.

Which leads me to what will prove to be an ultimately relevant digression on the American novelist, Thomas Wolfe (no relation to the contemporary journalist/novelist Tom Wolfe), who was to become the subject of my master's thesis in literature.

I had discovered Wolfe at an unusually early age. Perhaps nine or ten. I was laid up for five weeks with a kidney infection that demanded complete bed rest, and was devouring books my mother brought home from the library at a furious pace. To reduce time spent trekking back and forth, she started choosing longer books, and that was how I ended up reading Wolfe's massive, four-volume ode to America, beginning with the *bildungsroman* that brought him to public attention in a huge way, *Look Homeward, Angel*.

I adored Wolfe's magnificent prose style, even if I would later concede it was too florid for modern tastes, and I was riveted by his angst-ridden creative triumphs and tribulations. He opened a window for me on a bizarre new social planet through his faithful reconstruction of his histrionically dysfunctional Asheville, North Carolina family.

Everything Wolfe wrote was transparently autobiographical. His unsparing vivisection of his parents and siblings, his southern milieu, Harvard University in its pre-diversity days and later New York society, was a course in social American history no university course could surpass.

I was particularly fascinated by Wolfe's adventures with Jews, so few and marginal in his childhood, but so many and influential after he arrived in New York City in 1923. (The title of my thesis was "Thomas Wolfe, the Exile Motif and the Jews.")

There he taught English at New York University. Almost all his students were poor, first-generation Jews. His provincialism and received prejudices against Jews made life awkward for him. Wolfe didn't want to teach, but needed the money. That his students were almost all Jewish was a blow to his morale. "I teach! I teach! Jews! Jews!" he wrote to a friend.

It is hard for Wolfe at first to see his students as individuals or even as normal people. In his childhood he has seen Jews as "barbarians," and even engaged with friends in small-time pogroms for entertainment. Now at their service, he is made uneasy by their intellectual intensity, the "knowing" look in their eyes, their confidence, their sense of entitlement, their tribal solidarity. They aren't timid like other immigrants. They are already well-lettered, they are aware that they are intellectual scions of an ancient, book-based civilization. Socially clumsy, linguistically graceless (Yiddish their maternal language), they are vocal, demanding, competitive, striving. They exhaust him.

But once he begins to see them as individuals and form relationships, he comes to appreciate and respect them. (There is an affecting portrait of a brilliant, physically unattractive student whose polemical zeal initially repels Wolfe, but whom he ultimately befriends.)

Interestingly, Wolfe is the first American writer to treat Jews in fiction not as hybrid Americans, but as *full Americans*, and to acknowledge his anti-Semitism as a fault in himself – not in Jews – that he is bound to expunge. His description of 1937 Nazi Germany – his ancestors were German and he visited Germany to discover his roots – in his fourth novel, *You Can't Go Home Again*, is one of the most empathetic literary treatments of Jews I have ever read.

And it was as I wrote about Wolfe and his struggle to quell his default estrangement and contempt for his students that I did begin to wonder if my

11

gentile teachers at Forest Hill, some of whom probably grew up in small towns or neighbourhoods where Jews were a rarity or figures of suspicion, had felt something like the defensiveness and perplexity that had assailed Wolfe. Did any of them, I wonder, ever write to a friend: "I teach! I teach! Jews! Jews!"

* * *

At a time when something like eight percent of the general population attended university, with maybe a quarter of them girls, something like 80% of Forest Hill's kids went on to higher education. Most of our fathers had been forced into practical work, and many of them got rich selling insurance and running *shmata* factories, but that wasn't good enough for their children. Higher education for both boys and girls was not only a ticket to security, but a cultural status symbol.

Of course, there was a gendered difference in motive. Boys were preparing to become breadwinners; girls were preparing to marry them. Like most other Jewish girls of my generation and socio-economic privilege, I was encouraged to go to university and hone my fine mind. On the other hand, like most Jewish girls of my generation, I wasn't expected to apply its eventual stiletto sharpness to anything that might divert me from my real vocation as a wife and mother (although my mother, a great booster of my youthful scribbles, hoped that I would end up writing the great Canadian novel in my spare time). And it was well understood (and true) that the best place to snap up excellent husband material was at university.

So it mattered that I went to university, but it didn't matter what I studied. It is easy to see now where this untenable alliance was headed – to Betty Friedan and her 1963 book, *The Feminine Mystique,* that ignited the feminist revolution – but at the time it seemed not only reasonable, but a priceless gift. It meant that when I enrolled at the University of Toronto in 1960, I could study what I loved – literature – with no particular career in mind, if in fact "working" ever became an actual necessity at all.

To add to that gift, I was under no obligation to earn any portion of my tuition or expenses during school breaks. I took fun summer jobs or none as I pleased. Some years I did camp counselling, one summer I had a cushy job at the university housing service finding accommodation for out-of-town students, but one summer I just stayed home – with my parents' approval and indeed pride – to read all the great Russian novels, one after another, with no distractions.

Those were golden years. At that time, the government was flinging money at the universities, preparing for the post-war baby boom's future educational needs. If you were in an Honours course, as I was – for two years in *Latin with an English Option*, then in *English Language and Literature* – you never suffered the indignity of large, impersonal classes. And you had the best professors, the ones who had been actively recruited from all over North America and Britain to burnish the U of T's already lustrous reputation in English Literature. I don't remember a single dud.

And I don't remember being treated with a whit less respect by my male professors (all male, except for one marvellous Latin teacher) than the respect accorded to the boys. By the fourth year, our classes were almost all taken tutorial-style in small groups around tables in our professors' offices. No teaching assistants mediated between us and the profs. It was pedagogic heaven.

It was only now that I began to venture out of the privileged but sociologically stuffy bubble I had grown up in and meet people from other places and less advantaged circumstances in more than a superficial or surreptitious way. University College, where the Jewish students clustered, was the only secular arts college. The other three were affiliated with churches. But because there were so few students registered in my program, some of our Latin and Greek classes took place at Trinity (Anglican Church) and some at St. Michael's (Catholic). These forays to other colleges were a modest but for me memorable glimpse into a wider social world.

I was still politically naive. My professors were mostly middle-aged and older. They were not politicized. Or if they were, they didn't bring it to the classroom. Hewing to Matthew Arnold's rubric of culture – "the best that has been thought and said" – they taught the literary canon of dead, white European males (and deserving females like Jane Austen and George Eliot and Virginia Woolf) without apology, and without ideological annotation. I don't think they had any idea of the upheaval in their field – the triumphalist replacement of real literary appreciation by *Theory* – that was about to erupt.

Not only was I oblivious to the cultural iceberg our campus ship was heading for, I was literally singing and dancing my heart out as it hove upon us. During my first two years at U of T, my most absorbing extra-curricular interest was UC Follies, the (then) vaudeville-style musical review, some of whose famous alumni – Wayne and Shuster, Lorne Michaels – went on to international celebrity.

I have always been something of a ham. Perhaps a tendency to exhibitionism is something I should have added to my first paragraph's list of useful attributes for an opinion columnist. Not all opinion journalists actually enjoy performing on stage. In fact, many are visibly uncomfortable in their public appearances. But they enjoy it when their opinions cause a public stir. They even take satisfaction in being hated by some readers. In the parlance, they're "shy exhibitionists."

13

Exhibitionism, unlike journalism, is something I *did* come by honestly. My father was a handsome, charismatic man of unusual warmth and natural showmanship. He looked like Clark Gable, for those who remember that dashing icon of manly strength and charm. His birth niche, as the youngest of nine children (several born in Poland, the rest in Toronto), all vying for their harassed mother's attention, doubtless encouraged him to shine as an entertainer. A skilled raconteur in both his mother tongue, Yiddish, and English (which his parents never did learn to speak), he was hugely popular with both men and women, and the spark of every party. Of which there were plenty.

From the moment I demonstrated a talent for mimicry and a taste for applause, my parents encouraged me to exploit both. I took drama lessons, which led to a flurry of television appearances in minor roles. I always played the comic second lead in the Broadway shows that were a feature of the Jewish summer camps I attended. Once home from camp, my father would ask me to reprise those roles for the delectation of his friends. I also have a vivid memory of him waking me in the middle of the night to come downstairs and regale guests with a bleary-eyed impression of Jerry Lewis as the spastic foil to his suave sidekick Dean Martin.

I never said no, both because I enjoyed it and because I felt it would be letting down the side somehow to refuse. Both my parents left no doubt in our minds that entertaining others was not only a social virtue, but something akin to a tribal imperative. I know many other Jews like me, who reflexively adopt an "entertaining" mode in social situations. I am left to wonder if there was not some sort of atavistic Jewish instinct for pre-emptive ingratiation at work in my family's cultivation of personality power.

I'm not complaining. It took me a while to realize how terrible most people are at telling jokes. Thanks to my father's tutelage, my sisters and I are masters of comic timing, and our aptitude has stood us in good stead as a social ice-breaking mechanism and a prophylactic to boredom when social events fail to jell. When the three of us are together, we become more than the sum of our parts, spontaneously igniting into an act of sorts. We're funny and a social novelty for most non-Jewish Canadians. But I can see – I've been told, in fact – that for people from less wired backgrounds, we can be a bit intimidating, which, as I say, was probably the unarticulated idea behind our training.

UC Follies was a professional production. I revelled in the excitement and tension leading up to opening night, and in the romantic spin-offs I enjoyed with its brilliant writers and directors (Jewish, of course: otherwise I couldn't have dated them. Yes, still submitting to parental rules; still living at home). If I had been born 30 years later, my parents might have staked me to a bid for a show biz career, as many of my friends have done for their talented progeny. But that was then, not now, and the message then was: Enjoy the fun, but don't even think of taking it seriously.

*   *   *

At last, in my third year of university, in 1963, I began to hear the rumble of the cultural tumbrils. I had joined the UC's Literary and Athletic Society. One of our responsibilities was to oversee the election of a representative to the greater-university Student Administrative Council (SAC). Apparently nobody sought nomination to run, so I was offered the gig. I thought it might prove to be a lark, and accepted.

The SAC was more than a lark, although it was that too, with lots of socializing at the university's expense. It was my first exposure to my cohort's serious political junkies, and an introduction to the burgeoning student movement that in Europe and the U.S. was already revolutionizing campus life. During my tenure, on the cusp between top-down direction and actual student rebellion, relations with the campus administration were still very amicable. But student empowerment was in the air and often on the agenda.

I had no articulated opinions on any of this. I remember wondering what it was that students wanted empowerment for, since the university was already doing a bang-up job of educating us. Besides, I was sitting on the SAC by affirmative action, and felt outclassed in intelligence, knowledge and rhetorical skill by the others, who had actually been elected to serve on the basis of their competency and interest.

I met the best and the brightest from every arts college and faculty of the university. Several would go on to careers in the civil service or party politics. They came from different parts of Canada and the U.S., some from Toronto's WASP establishment and some from working class families in small towns. From my perspective they were a diverse group, even though, if memory serves, they were all white and mostly male.

Meeting a young woman representing St. Mike's on the SAC, who soon became a cherished friend, brought me into the orbit of her all-Catholic circle at St. Mike's. I was aware of being an exotic bird at her dorm, where I was apparently the first Jewish visitor in living memory. The sweetly welcoming nuns and many of the girls peered at me with near-anthropological curiosity, just as I had viewed my Protestant peers in first youth.

The social novelty of these encounters was intensely exciting, my first decisive step outside my cultural ghetto. It was exhilarating and a bit scary too, because I was old enough to be adventurous, but conservative enough to worry about where such "adventures" would lead. I was meeting attractive gentile young men whose difference fascinated me. I had assumed I would be married or

15

engaged by the time I left university, and inter-marriage was simply too radical an idea for me to contemplate. So these young men were candidates for adventure, but not marriage.

The Catholic president of SAC was handsome, charming and politically dynamic. He was leading the charge to topple old paradigms of student passivity. But I was not ready to topple personal paradigms of cultural conformity. We dated briefly, but the tension it caused at home was too much of a burden, and it fizzled out.

*　*　*

My older sister Anne married Ron, her high school sweetheart, a dentistry student, a month after she turned 19. Nobody thought she was too young. Most girls I knew married before they turned 21. By my last year of university I had dated some excellent prospects, brilliant young men who did go on to worldly success – with the proportions of men to women at university, a reasonably attractive girl had her pick of genuine suitors, by which I mean young men who knew that serious dating led to marriage – but none felt right for the long haul. I was still on the market, and more than a little concerned. I had no idea what I wanted to do after I graduated.

Then, within weeks of each other, I had a momentous choice to make between two exciting alternatives. A mild flirtation with a blond, slavicly handsome man from Montreal, working temporarily in Toronto, whose broad, squared-off shoulders reminded me of Jack Kennedy (our first date was the night JFK was assassinated), suddenly turned serious.

Shortly after, I was informed I had won a Woodrow Wilson fellowship – I had applied for it on a dare – that would guarantee my acceptance, and pay for my tuition and living expenses, at any grad school in North America. I hadn't even thought about going on to graduate school, but now obviously I had to. My parents were delirious with pride at the boasting rights "the Woodrow" bestowed, and I couldn't turn down such an opportunity.

Here was the crossroads where my future would be settled in a definitive way. Both choices presented as huge, life-shaping risks that might end in incalculable reward or spectacular disappointment.

If I went off to the University of Chicago or any of the elite California universities, my first choices, the romance with Ronny could not be sustained, and I would likely end up falling for an American and settling far from home. I had never lived anywhere on my own, not even a university dorm. The thought of being alone and responsible for myself in a strange city made my heart knock with fear. Needless to say, the option of Ronny changing the venue for the MBA he'd signed on for at McGill in order to follow me to the university of my choice never entered either one of our heads.

16

Marrying Ronny, as he proposed I do after a whirlwind courtship, would also be a risk, because we'd had so little time to really get to know each other, and it meant moving to Montreal. Predictably my parents preferred I marry rather than go off to the U.S. alone, where God knows what might befall me.

Even though they didn't know Ronny well, he was Jewish, from a respectable family and, with an engineering degree in hand and a business degree forthcoming, almost certainly slated for material success. He would do. My departure from Toronto to settle in Montreal would be a blow for them, but far preferable to my settling in remote California or even Chicago.

That we had only dated for a few months didn't faze them at all. They themselves had become engaged a week after they met, when my father was 20 and my mother 21. (They were married September 3, 1939. Their wedding party was dancing to big band music on the radio when the program was interrupted with the announcement that war had been declared, which promptly ended the festivities.)

Montreal itself made the decision for me. Ronny had invited me to a football weekend at McGill University that autumn. Walking up Peel Street from Central Station to the stadium on that crisp, sunny day, and taking in the beauty of the flaming leaves covering Mount Royal, I felt like Elizabeth Bennet in Jane Austen's *Pride and Prejudice* when she first sets eyes on Darcy's magnificent Derbyshire estate. Of course Elizabeth already loves Darcy, but Pemberley's beauty and situation seal the deal.

That's how Montreal struck me. I loved it at first sight. I would still be in Canada, not far from home, and yet in a much more lively and sophisticated city than I'd grown up in. And not alone, but under a man's protection, an old-fashioned phrase that sounds positively Victorian to my ears today, but didn't then.

As I got to know the city a little more, its physical beauty and bi-culturalism enchanted me after twenty years of humdrum Toronto's linguistic and WASP monolithism. Like Elizabeth, I would be near enough to my family to see them often, but not so near that I would be living in their volatile and subtly tyrannical pockets. I accepted Ronny's proposal and with a great sense of relief at having my future settled, applied to McGill University's graduate Literature program.

It was the conservative choice – again. And it meant I completely bypassed the counter-cultural turmoil in which I would almost certainly have been caught up if I had gone to the U.S. Instead, apart from my McGill grad studies – not at all onerous following on U of T's extraordinary undergrad program – I was almost completely absorbed by the novelty of housekeeping and learning to cook (I had never been asked to lift a finger to help at home and couldn't boil

17

the proverbial egg before marrying), in-laws boundary issues and making new friends.

*　*　*

One of my most vivid teenage memories has me seated with my sisters and parents at the dinner table in the mid-1950s. We were calmly discussing the pros and cons of building a well-stocked bomb shelter in our back yard to house us for a few weeks after a nuclear attack by the Soviet Union, a rational fear at the time, with bomb shelters quite a popular idea – and even occasional reality – amongst upper middle class people.

On the plus side were survival and diminished odds of severe radiation burns. On the minus side was the moral problem: We would naturally have to refuse entry to our feckless neighbours who had not had the prudence to build their own shelter, and they would be incinerated, if they were lucky, or irradiated and die an agonizing death. The bizarre disconnect between our ordinary dinner and the nightmare scenario we were painting was too much for me. I burst into tears and fled the room.

So although I was generally apolitical in my quotidian life, I was existentially preoccupied with one gigantic political idea: that the freedom-loving West was engaged in mortal combat with a monstrous totalitarian regime that wanted to take over the world. The enormous black mushroom cloud of Communism loomed over my inner life.

People now look back in amazement and often with bemusement at our Cold War hysteria. Yes, Joe McCarthy was a buffoon and the HUAC interrogations seem ugly out of context. But time has obliterated the constant, low grade psychological sense of impending doom we endured. Communism really was a deadly enemy aggressively seeking world dominion. About that big idea I was never a sceptic then or now.

I didn't come to my hatred of Communism via Karl Marx or Friedrich Hayek. I came to it by way of novels – George Orwell's *Animal Farm* and *Nineteen Eight-Four*, Arthur Koestler's *Darkness at Noon*, Ayn Rand's *Anthem* (not a patch for political gravamen on the others in this list, but compelling nonetheless) and Solzhenitsyn's *One Day in the Life of Ivan Denisovich,* not to mention Thomas Wolfe's hyper-patriotic *oeuvre* – and by positive exposure to capitalism.

I was proud of my entrepreneurial father's accomplishments. His immigrant family was so poor he never owned a pair of new shoes until he was old enough to buy them himself. He helped his father buy and sell junk from a horse-drawn cart (like in the 1960 film *Lies My Father Told Me*). Every penny he ever earned was the product of his own sense of family duty, initiative, risk and labour. He created jobs for others, and produced humble products – textiles, then utilitarian furniture – that people and institutions needed. I was always aware, from earliest childhood, that my soft life (and I always knew it was soft) rested squarely on my father's hardworking shoulders.

I had a personal fondness for the U.S. because I was, after all, half-American. My mother, born and raised in Detroit, was intensely patriotic and half my relatives lived in Michigan. The U.S. stood for ideals I cherished. Israel owed its existence to America's friendship. I believed in American exceptionalism. So when the rhetoric of moral equivalence between America and the Soviet Union began to surface on campus, my heart hardened against the intellectually feckless left.

At first, at McGill, I took no interest in campus politics or indeed any extra-curricular campus life. But Ronny did. His background had made him a passionate America booster and an aggressive anti-Communist. Russian by provenance, Ronny had been born in China just before World War Two. The most enduring memory from his childhood was the sight of liberating American soldiers in Jeeps rolling through the streets of Shanghai. (He only drives Jeeps to this day.)

His early life could not have been more different from mine. An only child of older parents, he arrived in Montreal when he was nine, speaking Russian and French, but not a word of English. He was automatically routed to an English school, according to Quebec's rigid distinctions between Catholics, virtually all francophones, and Protestants, virtually all anglophones. Jews were subsumed as Protestants for educational purposes. Isolated both linguistically and culturally, the only Jewish child in a sea of WASPs, he wasn't offered any special help adjusting; he was left by his teachers to sink or swim.

To add to his sense of cultural anomie, his parents immured themselves socially amongst other Russian *émigrés*. They seemed a generation older and in their formality and sobriety a half-century distant from other Canadian parents he met. He learned English at school, but spoke Russian at home until he was sixteen.

When Soviet leader Nikita Khrushchev banged his shoe on the table at the United Nations, Ronny was so embarrassed to be associated with such a thug, even by so tenuous a thread as a common language, he announced to his parents that henceforth they would speak English at home. And so they did for the next 50 years (until, in his mother's final decline, when English became laborious, he reverted to Russian.)

Many of Ronny's parents' relatives still lived in Russia. His parents were afraid to write to them or send them packages because they feared their relatives might suffer reprisals for their association with western capitalists. So Ronny's hatred of Communism was implacable, absolute, more visceral than mine.

19

As a representative of Graduate Studies on the McGill Student Council, with a portfolio in publications, including the *McGill Daily*, he fulminated against the Marxist editor and staff minions of the *Daily*. (He fully supported their right to editorialize from a left wing perspective. The problem was that the entire *Daily* was treated as an extended editorial pulpit for the dissemination of their radical views.)

I hadn't seen that side of him during our courtship. He was beating against a by now irresistible leftist current, but I was impressed by his courage in publicly adopting such an unpopular stand. Our personal relationship was bolstered by our mutual affection for America and our mutual disgust for Communist apologists.

* * *

Montreal had seduced me with its beauty, its *joie de vivre* and its biculturalism. I hadn't looked beneath the alluring surface, because I was eager to be seduced. I arrived in Montreal against a steady flow of traffic heading for Toronto. Ethnic nationalism was on the rise. A radical separatist group, *le Front de Libération du Québec* – the FLQ – had turned to terrorism to make its case for political separation from Canada. Between 1963 and 1970 the FLQ detonated over 95 bombs in symbolically anglo places – Westmount mailboxes, the train station, a RCMP recruitment centre, Eaton's department store, and most horribly in February, 1969, at the Montreal Stock Exchange, where 27 people were injured.

In October, 1970, when I was heavily pregnant with my second child, a daughter Joanne – our son Jonathan had been born in September, 1968 – the British Trade Commissioner, James Cross, was kidnapped by the FLQ. Shortly after, a cabinet minister, Pierre Laporte was kidnapped. The War Measures Act was enacted by Prime Minister Trudeau. A day later, Laporte was discovered dead. The city swarmed with army troops.

It was all quite surreal. My Toronto family couldn't understand why we were not fleeing back home. Strangely, although we were mesmerized by the drama and aware that we were living in something akin to a war zone, we were not exactly panicked, more paralyzed with astonishment that this could be happening in the peaceful kingdom of Canada.

Once the main FLQ culprits were rounded up and dealt with, a task made easy by the suspension of civil liberties, everything calmed down. In the aftermath there was a great deal of rhetorical blowback in the media against Prime Minister Trudeau for his decision to invoke the War Measures Act. Many innocent people had been arrested and detained temporarily on suspicion of involvement with FLQ members. This enraged Canada's liberal pundits, which is to say almost all of them.

I was confused and affronted by these Monday-morning quarterbacks. I don't think people outside Montreal had any idea of how serious the situation was. The FLQ were a small group, but they were mission-minded and committed to violence as a righteous political strategy. They were high on Marxist, revolutionary cant. Their grievances were objectively petty, but their swollen appetite for anarchy shamelessly seized on any handy straw. If they were not stamped out, I am sure they would have battened on the widespread sympathy for Quebec's allegedly oppressed situation amongst many intellectuals and other fellow-travelling grievance-collectors.

The Civil Rights movement, a truly righteous cause, was roiling America and separatists were envious of the attention and respect black activists received. One of their ideological gurus styled the *québécois* as "the white niggers of America." It was an obscene comparison, but as I was learning, for nationalist navel-gazing and outsized revanchism based in Freud's "narcissism of small differences," Quebec's ethnic-nationalist ideologues are a class unto themselves.

The War Measures Act did what it was designed to do. The FLQ was obliterated and never troubled us again. Those who critiqued Trudeau did not stop to contemplate how a less-than-definitive challenge would have ended. Terrorism was an ascendant trend in Europe's liberated colonies. Quebec intellectuals were far more influenced by violence-sanctioning activism from abroad than by intellectuals in the rest of Canada.

I could see that some radical Montreal intellectuals were sorry about the FLQ's wipeout. I began to understand that more than a few radically-minded intellectuals are excited when blood runs in the streets, as long as it isn't theirs. Decades later, when jihadists took down the Twin Towers on 9/11, and left wing intellectuals immediately looked to the "root causes" of their hatred, I was filled with disgust at their ignorance and even, in some cases, thinly-disguised admiration.

From the beginning of our return to Montreal, political and linguistic tensions have been an abiding presence in our lives. Tension, plus the loss of many anglo friends who couldn't see a future for themselves in a province where they weren't really wanted by a significant minority of the population. Within one year I lost my three best women friends, to Israel, Toronto and Seattle respectively. All stay-at-home mums, we had spent countless hours in each others' homes watching our babies grow into toddlerhood: cooking together, entertaining each other, babysitting for each other, sharing our hopes and dreams for our children, counting on each other. Those were precious times. Then poof! It was over.

We talked about leaving too. Ronny was in the financial sector and could have had a job in Toronto any time he wanted – indeed, he had some good offers, since so many of the head offices were starting to move to Toronto. But we couldn't leave his aging parents alone in Montreal. They had no other relatives here, our children were the great joy of their lives, and it would have been a cruelty to abandon them. Once we made that decision, we never seriously considered leaving again.

The separatist movement continued to surge after the FLQ crisis. The violent wing of separatism had been vanquished, but legitimate partisan strains swiftly emerged to form the *Parti Québécois* under René Lévesque's charismatic leadership. The call for a referendum on separation from Canada caught fire and from that day on, federalist Quebecers haven't known a moment's true political peace.

There was, however, a social upside to Jews arising from the insecurity that assailed all anglos.

A population of about 110,000, Jews made up a significant minority within the larger Montreal anglophone minority of 900,000. (Montreal's Jewish population now is about 90,000, thanks to the separatist undertow pulling our children away from us to more rewarding ports of call. Toronto, Vancouver, New York and Los Angeles became the principal destinations for many of our children).

Our community was long-established, well-endowed by a few extremely wealthy families, in particular the liquor-empire Bronfmans, and very well-organized. We ran – run – all kinds of agencies and institutions. Notable amongst them is the world-class Jewish General Hospital, founded in response to anti-Semitic exclusion in the medical profession. We also boasted a network of superb parochial schools (in one of which we enrolled our children). Jewish social service agencies and cultural organizations were serving the larger population as well as the Jewish community, which up to the 1960s was almost entirely Ashkenazi, Jews of European provenance.

Then a huge influx of francophone Jews from Morocco and other Maghreb lands where Sephardic Jews had long sojourned helped to stabilize the community demographics, even as it placed internal cultural strains within it (that have by now been almost completely resolved).

Even separatist governments acknowledged Jewish contributions to the common weal, so at the official level relations remained mutually respectful between the government and our community. Jewish community leaders, now chosen for their bilingualism as well as competence and smarts, had always had a remarkably sophisticated knack for diplomacy, walking close to the wall politically, making no waves, but through carefully nurtured behind-the-scenes relationships, advancing Jewish community interests. Funding for Jewish schools, ironically enough, is generous in Quebec, and our children's education cost half of what we would have paid in Ontario.

The Jewish community was also looked up to with respect and admiration by other anglos – and other less-entrenched cultural communities like the Italians and Greeks who identified with us politically – whose social self-confidence was rapidly eroding in the face of the rising nationalist tide. All anglos were now political bedfellows and, increasingly, social ones too. Misery loved company.

*   *   *

But there was a civic downside to our sense of Otherness. Elsewhere in Canada, completely integrated Jews were migrating into the political and cultural mainstream at a steady and frictionless pace, becoming involved in municipal and cultural affairs at all levels. We were never going to be part of a mainstream in Quebec.

Few anglophones, let alone Jews – apart from extremely well-heeled donors or a few bilingual "old-stock" types – could aspire to political engagement, or board-level involvement in our city's respected arts and charitable institutions. As for the civil service and provincial political affairs, those routes were closed to any but an anomalous handful of us.

Tokenism, for which one needed French fluency in any case, was not a feasible or palatable option for most of us, and we turned our backs on the civic institutions dominated by our political "hosts," concentrating on those institutions – anglo universities, the McCord Museum, anglo social service agencies and charities, and so forth – where a significant anglo and/or Jewish support base made our volunteerism welcome.

To add to Montreal Jews' gloom, the world outlook for Jews was far less sunny than it had been in my youth. After the 1967 war, anti-Zionism began to ramp up. By the 1973 Yom Kippur war, Israel's future looked grim. So Jews were even more inclined to turn inward to our own cultural and fundraising institutions. If we had stayed in Toronto, I don't think I would have felt the need to "huddle" within my community; the whole city, province and country would have been my oyster. But in those "siege" years, I found myself creeping closer to tribal fires. That sounds civically retrogressive, but in personal terms it worked out very well.

No need to chronicle the well-known facts about the arrival of the *Parti Québécois* to power in 1976 and the stampede down Highway 401 of capital, head offices and frightened federalists. Or the first referendum on separation from

Canada in 1980, soundly defeated. Or the protracted constitutional repatriation drama. Or the ever-tightening language laws resulting in Bill 101, or the emergence of the *Bloc Québécois* under Lucien Bouchard's charismatic leadership. Or the inexorable march toward the second referendum in 1995.

Canadians outside of Quebec were alternately baffled and enraged by what was happening here. And so it may seem strange to say this, but my life as a second-class citizen – and by any objective standards, that's what we were and are, though in an extremely benign form – was curiously exhilarating to the timid adventurer inside me.

Even if its language laws were fundamentally undemocratic in principle, and even if xenophobia quietly thrummed beneath the surface, Quebec was after all still run on predictable democratic lines. If you have no reason to fear illegal reprisals, or the midnight pounding on the door, as in lands where serious intolerance prevails, you are living a political adventure, not unwelcome after a lifetime of relative predictability. You are part of a velvet resistance movement. Your community feels unified against a common enemy. Your shared sense of righteous indignation is rarely dormant for long.

So paradoxically, I felt like the only "real" Canadian, because I was living our official biculturalism – what others pay lip service to, but never actually experience. I was *alive* to the world around me all the time. So I felt a kind of front-line superiority to, and pity for those in the rest of Canada who weren't toughing out Canada's existential crisis.

Which isn't to say that resentment didn't smolder within as well. Still, those of us who could have left, but stayed, had all consciously decided that outward accommodation was preferable to slinking away. We got on with our lives as normally as we could, every morning snatching up the *Montreal Gazette* to peruse news of fresh offences to anglos, and sharing our indignation with friends. As the cliché has it, we rolled with the punches.

One punch I felt we anglos deserved was criticism of our generation's laziness in acquiring good French. It's true that the school system in Quebec did not encourage real bilingualism. But there are many ways to acquire a second language, and the average francophone put us all to shame with his rapid acquisition of English through cultural osmosis alone.

My own French was functional, thanks to an excellent four years' grounding in grammar and other fundamentals at high school, but in conversation nothing to boast of. Ironically Forest Hill had given me a far better *formation* in everything but spoken French than anglos raised in Montreal. Immersion-language programs would make our children more competent, but we had to look out for ourselves.

Most people believe that it is easy to acquire a second language if you're living in a milieu where it is assumed to be the official language (constitutionally speaking, English is also an official language in Quebec, a fact most Quebecers are unaware of). But Quebec really is two linguistic solitudes, and there are areas where English is even today the unofficial *lingua franca*.

It is still perfectly feasible to live your entire life in English in Quebec if you confine your movements to a few square miles of Montreal, where francophones quite amiably and automatically switch to English to accommodate your dysfunction. I have many friends born and raised in Montreal or the anglo suburbs who still blithely subsist on their near-useless novice-level French.

(Sluggishness in acquiring French wasn't confined to my generation. My own son resisted learning French, in spite of every encouragement and opportunity. His exit from Quebec wasn't a political gesture, but a practical admission that his incompetency in French precluded any kind of decent career in Montreal.)

Even though I lived and sojourned in an almost completely anglo milieu, and even though all the francophones I knew were bilingual, I decided I would become fluent in French or bust. Over the last thirty years, I have probably put 10,000 hours into language courses, immersion weeks in Quebec City and rigorous self-imposed exposure to francophone media and books.

My goal was to comprehend and speak French with assurance simply to feel confident outside my cultural ghetto. I will never be completely fluent in French, but as it turned out, my vastly improved French has been a journalistic godsend. In October, 2012, I was able to hold my end up in an (edited-down) 90-minute interview/debate on anglo angst with a popular francophone TV talk show host. I rate that experience as one of the great triumphs of my life.

* * *

My life from the early 1970s until the mid-1990s was highly compartmentalized, but satisfying. My time was divided between domestic life, work, personal and intellectual growth and community volunteerism.

As an at-home mother, I was able to devote quality time to my kids' interests, especially my daughter's logistically demanding equestrian career in her teen years. Evenings I taught English literature and English as a Second Language part time at CEGEPs, Quebec's two (or three, depending on program) year educational bridge between high school and university. I also reviewed books on the active Jewish private study group circuit.

(I don't think I have known many Jewish women of my social class who are *not* in a book or study group of some kind. The mania for literary self-improvement amongst Jewish women didn't start in my generation, though. My moth-

25

er and her friends loved their book club too. Of course non-Jewish women also belong to book clubs, but not nearly in the same proportions.)

I became active in our synagogue – a small, unpretentious congregation affiliated with the Reconstructionist branch of Judaism – because its reason-based intellectual principles and traditional liturgy accorded with my own cultural mindset, and because I wanted to encourage my children's fidelity to Jewish peoplehood. That sparked an interest in bolstering my comprehension of Hebrew, sadly atrophied since my childhood years in afternoon Hebrew school, so I took Hebrew language and literature courses in McGill's Jewish Studies program, which I loved.

It was a good balance. I was always there for my kids. I kept my hand in professionally. The constant book-reviewing kept me reading and writing with critical purpose, and I even wrote fiction on the side for pleasure. Sitting on boards, I learned a lot about institutional governance, political jousting and how organizations process ideas into policy and events. To keep attuned to Quebec politics as it affected Jews, I joined the board of Canadian Jewish Congress, Quebec Region, the Jewish community's political arm, as it then was.

For long-term volunteerism commitment, I was drawn more to cultural institutions. For a number of years I sat on the board of a Jewish arts centre, but I found my most enduring personal reward came from involvement in the Jewish Public Library, the city's oldest Jewish institution, for 100 years operating in four languages – English, French, Yiddish and Hebrew (Russian is now a fifth official language) – and one of the few Jewish cultural sites that attracts the complete spectrum of Jews, from the Ultra-Orthodox to the completely secular.

On the library's behalf, I founded and for most of 25 years edited *First Fruits*, an annual anthology of creative writing in the original four languages by Montreal high school students (A prize-winning essay in *First Fruits* was my son's first, inspirational publishing venture.) Eventually I served as the library's president, so I learned a lot about leadership too.

But I always had time for friends and I always had time to read. I read novels, but more and more I read magazines and journals of political and cultural observation. The opinions I hold today began to take articulate form. Much of the credit for my journalistic point of view (or blame, depending on your perspective) has to go to the highly influential conservative, pro-Israel *Commentary Magazine*. I started reading *Commentary* in the early 1970s, when its famous editor and principal contributor Norman Podhoretz was in his prime (it is now edited by his son, John Podhoretz), and have never missed an issue since.

I read a lot and thought a lot. I couldn't have done most of what I have just described if I had worked full time or been consumed with career ambitions.

During all these years, feminism was gathering strength. At first it was a reform movement concentrated on achieving legal and economic-opportunity parity with men. I had nothing but admiration for these initiatives, which were overdue and sensible. But then it became a radicalized, revolutionary movement based in conspiracy-theory style distrust of men. All men.

Feminist anger didn't make sense to me. Betty Friedan had said, in *The Feminine Mystique*, that the women of her era lived in "comfortable concentration camps" in which they silently suffered the "problem that has no name."

Friedan wasn't talking about working-class women. She was talking about her fellow students who had graduated from a posh university: highly educated women married to decent, hardworking men. Like me, they had automatically made homemaking their priority, and like me could afford some household help. But unlike me, they felt they were under-utilizing their skills and knowledge.

The image feminism conjured up of the bitter, disaffected wife sitting idle at home with her brain withering away, and waiting for her husband to come home from his glamorous job downtown didn't jibe with my experience. For one thing, most men's work isn't glamorous or exciting. They may wear suits and ties and get out of the house all day, a situation to envy in the early years of child-rearing, but in the end it's mostly just work anyone else with the same credentials could do. For another, I have never met any woman of my generation and my socio-economic background who was bored or felt trapped in her home past her children's first few years of life.

Most of the stay-at-home moms I knew were at least as active in community volunteerism as I was. Many were engaged full-time in fundraising for Combined Jewish Appeal and other charities, or sat on boards of cultural organizations. They were accomplished public speakers and held in high respect by the men they collaborated with. They were culture-vultures, as we called them: belonged to book clubs; studied art; went to the theatre; took courses in "current events"; attended lecture series at their synagogues.

They were powerful in their homes. Their husbands deferred to them in all matters domestic and child-related. They were materially indulged insofar as a husband's budget could stretch. It was understood that if household help could be afforded for heavy domestic chores, so it would be.

In defending the way of life followed by most of my generation of women, I am not saying it was ideal, or that it is a prescription in perpetuity for all women. The world changes and people adapt. But I object to revisionist condemnation by theorists. I am just saying that for those of us who accepted at-home motherhood as a norm in that era, it was no hell on earth. It was mostly fun.

I sympathized with women who had burning ambitions they were held back from by wifedom and motherhood, but in reality, as I looked about me, such women were few in number. I did not see much quiet desperation in women of my class – that would be Friedan's class as well, and come to think of it, pretty well all professional feminists' class in years to come – that could not be assuaged by returning to school and finding part time work that was satisfying. Many did just that when their children were in school.

I am sure there were many less advantaged women in other communities whose gender-based grievances were real and pressing. But most Jewish women I knew and know have found their niche, whether it involves working, professional accreditation, creative endeavours or some other path to self-realization – without restraint or judgment by their typically uxorious Jewish husbands. Everyone was into *something*.

Most of the women I knew – exactly like Betty Friedan's worshipful demographic – harboured modest dreams that were realizable with a little patience and flexibility. Of course some of them had man troubles and personal issues, but so do many women today, just different kinds.

I was affronted by the steady downward estimation of mothering I saw in the feminist movement. I was often bored by my children, often irritated by the endless chores and routines, but the thought of paying someone else to raise my children for the better part of the day while I worked at some job anyone else with the same credentials could have done simply appalled me.

I know children do very well with mother substitutes, but I wouldn't have cared if they had better outcomes with nannies. They were *my* children, and *my* responsibility, and ultimately would be *my* source of pride or chagrin. I thought I was doing the most important job in the world. Still do. I was lucky, I think, that most other women of my generation felt the same way. If they hadn't, I would have been another lemming to the sea; I would have hired a nanny and worked. And I think – I am sure – I would have been unhappy away from my children.

Which isn't to say I think women should all stay home with their children today. It's a different world today. I accept that. My daughter and my daughter-in-law have worked full time since before they had children. They excel at high-level jobs and both are also excellent mothers. Their children are not suffering. I do regret, however, that women who want to stay home in their children's formative years, or who make mothering a priority until their children are capable of handling independence with confidence and self-possession, are made to feel guilty about that.

I concluded that women's self-worth and self-realization is largely a function of the esteem in which they are held and raised by their families and communities, as well as by the way sons are raised. If they are raised to respect and honour women as moral equals, they will. If they are raised to consider women inferior beings with no role other than produce sons, they will have contempt for them.

If both boys and girls are raised to believe that community engagement and support for worthy causes is honorable work and see the social capital that amasses to those who involve themselves in community advancement, they will consider community work a worthy endeavour. It's always about culture; I could see that.

Later, when I was exposed to the way women are raised in cultures where honour and shame are the prevailing motifs, I looked at the shocking contrast between my upbringing and theirs with astonishment and deep sadness. The disparity in outcomes for women from one culture to another led me to feel derision for the absurd reality-defying theories underlying both multiculturalism and feminism: the former for its insistence that all cultures are equal in value, and the latter for its insistence that men are inherently patriarchal, no matter what culture they've been raised in.

But even before I came to those conclusions through observation of women in my own community vis à vis others, and through critical analysis of feminist rhetoric and attitudes, I harboured a strong instinctive bias against feminism's growing, and very troubling antagonism to men.

When my older sister Anne, the one who married at 19, was completing her doctoral studies in history at the University of Toronto in 1972, she applied for the single job opening in the history department. She had long assumed that teaching was meant to be her vocation, and the natural outcome of her higher education. Her dissertation had received glowing tribute. And by now, feminism was already a strong presence on campus and beginning to penetrate popular culture. (*Ms. Magazine* began publication and Title IX, requiring equal sports resources and access for women as for men at universities, was passed the same year.) So she had very good reason to feel confident she would get the job.

Anne was up against two male candidates. The head of the department called her in. He told her that although her academic qualifications were superior to the other two, and he knew she would have made a great success of it, he was giving the job to one of the men. He was candid about his reason. Anne's husband was now a periodontist and making good money. She didn't need the job, but the men had to support their families. He was sorry, but that was how it was.

I include this episode because it had a huge impact on me. My younger sister Nancy and I are close friends, but she is almost five years younger than me. In our childhood and youth, this was an enormous gap, and although I may have influenced her somewhat, her activities and friendships and life choices did not influence me. But Anne is only eighteen months older than me. She has probably influenced my evolution as a woman more than anyone, even my mother. In retrospect, I see that Anne's response to her disappointment was a decisive milestone in my growing critical distance from the more militant strain of the feminist movement.

Anne always took her sisterly responsibilities seriously, and I in turn happily followed her around like a puppy, now and then nipping at her heels and being summarily cuffed back into line. On the few occasions that we were separated in childhood, I felt unanchored, adrift. (It came to me several years ago that almost all the people to whom I have gravitated as candidates for friendship are either oldest children or only children. I seem to enjoy being somewhat "managed" by my sister substitutes.)

I eventually struck out on my own educational path, and geographical distance added to my independence. But Anne remained a major force in my life. We were both swimming through the same cultural waters that were now out of our parents' depth. As I outgrew my mother's somewhat simplistic views on life, I became more and more reliant on Anne for life coaching and social mooring. Many of her friends became my friends, and vice versa.

I studied her winning social and academic strategies, some of which were based in personality and temperament traits I couldn't replicate. I didn't always follow her advice or her example. But I always knew she was one of life's winners, so attention had to be paid. And nothing she ever said or did failed to leave its mark.

If Anne had walked away from that interview with her department head harbouring a sense of gendered victimhood or bitterness about men's "privilege," my life might have taken a very different path. I might well have accepted the feminist catechism. But she didn't.

Anne knew she was herself a child of privilege. She could marry young and continue her studies because she and Ron had their parents' financial backing. It was true she didn't need the job, and it was true that men still needed jobs for reasons other than self-actualization. Those were realities of life at the time that deserved ethical consideration apart from one's own ambitions.

Besides, it wasn't in her to resent men who clearly bore more responsibility for their dependents than she did. As in mine, the men in her life – our father, cousins, teachers, rabbis, school friends and husband – had been upstanding, trustworthy people.

Fathers are important to children, but they're important to their daughters in different ways than they are to their sons. When I try to imagine my life without my father present in it, I don't see a confident woman emerging. Anne, Nancy and I all adored our father. He wasn't the most present or involved father as today's "new men" are – he would arrive home exhausted from work with little energy for engaged parenting – but his fiercely protective love for us and pride in our accomplishments shone forth. He was a heroic figure to us because of his stature in the community as an ethical businessman and philanthropic leader. When a new friend's parent would ask who my father was, and I told him, I would always see the same spontaneously spreading big smile. That's social capital of incalculable value to any child.

A man taking responsibility for his family was something Anne understood and respected. So there was no bitterness in her when she absorbed the rejection, only a period of reflection to consider what other channels were available through which she could divert her powerful sense of ambition. After taking stock of her options, Anne plunged into a volunteer political job that led to an opportunity for paid work, and thence to personal achievements and career heights few women in Canada can boast of.

In the early 1990s, when I had been teaching English part-time in the Quebec CEGEP system for many years, it was a tough job market for young teachers entering the field. One day I had a conversation with a young man who'd managed to get a few hours' teaching a week. His wife was pregnant, so he was desperately hoping it would become a secure, fulltime job.

As he confided his hopes to me, I thought about Anne's experience. I remembered that the closing of one door hadn't stopped her for long. She found work she loved because the qualities that make for success – a sound education, good work ethic, ambition and perseverance – are far more influential than the getting or losing of any single position.

Teaching had never been a burning vocation for me. And I didn't need the money. I knew full well that I taught because it was easy part-time work, and because, thanks to the deep penetration of ideological feminism into the general culture, I was embarrassed to tell people that I was primarily a homemaker and community volunteer.

Then I quit my job.

* * *

Now, as the *Bloc Québécois* (BQ) hoisted sail and made headway federally, I entered my political phase of life. I found it difficult to accept that even the "polite" nation of Canada could endorse the legitimacy of a federal party sworn to break up the country – a federal party with neither roots nor presence in any

31

other province but Quebec. To me the party's mandate was treason, *tout court*, and should have been ineligible for parliament.

You would have to have lived in Quebec during the second, yearlong 1994-5 referendum campaign to appreciate the dread we anglos lived with. It began on a level playing field, but once Lucien Bouchard took over the leadership of the *"Oui"* forces, it turned apocalyptic. Bouchard's personal charisma and demagogic power seemed to act on the population like a hypnotic spell.

He was everywhere. His thundering speeches created a kind of mass hysteria. I can never forget the sight, on television, of Bouchard making his way out of an auditorium and a woman in the crowd grasping his hand and bending to kiss it. My heart sank at the pitch of irrationality and even mania it represented.

We federalists felt completely abandoned. The prime minister, Jean Chrétien, was so unpopular in Quebec, he didn't dare intervene personally. He had totally miscalculated how close the referendum vote was going to be. But he or his advisors should have realized there would be trouble from the manipulative, tortured framing of the question. He should have realized – in polls it was made abundantly clear – that the average voter didn't even realize his 'yes' vote meant separation from Canada. The federal government had no plan, no strategy.

Montreal was hemorrhaging money and people. The separatists wouldn't have cared if every anglo in town scarpered and the economy collapsed. This was their moment, and it was worth whatever collateral damage a country of their own entailed. Most ordinary people didn't have a clue what was at stake or what the consequences would be.

People often say the *québécois* are canny, sophisticated voters. That is not my experience. I think most of them outside Montreal, except for the business people, live in a bubble, cut off from the rest of the world and ignorant of how the world works. Quebec is a nanny state, and the people assume the government will take care of them. If the referendum had passed, and the implications then made clear, half the people who had voted 'yes' would have been horrified by what they had done.

Only one thing kept the referendum from passing: the fear of partition: that is, the fear that an independent Quebec would itself be subjected to physical dismemberment on the same grounds that Quebec wished to dismember Canada. Prime Minister Trudeau had said, after the 1980 referendum, "If Canada is divisible, then Quebec is also divisible." It was an idea whose time had come.

I should here also add that there were a few courageous voices of sanity and reason that were a lifeline to intelligent observers. One I remember with affection was that of Canadian historian and journalist William Johnson, whose bold and deeply informed columns hammered away at the undemocratic and even unconstitutional nature of the referendum question and process. He was the first journalist in my life I ever contacted personally to thank, which resulted in a friendship and post-referendum activist collaboration.

Another was Stéphane Dion, a former sovereigntist turned federalist, then a professor of political science at the *Université de Montréal*. His quietly steely challenges to the separatist leadership, in media debates and a series of open letters, exposed the weaknesses and downright lies separatist leaders were feeding the public.

Finally, I remember with gratitude the superior rationality and debating skills of a young man from out west I'd never heard of before – Stephen Harper – who started appearing in televised debates, and who drove his opponents to rage with calmly defended ideas that would eventually become actualized when Jean Chrétien adopted them wholesale and entrenched them as the Clarity Act, a law that would in future forbid a 50% threshold for such a momentous national upheaval, and as well preclude the kind of snake-oil casuistry that tainted the entire 1995 referendum project.

A federalist group in Montreal drew up plans for a divided Quebec in which strongly federalist areas would stay within Canada, including half of Montreal. Then the Cree of northern Quebec announced they were holding their own referendum, which they did, with 95% of them voting to remain in Canada. They also noted with unveiled menace that the security of Quebec's massive hydro-electric installations in their territories was entirely in their hands.

The absolute shock and horror – almost comical in its naiveté – with which the idea of partition and the clarity of the Crees' gesture was greeted by separatists, even the intellectuals, I think reinforces my view of the *québécois* as politically rather simplistic. Partition was a logical response they should have seen coming a mile away.

When the reality that separation would not be a tidy parting of the ways sank in, even Lucien Bouchard's "magic wand" (he had actually said in a speech that the will for a country has the effect of a magic wand making everything come out right) wilted.

Nevertheless, the last weeks before the vote were pure agony. The photo finish – almost literally 50/50 – abetted by the outright theft of federalist votes in certain ridings, still an open wound in the memories of those who lived that near-death experience, ensured that the tension would continue, just as the hanging chads in the 2000 George W. Bush vs Al Gore presidential campaign hung over Bush's presidency, forever illegitimate in Democrats' minds, like a bad smell.

In his concession speech, the inebriated PQ leader, Jacques Parizeau, vented his bitterness in a diatribe against "money and the ethnic vote" as the cause of the separatists' loss. By "money" he meant Jews. By the "ethnic vote" he meant organized immigrant communities like the Italians and Greeks who lined up solidly on the No side.

There was truth in his statement, since francophones had voted majoritarily for the Yes, and it was a coalition of francophone federalists, anglos and allophones (as we call those speaking maternal languages other than French or English) that tipped the numbers into the No camp, but there was hostility in his heart, so overtly on display that he resigned in disgrace immediately afterward.

Parizeau and his cabinet henchmen, who harboured equally antagonistic views to Quebecers who weren't *québécois de souche*, of old ethnic stock, were denounced as racists, and perhaps they were. But most ethnic *québécois* are not, in my experience.

Living here for almost fifty years, I have naturally come into contact with innumerable old-stock francophones, and enjoy close friendships with a number of them. I find *québécois* to be a peaceable cultural group, warm, spontaneous and candid. Politically defensive? Of course. Who wouldn't be in their geopolitical situation? But racist? No. Xenophobic? Yes, many are somewhat xenophobic. But the difference between the two is significant and the line between them is usually blurred to the point of conflation.

When I sat on the board of Canadian Jewish Congress in the 1980s, the Department of Multiculturalism and Citizenship – I think that was the name – did a study on "Violence and racism in Quebec."

Some of the report's conclusions were obvious: that poverty and unemployment and political uncertainty and the lack of action by political leaders all contribute to making people feel marginalized, and that's why they blame minorities for their problems. But it got more interesting when it posed the question of whether Quebec was a racist society, as opposed to whether there were racist incidents, because of course there always are some of those. Was Quebec a more *inherently* racist society than other parts of Canada?

The conclusion was that Quebec was more *xenophobic* than the rest of Canada, but not more racist. Xenophobic means a fear of others, while racism, based in a sense of superiority, is a true hatred of others. The report noted that true racist groups in Quebec were imports, not homegrown. It cited Longitude 74 (the Montreal branch of the Ku Klux Klan) and the Aryan Resistance Movement, both of which advocated for racial segregation, actively recruited alienated youth and promoted racial conflict.

Xenophobic groups, on the other hand, were indigenous to Quebec. They were characteristically defensive rather than aggressive, based in insecurity rather than hatred. They put the emphasis on *l'Autre* – the Other – as an intruder rather than an inferior. And they expressed fear of economic and cultural takeover or fear of disappearance.

Examples were the now long-forgotten *Mouvement Pour La Survie de la Nation* and *Le Mouvement pour une Immigration Restreinte et Francophonie*. Considering its statements and activities, I would also have included the *Societé Saint-Jean-Baptiste de Montréal*, whose well-known hostility to the English language continually manifests itself in nuisance complaints, but so far without incitement to violence.

As I write in November 2012, shortly after the election of a PQ minority government, one feels the same vibe in the air as we did before the referendum, when these organized radical xenophobic clusters were active. Fear of the English language, insecurity, blame-laying on others: all these socially deleterious elements are in play once again.

When René Lévesque's first PQ government passed Bill 101, which made French the common language in Quebec, its preamble said that the law would be "respectful of the institutions of the English-speaking community of Quebec...", but today as I write, we have a PQ government pushing for French as the "language of use" in our private lives, and toying with restrictions on political candidacies that would virtually eliminate all but maternal-language francophones from public life. I don't believe Pauline Marois harbours any particular dislike for the English. But she is in thrall to a core xenophobic element in her party. There is an ugly imp sitting on this premier's shoulder. If she does not heed its tribalistic urgings, she will feel the pain of its sharp talons.

I seem to have come full circle in my half-century sojourn here. I arrived to tension; the tension subsided; the tension escalated; subsided again for what we assumed was "for good." But here we go again. And to my mind, because it is emanating from older sovereigntist veterans acting out of desperation with nothing to lose and a willingness to incite general hostility, this overt expression of hatred for the English language is more worrisome than ever.

Sometimes I feel guilty that we did not leave Quebec when our children were young. My son left Quebec because he could not see a career future here. But my daughter and her family stayed. They have good quality of life, but will my grandchildren? I worry about that.

* * *

It was in the post-referendum years, when feelings of rancour continued to run high on both sides of the sovereignty debate, that I became a journalist of

35

sorts. I began writing polemical pieces for publication in *Cité libre*, the political journal Trudeau had been active in founding in the turbulent 1960s. Long dormant, it had been revived as a journalistic champion of federalism under the spirited editorship of passionately federalist academics Max and Monique Nemni.

Trudeau's dual vision of official pan-Canadian bilingualism, with strongly protected individual rights, fuelled this enterprise. Whatever other reservations I had about Trudeau (and there are plenty), his position on Quebec sovereignty was an inspiration I was happy to pay homage to. It was invigorating – no, *cathartic* – to have such an outlet for my righteous anger. I felt young. My intellectual sap was running in a way I hadn't felt since university days.

That was the late 1990s. Then, by coincidence, my son Jonathan shocked us by announcing that he was joining the editorial board of Conrad Black's just-founded *National Post*. We knew he loved to write and had been proud to see his occasional pieces in print, but never dreamed he would segue from what seemed a settled career in tax law – he was then working for a Canadian firm in their New York office – into journalism.

Almost from the day Jon began working at the *Post*, I started pestering him about topics I thought the *Post* editorial board should be addressing. I was now fully engaged intellectually on a number of political and cultural issues: political correctness in the universities, feminism, multiculturalism and so forth, and delighted to have this filial conduit for my frustrations. Not that Jon followed my advice unless it jibed with what he and the other editorialists were thinking, of course. Still.

One day Jon said in response to yet another polemical nudge, "If you feel so strongly about these issues, why don't you write something yourself? I can't guarantee it will get published, but if it is half-decent, I will at least pass it along to the Comment editor." The rest, as they say, is my history. I wrote an op ed about Quebec. To my amazement it was published. It was a thrilling moment. I continued to send unsolicited op eds in for the next three years. An encouraging proportion of them were published.

Finally, in June of 2003, the Comment editor – in those days it was Natasha Hassan, who later decamped to the *Globe and Mail* – told me she liked my "voice." And did I think I could write something on a weekly basis? If ever there was a flood-tide risk in life that would never be offered again and was begging to be acknowledged and seized upon, this was it.

My heart knocking – for I certainly did not then believe I could turn out a weekly piece – my mind's eye glanced at the silver platter heaped with the blessings that had filled me with confidence in my youth. Then I calmly responded that yes, of course, I was *quite* sure I could turn out a weekly piece. So Natasha took a chance on me. And to my astonishment and delight it turned out that I could.

* * *

I love what I do. It feels natural to me, and my pleasure in writing has not withered with time and the familiarity of my 50-columns a year plus blogging writing routine. I opened by saying that I did not come to journalism by way of family tradition. But *opinions*! I don't remember a time when I did not feel compelled, daily as it seems to me, to impose, challenge or defend an opinion in my family circle and beyond.

Argument was the staff of family life. We argued about matters great and small – with each other, and with our parents, with our teachers, and even, in my later teen years, as I recall with a little embarrassment, with our rabbi, who took my callow cheekiness in good stride. We had no respect for each other's feelings if we thought we had the better end of the argumentative stick. Many arguments ended in tears, and I suppose we were reprimanded for extremism once in a while.

But on the whole, our parents looked benignly upon our clumsy verbal jousts, as a traditional Inuit father might smile at his son's wobbly struggles with a harpoon. With no other weapons at hand for most of our history, *making a case* – to kings, politicians, fellow students, the media – has evolved as a Jewish survival skill.

For me writing is not work. But it isn't quite play either – or not play as it is perceived by non-Jews. Jews are not a spontaneously lighthearted people; we can appear lighthearted, but we work at it. Until the last few hundred years, the whole idea of play – exercising one's body or mind for pleasure, "fun," or mere aesthetic gratification – was looked down on by Jews as the mark of people who were neither serious nor moral. Spontaneous play, organized sport – these are Hellenist inventions, eagerly snapped up by Christians – that completely bypassed Jews (and Jews it).

From the Enlightenment on, we Jews have naturally wanted to "play" like everyone else. But it still doesn't come spontaneously to many of us. (Our first novelist, Shalom Aleichem, evoked laughter that bled; our most artful modern novelists and entertainers – Bellow, Roth, Chabon; Woody Allen and Larry David – are steeped in mordant, moralistic angst.) As a consequence, when we modern Jews do engage in play, we cannot "just" play; we take play as seriously as we take everything else in life (this point was made to perfection in the 1981 film *Chariots of Fire*). We try, but we don't really understand activities that are ends in themselves. Even when we choose to be funny, it is humour with the bite of moral judgment or self-loathing.

Above all, we're not used to playfulness when we argue. Ideas are not something we juggle with for the entertainment or mere admiration of others. We don't boast the crystalline sparkle of an Oscar Wilde or a William F. Buckley. We take pride in the gleaming tungsten of Spinoza and Norman Podhoretz. Ideas are not just important to us, as they are to others. They are a matter of life and death. We have been tolerated because of ideas, hated because of ideas and decimated because of ideas. (We still await the idea that will make us lovable.)

So argumentation is existentially serious work for us, not a test of acumen or a "gotcha" political game. After three thousand years of continuous intellectual vigour and an equally long tradition of internal dissent over our destiny, we are trained to go for the jugular in debate. Our style is typically confident and aggressive, even belligerent. We seethe with special contempt for fellow Jews who disagree with us. Forbidden to use physical violence against them, we have become expert in savage internecine denunciation.

When I look back over the body of my columns, and note the topics that have sparked first my curiosity and then my compulsion to make a bulletproof case against the prevailing opinion, I see a superficial diversity of themes, such as fathers' rights, political correctness on campus, abortion, addiction, anglophone rights, domestic violence, anti-Zionism and pit bulls.

Under the surface though, there is one binding theme, and that is the Big Lie. The Big Lie has become a kind of cliché by now. It was first coined with reference to the Jews by Hitler in *Mein Kampf*, in which he advocated for the use of a lie so "colossal" that no one would believe that someone "could have the impudence to distort the truth so infamously." He correctly predicted that if you repeat even something unbelievable often enough and loudly enough, the gullible masses will buy it.

It may therefore seem pretentious and even inappropriate to apply the phrase to my niche subjects, except of course for the anti-Zionism inspired Holocaust inversion and Israel apartheid Big Lies, whose potential consequences are too dreadful to contemplate.

Nevertheless, in every subject that has aroused my writerly passion, there is at its core a Theory, an ideology or a racial imperative that in turn promotes a Big Lie sufficiently baleful to: withhold the constitutional rights of an entire class of citizens; ruin hundreds of thousands of fathers' and children's lives; blight neighbourhoods; quash freedom of intellectual inquiry and freedom of speech; deny tax-funded services to victims of violence on the basis of sex; and privilege the state over parents in the guardianship of children.

As a member of a people for whom the Big Lie is no abstract idea, but an eternally-present threat to physical survival, I know a Big Lie when I see one in all its irrational ingloriousness, even if it is not so colossal as to end in a massacre of innocents, "only" the massacre of democratic principles (although in the case of pit bulls, the unnecessary actual killing of innocents).

And when I see it, I feel compelled to *make the case* against it as if in fact my survival depended on it. Perhaps it is because my life has been so privileged that not a single one of the harms or injustices I write about has ever befallen me that I feel especially bound to pay my luck forward as aggressively as I can.

*　*　*

And now you know where, in the parlance, I am coming from. If appetite remains, you will find in the following previously-unpublished essays, reviews and public lectures a fair representation of the diverse cultural subjects that have kindled my interpretive fire for the past decade. If you read them all, you will note repetitions of certain statistics and statements that I regret, but that are unavoidable because of the overlap in themes.

My already-published columns are all archived, and continuously updated, on my website: www.barbarakay.ca.

Feminism's Impact on Society

This is the slightly updated text of a talk I gave at McGill University as a guest of the McGill Women's Alumnae Association in 2008. I almost didn't give the talk. A few days beforehand, two Womens Studies teachers lodged a complaint with the organizing committee against me, insisting I should not be given a platform because of what they considered to be my odious views on feminism.

The organizing committee was poised to cave in to their demand. I told them their choice was to have me speak to the 35 or so women who might attend, or withdraw the invitation and become the subject of a column I would write for thousands of Post readers. They sensibly stood by their invitation, and as I predicted, about 35 women attended. The security guard the committee had hired was unnecessary, but an interesting sign of the moral panic even a few disgruntled campus ideologues can arouse in these politically correct times.

In its earliest and most benign form – the political campaign to achieve equality under the law and equality in economic opportunities – feminism was a necessary and welcome reform movement. No rational person could be less than delighted to see barriers to a full range of educational and career options for women fall by the wayside.

The feminism I take exception to today is not the mild and blameless right of a woman to self-actualize that all women today absorb by osmosis. What I object to is the radical ideology that has come to dominate the movement's academic and institutional elites over the last 40 years:

41

This is an ideology that sees the relations between the sexes as a never-ending antagonistic power struggle, with women as eternal victims and men as eternal oppressors. It is an ideology that explains away the moral failings of women as the fault of a patriarchal "system", but holds men responsible for their actions. And most important, it is an ideology that short changes children by privileging the rights and importance to children of mothers over fathers.

That kind of feminism is so deeply entrenched in our society's cultural elites and the institutions they dominate – really it is the defining ideology of our era – that whether she wants to or not, no thinking woman can escape the necessity of negotiating some kind of relationship with its claims.

However intellectually objective we all try to be, each of us brings our own particular life experiences to the decision of what kind of relationship that will be, and I am no different.

So for full disclosure: I brought two relevant pieces of personal history to the table. The first is that I am the daughter – one of three – of a charismatic, entrepreneurial, risk-taking father. Having known the privations of extreme poverty in his youth, he was so obsessed with providing economic security for his family that he literally worked himself to a premature death.

Because he was a hero to me, I am well disposed toward the men I meet, unless I am shown good reason not to be, and as a result there are many wonderful men in my life, not least my husband of 44 years and my son and son-in-law, both supportive, loving husbands of high-achieving women and engaged, beloved fathers of two daughters each (update: my son has a third daughter born in 2012).

Everything in my experience with men points to the conclusion that different cultural values around relations between the sexes produce different outcomes. Normal, psychologically healthy men, raised in a society respectful of women, as Canada's heritage culture is, are governed in their relations with women by the instinct to protect them, not to hurt them.

The second element I bring to the subject is the fact that I am a Jew, and grew up at a moment of expanding acceptance of Jews as social equals, a direct result of the world's sympathy for Jews following the Holocaust.

Because of my people's unique history, I am instinctively wary of any group – whether a race, an ethnic group, a religion or a sex – that plays a dualistic hand, scapegoating an entire group to explain the unachieved goals of its own members.

For a scapegoating ideology always ends in grievance-collecting and a conspiracy theory of history. My people have been unusually vulnerable to conspiracy-theory evils over the centuries. It is presently in the midst of battling a particularly destructive and existentially threatening one.

Virtually all Arab and many other Muslim nations rely on Jew hatred to externalize an explanation for their own failures. It works very well. The world has not seen such a widespread and virulent strain of anti-Semitism dominating an entire region since the Nazi era. So I can say with the conviction bred of close scrutiny that I have no use for any ideology that lays all blame for the world's evils on any identifiable group.

* * *

I don't believe in re-inventing the wheel. In preparation for today's speech I decided to revisit my archives and trace the progress of those columns on issues in which I assigned direct or indirect blame for a social problem on feminist principles. So let me take you on a little stroll down my polemical Memory Lane.

I started writing intermittently for the *Post* in 2000, and on a weekly basis in 2003. For the first several years I wrote frequently about "bad girl culture": a column on children's hooker-wear – little girls dressing like Vegas show girls with the complicity and even active encouragement of their mothers; then one on young women at Ivy League universities starting porn magazines; and a few about the demeaning custom of "hooking up": guilt-free promiscuity with no emotional consequences, or rather none admitted.

I argued that what began for women as sexual liberation had degenerated into irresponsible, intimacy-anaesthetizing, sexual libertinism, an unhealthy trend for women and for society.

In its most delusional form, I cited what I considered a perfect media representation of the phenomenon: the 2001 movie *Bridget Jones*.

Bridget Jones was supposedly an update of *Pride and Prejudice*, Jane Austen's classic novel of a meeting of true minds. In the novel the dignified and witty Elizabeth Bennet captures the heart of the upright and gallant Mr. Darcy through her strong character, integrity and intelligence.

In the movie version Elizabeth has morphed into the ditzy Bridget Jones, an impulsive, chain-smoking slob of no discernible wit or understanding of human nature, available to any good-looking man who crosses her path. She is cute and sexy, nothing else.

Strangely, the modern Mr. Darcy character with whom Bridget ends up – completely unrealistically, of course because in real life such a man would never take her seriously – is in every way a faithful recreation of the original, an intelligent, refined man of taste, discernment and sexual restraint. My conclu-

43

sion: "Bridget Jones's and Mark Darcy's screen characters illuminate a curious postmodern gender disparity in moral standards…For the gentleman is a gentleman still, but the lady has become a tramp."

I moved on from there to the dramatic demographic consequences feminism has had on society.

As a result of feminists' promotion of career equity with men and unrestrained sexual experimentation over early and faithful commitment, women are having fewer children later, and many are having none. Consequently, birth rates are down in all western countries, in many below the replacement levels. Canada's 2010 fertility rate was 1.7 per woman, slightly ahead of China's 1.6.

Sadly, many women realize they want to have children, but too late. They were not warned by their Womens Studies teachers or by feminist commentators that a woman's peak fertility years are 15-25, or that late pregnancies carry elevated risks, or that induced abortions pose a risk of pre-term delivery in future pregnancies.

Abortion is now such a commonplace here that it is used as a backup form of birth control. Abortions in Quebec have doubled in the last 10 years: in 1998 16% of pregnancies resulted in abortion. Today 30% do. From 2000-2009, Statistics Canada reports that 491 late-term, born-alive abortions were performed in Canada. That means the intention was abortion, but since the baby was born alive and allowed to die, the actual procedure was something resembling negligent homicide. You don't have to be a religious Christian to find these facts disturbing.

All of these realities are directly traceable to feminist doctrine. Feminists' original goal may not have been the intention to preside over the actual demographic decline of western civilization. Their goal was to empower women. But as the old saying goes, when you are up to your neck in alligators, it's difficult to remember that your original intention was to drain the swamp.

I then turned my attention to the negative and far-ranging effects, of feminism on men.

Misandry, which is the female equivalent of misogyny (misanthropy is a hatred of humankind), is now entrenched in our public discourse, our education system and social services. Misandry flies beneath most people's radar, because we have become compliant in the acceptance of theories that have nothing to do with reality, and compliant in the speech codes that accompany that tendency.

Denigration of men in ways both casual and formal is a commonplace in society. Last Christmas I saw an advertisement for an "All men are bastards" butcher block knife holder in the shape of a man. The slot for the largest knife was placed in his groin. Hilarious? Imagine a knife holder in the shape of a woman and a knife slot at the vagina. Hilarious? Not so much. Once you become aware of the phenomenon, you will see it everywhere, trust me.

But misandry can also be implicit in what is not demonstrated in words or images. In March 2005, to give you a fleeting and seemingly trivial, but actually quite telling example, then Prime Minister Paul Martin eulogized four RCMP officers who had been slain in the course of duty. He said, "No matter the era, it seems that children always want to grow up to be police officers…It reflects a young heart's yearning to keep people safe and families whole."

This is of course nonsense. I wrote in a subsequent column: "If he had chosen his words for truth rather than gender-equity piety, Mr. Martin would have said, "No matter the era, it seems that *boys* always want to grow up to be police officers."

Little girls dream of many careers today, particularly the physically safe and prestigious fields of medicine and law and academia, but rarely of policing, or of any of the other "death professions," like fire fighting, military combat and construction. To "keep people safe and families whole" is a boy's life-risking ambition, and the tragic deaths of these four men cried out for acknowledgement of that noble male aspiration. But, to accommodate a politically correct falsehood, the PM simply airbrushed them out of their own narrative.

In fact there is only one day a year when men's heroism, gallantry and protective instincts are actively acknowledged and that is Remembrance Day. Even then the ceremony's wording is now gender-neutral, as if women and men made equal sacrifices on the battlefields of World War I and II, when in fact our female deaths in war under combat circumstances run in the single digits.

For overt misandry, one has only to survey the industry around domestic violence. You could be forgiven for thinking that domestic violence is a one-way street. That is certainly the impression one gets from the fact that there are innumerable tax-funded shelters for abused women, none for abused men, unlimited funds for campaigns to raise consciousness around abused women, none for abused men. There is not a single social services agency or charity in Canada advertising "family services" that offers counselling, shelter or legal services for men who have been physically abused by women.

And yet, as peer-reviewed community studies and Stats Canada attest, although under-reported, unprovoked violence by women against their domestic partners is equal to that of men in frequency and spontaneity, and almost equal in severity. Spousal homicides of either sex are so rare as to be statistically insignificant.

The tendency to violence in intimate relationships is bilateral and rooted in individual dysfunction. Men and women with personality disorders and/or family histories of violence are equally likely to be violent themselves, or seek violent partners.

But the academics who bring us these inconvenient truths are shunned. University of British Columbia psychology professor Don Dutton wrote the definitive book on intimate partner violence, *Rethinking Domestic Violence*, but after 25 years of impeccable scholarship, has yet to be invited to consult with any government agency or institution because influential feminist elites don't like his message.

When angry feminists adduce their mantra that only men are inherently violent and that women use violence only in self-defence, I bring up a question that is a forbidden topic in women's shelters: if men are the problem, how is it then that partner violence amongst lesbians is significantly higher than that found in heterosexual partnerships?

Moreover, if women are inherently non-violent, how is it that children are far more likely to be physically abused by their mothers than their fathers? And when they are, how can we justify a woman's right to take her children to a shelter to escape a violent husband when there is no shelter in the country that will accept a father with children fleeing an abusive mother?

I interviewed at length, by telephone and by e-mail, one woman with a degree in psychology who volunteered to help at a woman's shelter. She took part in a training program of some weeks' duration. She happened to be quite well read in the literature of domestic violence, and had in fact read Dr. Dutton's book. She attempted to raise the issue of bilateralism in group discussions. Her input was unwelcome. She told me that the supervisor became hostile to her, telling her, "You are too educated to work here," and she was asked to leave.

And thus, through institutionalized misandry and suppression of dissent, these questions are never addressed objectively or for that matter even raised in the media, and the truth remains hidden under a suffocating blanket of feminist correctness.

On the domestic violence front, nothing has provoked me to greater indignation than the exploitation by feminists of the 1989 Montreal Massacre of 14 women at the Polytechnic by sociopath Marc Lepine.

In 2006 I wrote:

> *In the massacre's wake, ideologues elevated Lepine's rampage from a random act by one disaffected individual into the gender equivalent of Kristallnacht or 9/11. A narrative evolved in which every woman be-*

came a potential victim of an organized, hate-driven enemy – like the Nazis or al-Qaeda – with the massacre as an ominous harbinger of more aggression to come.

Both male and female feminists colluded in promoting the myth of lone killer Lepine as the symbol of all males' innate hostility to women, however dormant it might be.

In a shameful, inflammatory broadside affirming generalized male responsibility, for example, a group called Montreal Men Against Sexism responded to the massacre with self-hating stereotyping inconceivable in the context of a similar crime committed by, say, a black or a Muslim: "Men kill women and children as a proprietary, vengeful and terrorist act ... with the support of a sexist society ... As pro-feminist men, we try to reveal and to end this continuing massacre."

What "continuing massacre"? Where are the copycats? There never was a female-only mass killing before Marc Lepine and there hasn't been one since. Women have been subjugated by men throughout history, but organized massacres of women by their own culture's males? Never.

Amongst other unjust and gender-divisive consequences of the massacre, the "White Ribbon" educational movement, initiated in 1991 as a direct response to it, and now integrated into more than 100 schools across Canada, sponsors a biased, error-riddled curriculum on domestic violence (read "violence against women by men").

A freak tragedy has thus become the misandric lens through which many Canadian children are taught to perceive gender relations.

Ritualized violence against women, such as wife beating, bride burnings or honour killings, is learned behaviour, a function of retrograde cultural notions of sexual relations. If such abhorrent behaviours were officially tolerated or encouraged here, then politicizing a particularly egregious example would be justified in order to end the practice.

But the complete reverse is the case. Officially and unofficially, virtually to a man and woman, Canadians schooled in our heritage culture utterly repudiate violence against women.

Ironically, the Montreal Massacre commemoration industry, whose emotive effect depends on scapegoating men, is having the opposite effect: For the sins of a few, the nature of half our polity is often falsely maligned, breeding suspicion and hostility in women, needless shame and guilt in all men, and mutual resentment and mistrust between the sexes.

47

Anti-male bias that affects men is of course morally wrong. But institutionalized bias that inculcates shame in children on the basis of their sex is scandalous and, when abetted by school boards and Children's Aid Societies, a serious stain on any democratic society.

In 2000 the Peel School Board in Ontario accepted a grant from the Ontario Ministry of Education and the Ontario Women's Directorate, specifically tied to programming around violence against women. Called *Breaking the Silence,* the project was construed as a teacher's guide for identifying and helping children who witness violence in the home.

If the teachers followed the guidelines, however, they would only be alert to children whose fathers abused their mothers – not the other way around – as witness the following representative statements from the pamphlet: "Women abuse is a serious problem"; "Violence against women is a crime; it is never justified or acceptable"; "Woman abuse is about a husband or partner controlling a woman's behaviour and may condemn a woman and her children to suffer in silence"; "Children who witness violence in the home may feel guilty for not protecting their mother"; "In Ontario, as many as six women are murdered each month by their current or former male partner."

Did you believe that last statement? That absurd "statistic" symbolizes the fecklessness of the entire enterprise, implying that Ontario saw "as many as" 72 women murdered by their male partners in 2000. In 2000 the *national* spousal homicide total was 67!

So where did the Ontario Women's Directorate's one-sided findings on domestic violence come from, which the board accepted for the pamphlet without demur? Not from peer-reviewed community studies like Don Dutton's or from StatsCan.

No, the Peel Board simply downloaded information provided by three women's shelters about whom the most charitable thing one can say regarding their bogus "research" is that it is uncredentialed, guilty of selection bias, ideologically driven, patently skewed, and utterly unreliable.

Breaking the Silence encourages teachers to assume – and in a trickledown way, communicate to children – that females won't be held responsible for any violence they initiate, that males' characters are inherently worse than females', and that the pain of all children who witness abuse of their father by their mother, or who themselves suffer abuse by their mother, is socially inadmissible. *Breaking the Silence* is the misandric equivalent of racism: "We" are blameless; "they" cause trouble.

For another example, last September I wrote about RUCS – Routine Universal Comprehensive Screening – a protocol now in place in 25 Ontario health units. According to this protocol, girls of 12 or older are routinely asked when they enter these units for any reason whatsoever whether they have been sexually abused, in order to pro-actively offer them therapeutic help. But boys are not asked the same question, even though boys are sexually abused as often as girls in childhood.

The protocol has even won the recognition of the Registered Nurses' Association of Ontario as a "best practice." I asked the nurses' spokesperson why they didn't serve boys. I got nothing but evasive responses. In one case the spokesperson said the sexual abuse of boys was "understudied." In my column I wrote:

> *Yet after a brief Google search I had no trouble finding credible peer-reviewed research that attested to the fact that boys are abused but tend to under-report it, and that it is unprofessional not to offer help. Boys desperately need the therapeutic outreach RUCS only offers girls.*
>
> *Don't the 137,000 registered nurses of Ontario have sons, brothers, nephews? How is it that not one of them felt shame enough to object to this blatant discrimination? How can any public institution in conscience allow an entire sex to be disqualified from a possibly helpful therapeutic encounter in the full knowledge that these boys are equally liable to abuse as girls – and not only from males; about 20% of sexual abuse of boys is perpetrated by women. Again, is there any other identity group one can think of in society against whom such an insult would be tolerated?*

One final note: The legal definition of a child is anyone under the age of sixteen, and the CAS is mandated to protect all children's rights. Yet the London CAS director sat on the task force that recommended RUCS, and no CAS voice has ever been raised in opposition to it.

Finally I want to talk about the implosion of the traditional family, which can be directly traced to feminism's repudiation of normative marriage and the role of fathers as vital to a child's psychological well-being.

In June 2006 I wrote about the imbalance, in women's favour, in the family law system: the vast majority of contested custody suits end in sole custody awarded to the mother. Even when the mother is not awarded sole custody, she is often awarded *control* over the children. On paper there seems to be more equality. But in fact there isn't.

For example, when you see the words "joint custody," you may be inclined to think that both parents are contributing to decisions around the children and are spending equal time with the children, but that is not the case.

The words "joint custody" are followed by "with primary residency," which almost always means the children are living with the mother. That also means the father has "access" rights, but not the right to decide where the children go to school, or what sports they take part in, etc. In other words, the *language* has evolved around custody, but the new words do nothing to equalize "control" of the children; mothers still control the children in about 90% of cases. Only "shared equal parenting" – a policy long promised, but not yet actually realised – conveys the reality of two parents with equal input into their children's lives.

The family law system is now systemically colonized by radical feminists. Their goal is the incremental legal eclipse of men's influence over women's spheres of "identity" interests, which includes children. To that end the custody issue has become a front line in the gender wars, supported by all feminist academics and institutional elites, by supine cabinet ministers and by feminist judges.

To illustrate with just a few examples:

- Supreme Court of Canada chief justice Beverley McLachlin: "We have to be pro-active in rearranging the Canadian family";

- Feminist psychologist Peter Jaffe, a social-context educator of family court judges: "[J]oint custody is an attempt of males to continue dominance over females";

- And most egregiously, this from the National Association of Women and the Law: "Courts may treat parents unequally and *deny them basic civil liberties and rights, as long as their motives are good.*"

Here we are truly in George Orwell country. In simple words this statement means "The end justifies the means" and there is not a totalitarian regime in the world that does not espouse that exact excuse for their denial of rights to their citizens.

In our courts the "good" that motivates them is supposedly the child's "best interests," but in fact it is virtually always the mother's happiness. Indeed, Justice Rosalie Abella is on record with her definition of the "best interests of the child" meaning whatever makes the "residential parent happy". Surely if we are really considering the "best interests of the child," we would turn that dictum on its head, affirming that whatever makes the children happy should make both the residential and the non-residential parent happy.

Their efforts have not gone unnoticed. Eminent lawyer and civil libertarian Eddie Greenspan notes: "Feminists have entrenched their ideology in the Supreme Court of Canada and have put all contrary views beyond the pale"; Liberal MP Roger Galloway, who chaired the 1998 Report of the Special Joint

Committee on Child Custody and Access, has commented that "Justice, if it occurs in a divorce court, is accidental."

Misandry in family law arises from an ideology that views children as the property of women, even though many peer-reviewed studies show children want and need both parents, and no studies show sole parenting by a mother serves children's best interests.

This ideology is instilled in judges during training sessions devised at the National Institute for Justice, featuring feminism-driven materials, and subsequently often plays out as an unaccountable kangaroo courtroom.

The result is that an adversarial mother who initiates a divorce against the will of the father – however indifferent her parenting skills, however superb his, and even if the children spend their days with nannies or day care workers – pretty well has a lock on control of the children.

If a woman makes a false allegation of abuse in order to have a man barred from the house, or denies rightful access to the father, she will never be punished at all. This happens regularly; any unsubstantiated claim of abuse or *even voicing her fear of abuse* by a woman will be acted upon instantly by the police and the courts with no recourse for the man.

Conversely, if a man withholds support money, even if he has lost his job and has no other means of paying, he will be criminalized. His picture as a "deadbeat dad" may appear on government-sanctioned Internet sites, and if he goes to jail, as is likely, he will serve a longer sentence than cocaine dealers. The sentence for both is 30 days, but the cocaine dealer usually serves only two thirds of the sentence, while dads in arrears automatically serve the whole sentence.

The family law system is premised on the feminist theory that fathers are of no special importance to children. And yet every credible sociological study on record demonstrates without ambiguity that if there is a single sure indicator for success in adulthood, it is the presence of a father in a child's life from the time he or she is old enough to negotiate a path through the world beyond her doorstep.

If there is a sure indicator of failure – dropping out, drugs, promiscuity, crime – it is not poverty, it is fatherlessness in later childhood and adolescence.

But ideologues don't care about statistics, and they don't pay attention to the United Nations Conventions on the Rights of Children, which states that every child has the right to know and love his biological father and mother. Ideologues care about theory, and according to the one they favour, women don't need men, and children don't need fathers.

Children, on the other hand, are natural conservatives and are impervious to ideological brainwashing. They mourn the lost connection to their fathers. I get a lot of mail from heartbroken fathers who have lost their children to women-friendly courts that heartlessly and self-righteously, thinking they are doing good, cut fathers out of their children's lives. Reading these tragic narratives is the toughest part of my job. Their stories haunt me.

In one story a social worker asked a child in an assessment interview (the following was read to me from an actual transcript): "What's the best thing and the worst thing about your father no longer living [at home]?" The best thing? Why this leading question? Can you conceive of a social worker asking that question about a mother of a child being raised primarily by a father?

Fortunately children don't read or care about feminist scripts. As the "worst thing", that particular pre-adolescent girl responded, "I don't have a father." And the "best thing"?

"Nothing."

Peter Jaffe, the feminist psychologist I mentioned earlier, makes a very good living from sitting on feminist task forces, collaborating on writing feminism-driven guidelines for judges, keynoting conferences on domestic violence against women and so forth, because he says the things feminists (and therefore governments) want to hear.

Jaffe sat on the 2001 task force that recommended the girls-only RUCS protocol, even though he is also an expert on the sexual abuse of boys, and better than anyone understands the injustice of the protocol.

I interviewed him and asked him – a father of four boys, by the way – about this apparent conflict of interest.

He admitted that he would not have sat on that task force today, as he no longer agrees with the outcome. Did he think that the feminist pendulum had swung too far, I asked. Yes, he said, and I quote, "Men find themselves today very much in the position that women used to."

I said to him, "You know, Peter, you are respected by feminists. You would do the men of this country a great service if you wrote a letter to the editor when my column appears and say to all of Canada what you just said to me."

Of course he didn't, and I regret his cowardice, for such a letter might have gone far to effect a necessary reconciliation between the sexes in this country.

There is a Yiddish expression my mother used to invoke with a philosophical sigh, "The 'reidele dreht sich'" – the wheel turns. A hundred years ago, it was homosexual love that dared not speak its name. Today homosexual love roars, and it is manliness that whispers in the shadows.

Goethe said: "All theory is grey, but green springs the golden tree of life." The time for zero-sum theories – if your sex wins, mine loses – is past. Men's voices needn't be silenced for women's to be heard. We need more conversation, less monologue.

Only one voice should be privileged by everyone: the still, small voice of conscience. Conscience leads away from sexism and toward humanism. Humanism leads to mutual respect and trust between the sexes. And collaboration between the sexes leads to the "golden tree of life" we should all be striving toward – a healthy society.

The Pro-Life Movement's Communication Problem

I delivered this talk at Western University to the Kings College "Live for Life Club" December 5, 2008.

Thank you for the honour of the invitation that has brought us together. This is the first time I have ever addressed a pro-life group, and I am grateful for the opportunity to exchange views with you.

When Anne [Culligan] first approached me about a speaking engagement, I was quite taken aback, as I naturally assumed that a pro-life group would not wish to listen to someone who doesn't unequivocally share the group's ideological position on abortion.

Then it occurred to me that she was not aware of precisely what "camp" I represent. I don't allude to my own beliefs in my abortion-themed columns, because they are more about freedom of speech and conscience and the injustice of allowing one "correct" view to dominate the public forum than about the morality of abortion.

But, since few journalists are sympathetic to pro-lifers, I realized I might have given the impression that I was ideologically partisan simply for defending pro-lifers' right to be heard.

In my several columns on abortion this year, I condemned Canada's (historically unique) lack of any abortion law. In one I drew attention to the ignorance around the physical effects of abortion and women's right to informed consent, which they do not presently enjoy; in another I denounced the Ontario Human Rights Commission for demanding that physicians "leave their personal

55

beliefs outside the surgery" as unacceptable coercion of the private conscience of the individual; and in a third I spoke against the ideology-driven awarding of an Order of Canada to a fanatic who not only enjoys (what should be) demoralizing work far too much for most Canadians' comfort, but one who has profited hugely in material terms from his political activism.

But in fact, although I am sympathetic to the frustration felt by pro-lifers whose voices have been suppressed on campus and ignored in the media (except for negative exposure), I am by no means an activist for ending legal abortion. I made this clear to Anne, extending her the opportunity to withdraw the invitation with no offence taken on my part.

Instead she graciously accepted my offer to speak of common values between pro-lifers and cultural reformists like myself. I say "cultural reformist," but in fact people like me – and there are millions – have no name, and we aren't organized into a movement as you are. Many amongst us have not even articulated our feelings.

What we do know is that we are disturbed by a culture that has become so detached from natural law and common sense that it sets its highest value on women when they repudiate their defining contribution to the world, and implies an adversarial relationship between women's self-realization and childbearing.

When I say "detached from natural law" I speak of a detachment from basic moral principles such as the respect for life – one's own and others – that constitutes the founding principle of our heritage culture, a principle that precedes all political authority and speaks to our inherent sense of justice.

We have watched with dismay as what used to be a matter of conscience, undertaken with emotional anguish and a heavy heart, has now become dumbed down to a service of convenience, often a form of retroactive birth control, to which no real thought or moral consideration is given.

We would like to see legislative constraints on abortion – beginning with an outright ban on the abomination of partial-birth abortion. Ideally we would like to be part of a society in which abortion is rare and regretfully undertaken – in short, a culture of life.

So I am here to talk about our common ground. As you make progress in promoting a culture of life, so will we. But if we are to join forces at any level, we need to share a communications template acceptable to both of us for expressing our common views in the national forum.

I began to take a serious interest in the abortion debate because of a personal experience.

Our dear friends' daughter had her first baby almost four years ago. Two years later, she became pregnant again, but her 12-week ultrasound showed no heartbeat. The fetus had died, but she had not miscarried.

She then underwent an induced abortion, which is the standard procedure for that situation. Last year she became pregnant again but it was not an easy pregnancy and she spent most of it on bed rest. She was told she was at high risk for a premature birth.

Curious, I started reading up on premature birth and to my surprise discovered that a previous induced abortion raises the risk of a premature birth in a subsequent pregnancy. More than one induced abortion significantly raises the risk for extreme premature birth. And extreme premature birth – delivery at fewer than 28 weeks gestation – is irrefutably associated with the risk of Cerebral Palsy.

Meanwhile, a friend of this young woman in the same situation *had* done her research and refused to have an induced abortion when her fetus died. Instead she waited to miscarry, because she knew about the link between induced abortion and the risk to future pregnancy.

Our friend's story had a happy ending – against almost all odds, their daughter carried to term and they have a beautiful eight-month old healthy baby granddaughter – but their anger – and by extension mine – over their ignorance did not go away.

Why wasn't this common knowledge, I wondered. I checked on pro-choice and abortion clinic websites. There is no mention of this link.

So I sent a young woman posing as a potential client to the Morgentaler Clinic as well as another abortion clinic to see if any doctor there would mention it. But even though she asked again and again if there was a risk attached to the abortion (she had trouble getting a doctor even to consult with her at all), she was assured that she could have multiple abortions with no risk to a future pregnancy.

It was then I realized that ideological fervour in the feminist movement was actually suppressing information that women have a right to know. It was then I realized that unlike all other medical procedures, women were submitting to abortions without informed consent.

The more I researched, the more physical and psychological risks to women I discovered associated with abortion that abortion providers do not tell their patients. It dawned on me that abortion is the only surgical procedure in which the practitioners are not disinterested; quite the opposite.

So even though I cannot join you in demanding the complete abolition of abortion, we both feel indignation over abortion's misrepresentation as safe and innocent by the abortion industry.

Up to now your campaigns have been of the purist variety. Basically your message is: "Abortion is morally wrong. Stop doing it." You haven't made much headway with that message. You haven't engaged the attention, let alone the sympathy, of the 95% of Canadians who don't believe, like you, that abortion should be "illegal in all circumstances."

Two clichés spring to mind here. The first is that politics is the art of the possible. Outlawing abortion altogether is impossible in this country for the foreseeable future. And the other cliché is that perfection is the enemy of the good.

So today, while appreciating that your efforts have been bent on realizing your ultimate wish – perfection – that is, to see abortion prohibited, I want to speak to you about achieving what is both possible and good.

Achieving what is possible and good does not mean compromising your beliefs. I respect them. Those of us who claim to believe in the sanctity of human life, yet condone abortion, even those of us who only condone it under narrowly specific circumstances, must admit that your view is the only purely intellectually consistent position. Ours is not, and in recent years scientific advances have removed the complacency that used to accompany our inconsistency.

In the old days pro-choicers comforted themselves with the notion that sentient, or recognizably human life only began in the second trimester. Now, between the revelations of DNA – every fetus's DNA is unique – and ultrasounds, we can no longer entertain that myth. It is settled fact that life in the scientific sense begins at conception. So we agree on that.

Here's where it gets a little murky. Your instinct is to explain God's contingent-free wishes to man. My instinct – and I think I probably speak for many others – is to explain the complexity of life here below, never contingency-free, to God.

It is a natural instinct to think first of ourselves, then of the well-being of those whom we love and who love us back, before we consider our allegiance to those we can only imagine as future intimates, but who cannot imagine us back.

We see the indifference and apparent randomness with which nature ends life in the womb. We are creatures of limited imagination: The child is real, the fetus is abstract.

None of you have children yet, I presume. It is only when one actually becomes a parent that one begins to appreciate the excruciatingly fierce attachment that develops between you and your child, an attachment that begins with the fetus *in utero*, then soars beyond our previous ability to imagine after birth. You thought you loved your fetus; only when you are holding a born child do you see the chasm between the two loves. It is very sad to miscarry a fetus; but it is an unbearable and lifelong grief to lose a child.

It is humanly natural to act according to a hierarchy of virtue that takes its ethical cue from *the circumstances in which we find ourselves at the moment of decision.*

Like you, we consider all life to be sacred as a general rule, but unlike you, we recognize that holding a principle sacred does not eliminate the need to make difficult choices.

For example, in wartime, we do not consider the killing of enemy soldiers murder. Even the targeted killing of terrorist leaders is now an uncontroversial commonplace. And until recently our western civilization was comfortable with the death penalty as justice for those who took human life.

History constantly reminds us that desperate circumstances prompt desperate choices.

In their nomadic days the Inuit abandoned the frail and aged in order that the others could go on without encumbrances that might endanger the entire group. Perhaps you have heard stories of babies in the Holocaust who were suffocated by their mothers' hands so their cries would not draw the attention of storm troopers to their hiding places and expose all who were there to certain death.

Comrades in arms answer to an exceptional ethical imperative under certain circumstances. A mortally wounded soldier asks his buddy to kill him so he won't be tortured as he is dying by the enemy. His buddy, who can rescue himself, but not his comrade, complies in a mercy killing. Dare we call him immoral?

These examples tell us that the principle of the sanctity of life may be absolute in theory, but that life is messy. Bio-ethical quandaries abound.

The touchstone is the word "survival." When another individual's survival threatens your own or the survival of those you owe a prior duty to, we see an ethical dilemma that must be settled according to the individual conscience. And this – the lesser of two perceived – I won't say evils, rather I would call them perceived intolerable outcomes – is the position most religions take too.

And for us, in exceptional circumstances, that may lead to privileging one's own "survival," however that is interpreted by the individual, as ethically admissible. Oh yes, there is that famous slippery slope, which we are on for precisely that reason, precisely because of the temptation to subsume transient and trivial desires into the word, but that is what legislation is for, and that is why we need an abortion law.

These are perceptions leading to moral distinctions you may disagree with, even be repulsed by, but if you are not prepared to grant some degree of respect to those who accept a hierarchy in the sanctity of human life, the point of view of most Canadians, you will remain outliers in the national discussion.

As a Jew, I perhaps come at the question of abortion with a kind of built-in difference of perception. One reason may be that the Old Testament, as you would call the Bible, makes no mention of abortion. There are 613 commandments in the Torah, the Five Books of Moses, with more than half of them negative prohibitions, yet none proscribes abortion. True, there is the proscription not to commit murder, but not a single rabbi in the history of Judaism has ever applied that injunction to a fetus.

Historically Judaism sees life beginning at birth, and even then – because the mortality rate for infants was so high before modern times – a newborn was not granted legal personhood. As a matter of fact, according to Jewish law, a stillborn baby is not given a funeral. Only a baby that dies after 30 days of life is granted the legal distinction of personhood, and accorded the ritual ceremonies of a community member.

So there is an irony in my culture. For Jews life is paramount, and saving a life – *pikuach nefesh* is the actual Hebrew phrase – overrides all other commandments and proscriptions. But a "life" always means the one who is already living. Thus in Jewish law there is never a conflict between the life of the mother or the fetus; it is always the mother's life that is privileged.

Interestingly, abortion is a kind of orphan topic in the Jewish community, and virtually never discussed from the pulpit. I have attended Orthodox, Conservative and liberal synagogues all my life, and never once heard the topic addressed by a rabbi in a sermon.

So, as an aside, preparing for this talk has encouraged me to consider writing about that strange lacuna. For example, I discovered that according to Jewish law, partial-birth abortion is impermissible, because if any part of a baby is born alive, then it is against Jewish law not to make every effort to save the baby.

Why have rabbis not spoken out against this practice? I will pose that question in a future column. My theme might be that here is an interesting possibility for an alliance on a single issue – abortion carried out during a live birth. (I would encourage you to petition Orthodox rabbis to stand up for the abolition of that practice.)

Given that it is impossible to re-criminalize abortion, what are the best uses of your time and resources as an advocacy group?

My advice would be to redirect your efforts toward a goal that is possible: going positive. You remember the fable of the Sun and the Wind and their bet about who could make the man take off his coat. My advice would be to aim at being the Sun rather than, as you are perceived now, as the Wind.

I want to conclude with the Sun – our common ground – so let us first get the "Wind" out of the way. In terms of being the wind, making people wrap their coats more firmly against you, I cannot think of anything more damaging amongst educated observers to the pro-life cause than the Genocide Awareness Project (GAP) campaign, which draws a moral equivalence between abortion and the Holocaust.

I know that your goal with the GAP campaign is to force people to see the shocking nature of the violence done to the fetus in the act of abortion. Personally, I feel quite sure that you turn off more people than you persuade with this technique, but it is your right to show these images and admissible as freedom of speech. What is not ethically admissible is rhetorical distortion.

What is not admissible is to co-opt as a parallel to your cause for emotional effect a tragedy that offers neither logical nor moral nor historical basis for such linkage. You cannot build an argument on an analogy alone. In any debate emotional arousal must be subordinated to rational persuasion.

Why is the GAP campaign intellectually flawed? Because it extrapolates one detail from the Holocaust – numbers killed – the most inconsequential detail, by the way, and on that basis alone proclaims a moral equivalence. It puts you in the same dubious camp as PETA, whose analogy of the slaughter of cows and chickens for food with the Holocaust is, I am sure you would agree, extremely offensive. But they defend their campaign on the same grounds you do – that a lack of respect and empathy for any form of life can lead to a coarsening contempt for those we consider inferior beings and from contempt to indifference to their suffering.

The point of the Holocaust is not the number of lives extinguished. Genocides come in many numbers. Six million, three million, one million, 50,000: It isn't the numbers that make it a genocide. It is ideology-based *hatred* – unchecked hatred and its consequences that is the point of genocide, the hatred of innocent people whose only crime is their tribal, racial or religious identity. It is the hunting down and systematic extermination of one group of people by another. It is the support for that hatred and extermination by the followers of the murderous group in power.

On what basis can we compare the Holocaust to abortion? Fetuses do not belong to an identity group. Nor are they hated as a group by another group.

There is no politically sanctioned "order" to kill all fetuses of a certain size or weight or characteristic. Every single abortion in this country is an individual choice made by an individual woman. There is no public, central killing ground where the violence against the victims is used as a bonding agent for the persecutors.

A woman who aborts a fetus is not cheering on the killing of other fetuses. Nor does she "hate" her own. What she hates is the burden of responsibility the fetus represents for her future. She is simply choosing her particular interests over that of the fetus. In the Holocaust it served nobody's interest to eliminate Jews. They weren't a burden to the state, they were valuable contributors to the state. Their extermination served only to satisfy the sadism of viciously anti-Semitic Nazi elites for whom Jews were vermin polluting the Aryan racial strain.

Furthermore, most women who have abortions do go on to have children that they love. If it were all fetuses they hated, no woman who aborts would ever have children. Nazis did not kill some Jews, and cultivate friendships with others.

You are not only describing the action of abortion as evil in this comparison, you are comparing the women who have abortions to Nazis. Naziism is an evil ideology, and Nazis were not just wrong, they were the embodiment of evil. There is neither truth nor dignity in accusing women of such moral turpitude.

So you see, there is not a single moral parallel between the situations. And that is why it is not in your interest to pursue it. Or in our mutual interest, because it stands in the way of an alliance between us.

I wonder if those who think the GAP campaign is a good idea have really assessed the damaging image it creates in intelligent observers' minds. It marks you as people who feel passionately, but who do not think clearly. Feeling deeply and thinking irrationally are the marks of extremists and conspiracy theorists.

The result – and I think this is a very grave consequence for any movement – is that thoughtful, educated people do not take you seriously. They do not respect your strategies for persuasion. You must consider whether the shock and emotional impact of your message is so important to you that it is worth burning the narrow but sturdy bridge you could be using to reach people like me.

By contrast, if you made the analogy of a genocide to abortions done in the name of sex selection, you would be on firmer ground, because sex selection is a form of bias – arguably even a form of hatred – against an identifiable group.

Immigrant groups here in Canada are more or less openly practicing this gendercide, and it is widely practiced in other countries. Feminists are conflicted about condemning the practice without seeming to deny women their precious "choice." By exposing their cowardice and hypocrisy, you would be addressing a serious moral crime most Canadians would be happy to see legally constrained. Here is an area you should press hard on.

*　*　*

What does it mean to be the Sun? It means that you would concentrate on issues that do not pit you against pro-choicers on moral grounds, but on rational, scientific grounds. You would shake women from their passivity on the subject and "warm" them into taking an active role in their reproductive health.

So it seems to me that this is where your communication efforts should go. Away from the rights of the fetus, which arouses defensiveness and hostility, and toward the rights of women, which up to now has been staked out as the moral high ground of the pro-choicers.

Pro-choicers talk about "A woman's right to choose." This is rhetorically a very strong position, because "rights" is a very charged word. So to be against abortion is to be against women's rights, or at least that is how the debate is currently framed.

But the cooptation of "rights" as the issue is a vulnerable one, because it implies that women have only one consideration at stake: choice or no choice. In fact, there should be many rights in play, some of which conflict with the pro-choicers' message, rights that you are ideally placed to address.

Therefore I believe that your message should take back the word "rights." You should counter "A woman's right to choose" with: "A woman's right to informed consent," "A woman's right to optimal reproductive health," "A woman's right to self-respect," "A woman's right to avoid regret" – and I am sure you can think of many others.

The beauty of such a campaign is that it is one I – and many others for whom fairness is an important value – would willingly join you in promoting. This would raise your profile in the community as cooperative consensus-builders rather than as anti-women extremists.

How can any campus union have the gall to stop an information session that positively frames its message as concern for women's health and well-being? If you focused the debate on women's health, you would then occupy the moral high ground feminists claim as their particular precinct.

Feminists are making the claim that abortion is good for women, because they only attach one virtue to it – abortion gives a woman her freedom from responsibility – and yes, it certainly does that.

But what if women who assume abortion is a safe option knew the long list of known and suspected health deficits – physical and psychological – that are associated with women who have even one abortion, as well as the known risks for the wanted children in future pregnancies?

So that is the principal strategy I would suggest. Shift the discussion from sympathy for the rights of the fetus to sympathy for the rights of *women* who are presently being kept ignorant and who are in fact being used as guinea pigs.

Aspiration abortion – the most common method for abortion – uniquely amongst surgical interventions, has never been tested for safety on animals. I think many women would be quite bothered by that fact. We should call upon abortion proponents to open the door to this crucial information. If you did that, you might find that objective media observers, and not only Christian ideologues, would support such an initiative. I certainly would.

Of course there would be a backlash. Of course feminists would attempt to discredit your sources. Which means that you must have available only the most unassailable evidence: all peer-reviewed, all credible sources. But you do have that.

Focus too on the *"Juno"* approach. In that movie we saw a very positive message – that there is no need to have an abortion where there is no shame, and that carrying to term is a gift for a loving would-be mother.

Before 1970 an unwed pregnancy could literally ruin a girl's life and make her a social pariah, not to mention stigmatizing the child's life. I remember those days, and some girls at my school whose lives were devastated by an unwanted pregnancy. That used to be the one unassailable argument for legalizing abortion. But, as this movie in which a young girl's parents, friends and community accept Juno's pregnancy with equanimity makes clear, that era is long gone.

Not only is there no shame in having a child, single motherhood has become chic. We need not approve of that, but the point is that if there is no shame, where is the pressing need? We saw this reality exemplified in the case of the pregnant daughter of 2008 Republican vice-presidential candidate Sarah Palin. In the old days, that pregnancy would have been a barrier to her mother's political candidacy. At the very least, the daughter would have been whisked out of sight, possibly sent to an Unwed Mothers' home, as they did in my youth.

But there she was, not in the least bit embarrassed, front and centre, greeting all America, accepted by her family and the entire Christian community. In her case, she chose to marry the father. If she had chosen to adopt out the baby, that decision would also have been supported.

We should be calling for better pre-natal and post-natal care for women who carry to term and adopt out their babies. They should feel the warmth of social approval. We should work towards advancing the image of the pregnant woman who carries to term as heroic, socially useful and admirable.

In short, be the Sun, not the Wind, and let your warmth draw Canadians like me closer to your cause

Anti-Male Bias in the Media

This was my contribution to a March, 2009 panel discussion in Ottawa entitled: "Freedom of Speech: Restoring respect, truth and civility to the public square," sponsored by the Neeje Association for Women and Family.

Media bias is not a unitary phenomenon. Some media bias is good: when, that is, it is confined to the opinion pages or one-sided blogs or openly dedicated advocacy magazines, cable channels and so forth. A healthy society welcomes a variety of biases freely expressed in the appropriate forums.

The kinds of media bias that we should find disturbing are: unintended bias through ignorance which results in misleading or unfactual statements presented as objective truth; routine negative stereotyping presented as received wisdom; intended bias presented as objective reporting rather than as opinion; and bias springing from an absence of information – intentionally or unintentionally – that results in discriminatory treatment of an individual or group.

Misandry in the media is well represented on all those fronts, and most of my talk will simply be examples that speak for themselves.

I've chosen to speak of this particular area – bias against men in the media – for several reasons: Because the general topic of media bias is far too vast a subject for a single panel presentation; because it is a subject I have come to know very well and one I monitor closely; and because other kinds of bias – liberal, conservative, anti-American and other political types of bias – are already widely commented on. Misandry is a subject that flies well below the mainstream media radar, and in fact is what you might call an orphan topic.

67

We live in an age in which the media are scrupulously rigorous in self-censoring when it comes to the terrible social crime of offending women, gays, people of colour and natives. Only one identifiable group – white heterosexual men (if they're Christian, so much the better) – is considered fair game for overt collective prejudice.

Except for radio talk shows, where real people with no ideological axe to grind control the agenda, misandry is ubiquitous in the media – and by media I mean all kinds: advertisements, sitcoms, films, political ads, TV talk shows, social service agency websites and billboards, and of course the punditocracy.

Sometimes the prejudice is benign, sometimes it is actively hostile.

For a benign example, take health issues. We're inundated with breast cancer ads in hugely disproportionate numbers to prostate cancer ads, which is highly preventable when caught early and kills in equal measure. One could argue that the popular media's imbalance of articles towards women's health is a question of supply and demand, but a search of more than 3,000 medical journals – and professional journals also count as media – listed in Index Medicus found that for every one article on men's health issues, there were 23 articles for women's health issues.

For an overtly hostile example, here is mainstream writer Nora Ephron, ironically a revered romantic comedy writer – she scripted *When Harry met Sally*, and *Sleepless in Seattle* – pontificating April 20 in the *Huffington Post* blog on the subject of the American political primaries:

> *"This is an election about whether the people of Pennsylvania hate blacks more than they hate women. And when I say people, I don't mean people, I mean white men…the outcome of the general election will depend on whether enough of them vote for McCain. A lot of them will: white men cannot be relied on, as all of us know who have spent a lifetime dating them…"* It goes on in this vein.

Her claim is absurd. Blacks and blue-collar white women vote as bloc-ishly as white men, so why the anger at white men? It's unseemly, and yet it went completely unremarked. Apply the same words to black men or women and watch the sparks fly. Of course no mainstream writer would ever say these things of blacks or women. They know better.

As a print journalist, my particular interest is my own peer group, many of whom echo Ephron's gratuitous contempt for men. While most male writers take up journalism because they are news or political junkies, a good many women journalists have entered the field specifically as women with a feminist axe to grind.

That's not quite the same as spreading a conservative or liberal or libertarian message, where you attack a line of thinking, not actual people. Urging feminism on readers and viewers is tantamount to spreading misandry, for feminism as it is ideologically conceived and played out in society today evokes zero-sum thinking and the conspiracy-theory temptation. When women succeed, it is because they are superior; when they fail, it is because they have been thwarted by men.

Male writers who try to defend men from anti-male bias or who criticize feminist ideology find it a very impolitic career move if they are not already well established. I personally know two excellent male writers, probably Canada's most under-utilized researchers, who can't get a media foothold because they critique feminism.

But there is virtually no public awareness of the hostility on overt display, which is another way of saying that misandry is such an acceptable form of cultural bias that people fail to perceive it when they hear it, read it, or see it.

Identifying active misandry is easy. One has only to imagine the same words, image or falsehood or failure to report attached to any other identifiable group, and the imbalance becomes clear.

Once you decide to take conscious notice of the problem, media bias in a myriad of forms leaps out at you. Positive images of women are ubiquitous; positive images of manly men are uncommon. Generally speaking, men are portrayed as objects of scorn or wrath.

The cumulative message the media sends is that if men try hard to meet criteria established by women as lovers, husbands and fathers, they can hope to achieve status as contributors to women's and children's happiness, though on the whole unnecessary to it.

But all too often they are portrayed as active agents of women's and children's unhappiness. Women who rid themselves of these bad eggs are portrayed as heroic. Promiscuous women in films like *Bridget Jones* and TV sitcoms like *Sex and the City* present as warm, loyal and liberated. The promiscuous men in these stories are depicted as shallow, untrustworthy and opportunistic.

When men are characterized as heroic fathers in films, it is usually because the woman has fled the scene or died, a paradigm that debuted with the 1979 film, *Kramer vs Kramer*. That is, men are only allowed to present as good parental role models when they are desperately trying to fill the shoes of a mother. It is a role they must learn. In movies with couples, it is rare for the father's parenting skills to outshine the mother's, whose commitment and skills present as inherent.

69

The past few years have seen a spate of "baby" movies: *Juno, Waitress, Knocked Up, Baby Mama, Then She Found Me*. All have in common women protagonists challenged by fertility issues or inconvenient pregnancies they choose not to terminate. In every case the elective mother may have foibles, but she is on the whole mature, smart and responsible.

The men are undesirable parent material, lumps of animated clay to be tossed away, or spun and shaped by a woman potter into a domestically useful artefact. These potential or accidental fathers range from the merely wimpy to infantile to explicitly abusive. None of the films express reservations about a child's future with no father.

The most disturbing aspects of media misandry revolve around the issue of domestic violence, which is, apart from custody, the hottest of the hot button issues for demonizers and myth busters alike.

The Ontario Human Rights Code bars "discrimination via signs or symbols," but I doubt any charges of discrimination will be laid against the Canadian Womens Foundation, which last year carpet-bombed the media with this misandric ad:

One sees here a family – divided on a sofa – a sullen, rather menacing father staring defiantly at the camera on one side, a waifish, stressed-looking mother shielding anxious children on the other.

The written message is: "No one should have to live with abuse." But the real message is "No *woman* should have to live with abuse." This is received wisdom in the media: Domestic Violence is only perpetrated by men, who are by nature disposed to controlling behaviours, while women and children (an inseparable unit) are always innocent victims.

The ad represents a half-truth and therefore a lie. The truth, established by all credible, peer-reviewed research, including StatsCan, is that unprovoked intimate-partner violence is about equally split between men and women.

Imagine another ad based on a half-truth: a woman on one side of the sofa, a man protecting children or even his aged mother on the other, because women abuse the elderly and their children more frequently than men do. You never will see such an ad. Media bias against men is as notable for what you don't see and hear as for what you do.

(Update: in the fall of 2012, the Canadian Women's Federation ran another fear-mongering ad featuring a baby shower gift of a "rape whistle" that claimed *one in two* women would suffer sexual or physical assault in her lifetime. I was the only journalist to challenge that absurd and contextless figure.)

The propaganda machine is abetted by feminist politicians. A case in point is a recent Quebec ad sponsored by the provincial government which perpetuated the false claim – based on a poll about *perception* of risk rather than actual incidents – that one in three women will be the victim of a sexual assault in her lifetime, not much more credible than the Canadian Women's Federation figure, but still wide of the real mark, which is more like one in seven, with one man in six running the same risk. This debunked figure reappears time and again, recently in a *pro forma* public letter by Michael Ignatieff to commemorate the Montreal Massacre.

The worst case I have yet seen of blatant Domestic Violence-related aggression in the media is some bus ads that appeared on and inside Dallas Area Rapid Transit buses last November (2008). In one panel a little black girl staring sombrely out at the viewer says: "One day my husband will kill me;" in another a young white boy says: "When I grow up, I will beat my wife."

All news stories of violence against women are seized upon as proof of what feminists see as a pandemic. No event was more successfully parlayed into the campaign than the Montreal Massacre of 1989, when 14 female engineering students were mowed down by a crazed gunman.

With the media's facilitation, an entire industry has been built on the Montreal Massacre, a tragedy – unlike male gendercides, which frequently occur in war – that has no historical precedent or sequel. The weeks before every December 6th anniversary produce a media orgy around domestic violence against women, with killer Marc Lepine, a solitary sociopath, touted as a mere exaggeration of typical male drives.

Conversely the media treatment of Remembrance Day, the one day a year feminists tacitly lay off men, no longer celebrates the specifically manly trait of physical courage. If you'll notice, Remembrance Day now is played out in gender-neutral programming, with combat-non-combat lines blurred to equalize the contributions of men and women.

While the plight of abused heterosexual men is ignored in the media, whatever afflicts gay men is instantly picked up on. When StatsCan released figures last year indicating intimate partner violence was disproportionately high amongst gay and lesbian couples, the *Globe and Mail* immediately commissioned a feature article – "A Skeleton that's Still in the Closet" – for their April 12/08 Focus section.

The violence scenarios described in the selected gay-couple examples are exactly the same as those in straight couples, reinforcing objective research concluding that partner violence is gender-neutral, a function of individual pathology. Yet unlike hetero male violence, for which no explanation other than an inherent urge to control women is ever offered, this article falls over itself finding reasons to excuse violent gays' behaviour.

71

In their treatment of men, a lazy perpetuation of falsehoods, an incurious acceptance of bogus studies and statistics, and an eager willingness to recycle superannuated stereotypes constitute the present media template.

I mentioned the Ontario Human Rights Code. I will end with it as the central motif of a seemingly trivial but memorable example of misandry that was brought to my attention by a vigilant reader.

In 99% of funded social services in Canada, even those advertising "family services," counselling and other forms of help are only provided to women victims of domestic violence. Here is how the Crouch Neighbourhood Resource Centre in London, Ontario provided itself with bogus moral high ground for refusing funded psychiatric help to men in crisis on their website:

"We at Crouch want to ensure that all our programming [is] accessible to all. The Ontario Human Rights Code states in section i: Every person has a right to equal treatment with respect to services, goods and facilities without discrimination because of race, age, ancestry, place of origin, colour, ethnic origin, citizenship, creed, sexual orientation, age, record of offences, marital status, same-sex partnership, family status or disability."

Sounds official, doesn't it? But in the *actual* Ontario Human Rights Code, between the words "creed" and "sexual orientation" is the word "sex." Its omission was no accident. I called the director of the centre to inquire about it. She was aware of it, but blamed the discrepancy on their website manager.

That is hard to believe. I am morally certain the website designer would have copied and pasted the quotation, not rewritten it, unless ordered to. I suggested I might be writing about it. It was removed the next day. But I was left rather dumbfounded by what struck me as an act of wilful duplicity. To accommodate an ideological bias, this website, in my opinion, *deliberately falsified the Ontario Human Rights Code.* The excision of those three letters was, for me, in its Orwellian implications, the most chilling example of media misandry of all

Pseudo-Learning in Our Universities

This is the updated text of a guest lecture I was invited to deliver in March 2011 to a McGill University undergraduate class in Conservative Studies, taught by Adam Daifallah, presently a partner in the firm of Hatley Strategic Advisors and part time lecturer at McGill.

What is the purpose of a university? The counter-culture of the 1960s drew a bright line between all past understandings and the present understanding of what universities were for. Standing on one leg, one might say that in the past universities felt it was their mission to teach students *how* to think, and in doing so it was considered natural to use as a teaching guide, as Mathew Arnold put it, "the best which has been thought and said" in our culture.

For the last 40 years, universities have considered it their mission to teach students *what* to think, and our western civilization's cultural canon is the last place to look for the content they wish to convey.

In a word, the universities, formerly independent custodians of objective knowledge governed by the rubric of free academic inquiry, have become politicized engines of social change. Intellectual investigation has been subordinated to non-intellectual and even anti-intellectual imperatives.

In his essay, "What are universities for?" philosopher Leszek Kolakowski said: "The greatest danger is the invasion of an intellectual fashion which wants to abolish cognitive criteria of knowledge and truth itself. The humanities and social sciences have always succumbed to various fashions, and this seems inevitable. But this is probably the first time that we are dealing with a fashion, or rather fashions, according to which there are no generally valid intellectual criteria."

The catalyst for all the hand-wringing of the past two decades was Chicago professor Allan Bloom's 1987 book, *The Closing of the American Mind*. In it Bloom denounced the academy for its indulgence of a viral political correctness that has infected higher education, resulting in curricula whose animating theme is cultural self-hatred, a phenomenon unique in world history. Bloom made the case for a strict separation between the pursuit of truth in the classroom and the quest for political advantage outside it.

Since Bloom began the trend of denunciation, the requiems have tumbled forth. I myself own an entire bookshelf of them, and a random glance at their titles tells the tale: *Zero Tolerance, Humanism Betrayed, Brainwashed, The Betrayal of Intellect in Higher Education, Petrified Campus, Education's End: Why Our Colleges and Universities Have Given Up on the Meaning of Life, Ivory Tower Blues*, and many more.

Universities are diverse in all that touches race, ethnicity gender. What is lacking is intellectual diversity, virtually proscribed in the academic community. From their ivory towers our leftist ecclesiastics rigorously monitor the four credos from which no dissent is permitted: relativism (each to his own "truth" except the truth of relativism, which is absolute), feminism, postcolonialism and multiculturalism (the rights of cultures trump the achievements of civilization).

To this effect: Inscribed over the portals of the humanities and social sciences departments in most Canadian universities should be the words: Abandon critical judgment, all ye who enter here.

Professor Stanley Fish, a well-known academic scholar and political liberal, who recently retired as Dean of the Chicago campus of the University of Illinois, wrote an article on this subject that appeared in the *Chronicle of Higher Education* and then became a book, *Save The World On Your Own Time*.

Fish notes that a perusal of mission statements of universities across the land reveals a belief that their main task is to promote social justice and form moral citizens. If that is their objective, then they are practicing without a licence something other than teaching. His book promotes a "narrow sense of vocation." Intellectual work is not politics by other means. It is not about joining movements or parties; it is about constructing evidence-based arguments, not celebrating or embracing causes.

Fish writes: "Teachers should teach their subjects. They should not teach peace or war or freedom or diversity or uniformity or nationalism or anti-nationalism or any other agenda that might properly be taught by a political leader or a talk-show host...The only advocacy that should go on in the classroom is the advocacy of what James Murphy has identified as the intellectual virtues, 'thoroughness, perseverance, intellectual honesty,' all components of the cardinal academic virtue of being 'conscientious in the pursuit of truth.'"

In other words, teachers should approach controversial issues that are relevant to the courses in which they have expertise, as disinterested scholars. They should present their students with two or more sides to any controversial issue, and not urge on them any particular side. They should teach them what the evidence is, how to assemble it, and how to construct an argument. After that, they should leave it to students to form their own conclusions.

The colonization of intellectual life by politics cannot help but degrade a liberal education. If I sound bitter it is not because the universities have been politicized in a way that privileges left-wing activism; I would be equally unhappy to see conservatism promoted as a given in academic discourse.

In his 2012 book, *The Victims' Revolution: The Rise of identity Studies and the Closing of the liberal Mind*, Bruce Bawer recounts his adventures visiting identity studies conferences all over the U.S.: Women's Studies, Black Studies, Queer Studies, Chicano Studies, and others. Bawer explores the evolution of all these disciplines and examines their principal texts and purveyors of ideas. He concludes that their influence has been almost entirely negative. Most helpfully, Bawer traces the problem in the humanities back to their intellectual source in three seminal texts: Antonio Gramsci's *Prison Notebooks*; Paulo Freire's *Pedagogy of the Oppressed;* and Frantz Fanon's *The Wretched of the Earth.*

Gramsci, born 1891, is famous for introducing the notion of "hegemony," so liberally scattered in the discourse of all identity studies programs. According to Gramsci, people may believe they are free in western democracies, but that is an illusion. In fact, Americans are less free in Gramsci's view than the Soviets under Stalin! The notion of hegemony gave academics a cudgel to beat up their own nation as the fountainhead of all wickedness.

Freire, born 1921, began his career teaching underprivileged children in Brazil, then taught illiterate labourers to read and write. His book, published 1968, brought him international fame and a teaching contract at Harvard. He ended up as an icon of the pedagogical world, with his book the lynchpin of teacher-training programs everywhere. *Pedagogy of the Oppressed* is a Marxist credo that calls for the overthrow of capitalist hegemony and the creation of a classless society. Freire did not believe in actual *teaching,* since that is in his view an act of oppression. Teachers and students were to be absolute equals. "Revolutionary leaders" (i.e. teachers) were not to be "masters," but "comrades." Freire was a great fan of Mao and his "cultural revolution."

Fanon, born in Martinique in 1925, became a psychiatrist, who believed westerners were colonizers and evil (at the time many were, to be sure), as opposed to the non-western oppressed who are all virtuous. Like Freire, he was sympathetic to violence that sprang from politically correct sources, such as "natives," believing that "The practice of violence binds [natives] together as a whole, since each individual forms a violent link in the great chain, a part of the great organism of violence, [which] is a cleansing force."

Taken together, the influence of these three men has been disastrous for the humanities. They all teach contempt for the West – the fountainhead of capitalism, colonialism and imperialism – as irredeemably evil. Forgotten in their writings are the great achievements of western civilization. All concentrate on discrediting the legacy our universities were founded to celebrate.

For a glimpse into the epicentre of the revolution against objectivity, we might also revisit the words of political theorist, sociologist and "father of the New Left" Herbert Marcuse: In a 1965 essay entitled "Repressive Tolerance," Herbert Marcuse inspired a generation of teachers and students to embrace a principle of epistemic subversion. "The restoration of freedom of thought," Marcuse argued, "may necessitate new and rigid restrictions on teachings and practices in the educational institutions which, by their very methods and concepts, serve to enclose the mind within the established universe of discourse and behavior." By "restrictions," of course, Marcuse was thinking selectively – he meant imposing a moratorium on conservative thought and teaching. Leftist and socialist doctrines were given carte blanche.

And what have students been learning and what are they still learning? Students soon internalize the catechism: Western civilization thrived on white, Christian, Euro-centric aggression against Others; Western literature and art are the patriarchy's handmaidens; the university's mission is not about disinterested knowledge, but achieving the just society and empowering the wretched of the earth; objective "knowledge" is a tool for one dominant race, gender and sexuality to oppress the powerless; reason is but one "way of knowing"; (So if aboriginals' "story," that they have occupied Canada since time immemorial, resists the historical truth that their ancestors crossed the Bering Strait 10,000 years ago, then aboriginals' "truth" must be privileged over actual history); any opposition to identity politics and multiculturalism is racism; there are no hierarchies in cultural values – in matters of gender, art and family, all manifestations are equally valid.

Most insidiously, acknowledging and rewarding objective merit is considered an "institutionalized form of racism and classism."

Strategies for eliminating intellectual debate on campus are manifold. Amongst them: disinviting or disrupting the speech of politically incorrect speakers (right wing speakers, pro-life activists and pro-Israel speakers often need tough security on campuses, but never the other way around); eliminating neutral survey courses, but sanctioning group identity courses designed to promote activism ("Womanhood: Black Feminists" as an English Literature course, for example); stifling speech codes to punish "offensive" language to women and minorities; and preferential hiring by ideology and group identity rather than academic accreditation. (On this last point, for example, a few years ago, Simon Fraser University advertised for a professor with these qualifications: "extensive experience in academia, *or as an activist.*")

Especially pernicious is the suppression of conservative voices in reading lists. My great-nephew is studying Political Science here at McGill: on his reading list is Karl Marx but not Friedrich Hayek's 1944 *Road to Serfdom*, or Adam Smith. In the U.S., according to Bawer, a majority of universities obliges students to read self-proclaimed socialist Barbara Ehrenreich's 2001 book, *Nickel and Dimed*, but not Adam Smith.

Economics seems to have lost interest in its seminal intellectual history. Most of today's undergrads have no classroom forum where they learn the philosophical and historical foundation on which western capitalism rests. A Council of Economic Education survey found that most college students are grossly misinformed or uninformed about how the market system works, or why its advocates believe it produces better results than other economic systems in creating general prosperity while respecting personal freedoms.

But with a few notable exceptions, all the liberal arts are in the same boat: the entire rich tradition of conservative thought, including the disinterested study of religions and their complex intellectual legacy is AWOL on campus.

Speaking of reading lists, I found it interesting, in the course of research I did for a column on conservative content in public and university libraries, that librarians are extremely liberal. Much was made in the 2004 presidential election of the 11-1 ratio of university professors' donations to Kerry's campaign over Bush's. Compared to librarians, however, academics are Rush Limbaugh's fan club, for the Kerry-Bush ratio of librarians' donations was a stunning 223-1.

Are Canadian librarians less ideologically monolithic than their U.S. colleagues? I could find no statistics to make such a case. Still, at the Toronto Public Library, Canada's largest, *The Bush-Haters Handbook* is readily available, but not [Mark] Steyn's *The Face of the Tiger*, which, by the way, was not at the time of my inquiries two years ago carried in the public libraries of Winnipeg, Montreal or Fredericton, or in the university libraries of Toronto, British Columbia and McGill.

A few years ago I wrote about the politicization of campus teaching in a column, and asked students and teachers to report back anecdotally on their experiences. I received over a 100 responses, detailing personal experiences in the classroom that would have been unthinkable in my day:

i. Comparative Politics teachers wouldn't admit *The Economist* (in one case) or Fraser Institute reports (in another) as source material because of their "right wing, biased writers";

ii. An International Relations professor pronounced political realism as a method of inquiry "dead" and inadmissible in argumentation;

iii. Political Science students taught by a feminist were not permitted to use statistics to bolster an argument because "mathematics is a male construct for a male-dominated world";

iv. A professor in a course on terrorism said: "No educated person can support Israel ... educated people don't have those kinds of views";

v. A feminist teacher in a school of nursing insisted that her male students participate in a Montreal Massacre commemoration. When one refused (on the grounds that he is no more responsible for Marc Lepine's sins than his teacher is for Karla Homolka's), he was made to submit to corrective counselling;

vi. Several years ago, a McGill student took a semester-long course, "Canadian-American Relations since 1939." His instructor, a PhD candidate, the student wrote me, was "the most gifted teacher I've encountered at McGill ... I haven't the faintest idea where he stands politically.... and that's exactly how it should be.... he received outstanding evaluations." He goes on to say that the gifted teacher was replaced [the next] semester by a "more qualified" teacher who said all Canadian-American relations since 1939 would be viewed "through a gay/lesbian/transsexual lens" and that they would devote part of the course to "lesbians who are claiming refugee status in Canada after Bush's re-election."

To be fair, my methodology is guilty of selection bias and doubtless these truly absurd examples may not be said to be representative of all academic life in Canada. I have a young friend doing a PhD in Canadian history who assures me that the general mood in academia in his field is not nearly as extreme as it was in past decades, and that centrism and non-partisanship is the order of the day. But that they happen at all is disconcerting.

What is common to all the anecdotal examples is evidence that the teacher sees his role as an advocate rather than as a dispenser of knowledge. The words academic and scholar are no longer interchangeable. To a scholar his subject matter is of interest apart from what is at stake for any particular group. Scholars have their own biases, of course, but when engaged in teaching their discipline, they are careful to monitor the possible intrusions of their biases into the field of study.

Social policy and other applications of the knowledge derived from real scholarship should not be the scholar's purview.

But if you look at the humanities today – literature, psychology, sociology, anthropology – they are dominated by a dual message of social mission and cultural blame. Let me give you a few examples.

In the fall of 2007, the University of Delaware inaugurated an ideological orientation for freshmen. The "treatment," as even the administration dubbed it, probed students' private lives, asking, for example: "When did you discover your sexual identity?" The course taught that the epithet "racist" "applies to all white people," and "people of colour cannot be racists." After publicized protests, the program was de-activated.

For a Canadian example, there is a course at Ryerson University called Immigration and Settlement Studies. In one obligatory course, students are asked to participate in an exercise of "social location," which is overtly designed to elicit confessions of racism or sexism. The course outlines states: "you are expected to self-reflect on your own social location (i.e., class, race, gender, sexual orientation, ability/disability) in relation to a particular population group (immigrants/refugees)."

One student who balked at talking about her sex life was given a very hard time that eventually involved threats of her being taken to the Human Rights Commission. To my knowledge, this "treatment" has not been de-activated.

"Social location" and confessions of white privilege or male privilege are also common in gender studies and social work curricula. They have an air of show trials about them, these forced confessions, what psychology professor John Furedy has labelled "velvet totalitarianism" in his writings about the politicization of the campus.

Brandeis University, for instance, has, as of November 2012, yet to recall a finding of racial harassment against Professor Paul Hindley for explaining the origins of the word "wetback" in a Latin-American Studies course. Mind you, Indiana University *did* apologize to a janitor who was found guilty of racial harassment for a book he was reading (its title was noticed by two black colleagues) that *celebrated* the demise of the Ku Klux Klan.

But how can such absurd charges be laid in the first place? In almost every one of these and a myriad of similar cases, they are dominated by Marxist thought, the idea that all identity groups are one or another kind of oppressed group struggling against a powerful oppressor group. And what happens when a group circles around a sacred principle is that it evolves into a tribal unit. They embrace what supports it, reject or distort what threatens it.

One of the greatest sociological scandals of the 20th century was the shunning of (Democrat) Daniel Patrick Moynihan, an academic turned politician. In 1965 he wrote a forceful essay warning about the disintegration of marriage and the family amongst poor blacks, prophesying (accurately) that single motherhood and reliance on welfare would lead to total dysfunction in poor black communities. He was shunned at Harvard as racist. Open-minded inquiry into the problems of blacks trapped in poverty cycles was simply shut down and only in recent years have liberal sociologists grudgingly acknowledged that Moynihan was 100% right.

Or take a fairly new discipline called Disability Studies. On its face, it's an excellent idea. The whole human history of attitudes and beliefs and treatment of the disabled is a rich mine of knowledge waiting to be organized and explored. Disability in literature and religion, disability in family dynamics, disability in sports, disability in political leaders – the possibilities for a scholar are really quite exciting.

But what has actually happened to this nascent discipline? It has been taken over by the Marxists, and at its core is once again advocacy rather than discovery. You'll find in its literature all the buzz words: "progressive," "oppression," "bourgeois," "empowerment," "rights," "social justice," "socially constructed." I've read a few papers in the discipline and I see stuff like: "At the heart of disability studies is a recognition that disability is a cultural construction; that is, that 'disability' has no inherent meaning'"; and "The exciting thing about disability studies is that it is both an academic field of enquiry and an area of political activity...involving the classrooms, the workplace, the courts, the legislature, the media, and so on"; and "Social justice is at the heart of disability theory and changing morality in the Western world."

In other words, rather than studying disability as a phenomenon, the academics have designated the disabled as one more oppressed minority: University of Toronto Disabilities Studies says it "aims to examine and deconstruct ableism." Ableism? In addition to feeling guilty about being white, of European provenance, heterosexual and Christian, here is one more thing you need to do penance for.

Turning to anthropology:

In the field of anthropology, we have this astonishing 2004 statement from the [American] Anthropological Association, an overt endorsement of same-sex marriage: "[T]he results of more than a century of anthropological research on households, kinship relationships, and families, across cultures, and through time, provide no support whatsoever for the view that either civilization or viable social orders depend upon marriage as an exclusively heterosexual institution."

Peter Wood, an association member of the AAA for more than 25 years, labelled this statement "a breathless lie." In fact, he wrote at *National Review Online*, "Some 250 years of systematic inquiry by anthropologists leaves little doubt that heterosexual marriage is found in nearly every human society and almost always as a pivotal institution. Homosexual marriage outside contemporary Western societies is exceedingly rare and never the basis of 'viable social order.' That might sound like a still-vibrant debate, but the Anthropological Association has declared the matter settled."

And social work (Source: John Leo, *Townhall*, Sept 11, 2007):

> *In 1997, the National Association of Social Work (NASW) altered its ethics code, ruling that all social workers must promote social justice 'from local to global level.' This call for mandatory advocacy raised the question: what kind of political action did the highly liberal field of social work have in mind? The answer wasn't long in coming. The Council on Social Work Education, the national accreditor of social work education programs, says candidates must fight 'oppression,' and sees American society as pervaded by the 'global interconnections of oppression.' Now aspiring social workers must commit themselves, usually in writing, to a culturally left agenda, often including diversity programs, state-sponsored redistribution of income, and a readiness to combat heterosexism, ableism, and classism.*

The National Association of Scholars protested in a report called "The Scandal of Social Work": "[T]hese programs have lost sight of the difference between instruction and indoctrination to a scandalous extent. They have, for the most part, adopted an official ideological line, closing off debate on many questions that serious students of public policy would admit to be open to the play of contending viewpoints."

On some American campuses, distaste for conservatism has escalated into fear and loathing: In the 2007 film *Indoctrinate U,* we meet Laura Freberg of California Polytechnic, a "closet" conservative academic. Then she is outed. Her colleagues are aghast: "We never would have hired you if we'd known you were Republican." In spite of her impeccable academic credentials and stellar teaching ratings, Freberg was removed as department chair, and a swastika burned on her lawn.

Okay, these are American examples and thinkers, and no academic has had a cross burned on her lawn here for voting Conservative. But in western academia there are only differences of degree. There is no substantive difference in the philosophical and ideological perspectives. The politicization of the social sciences knows no boundaries in the West.

The natural consequence of a monolithic view of the academic mission is a concomitant determination to censor opposing views. After all, if there is no question whatsoever that the prevailing wisdom is the only "correct" version of history, morality or policy, then logically to offer space to countervailing discourse is a dereliction of academic duty. Thus, the suppression of politically incorrect ideas comes to seem not only justifiable, but admirable.

In October, 2012, the Justice Centre for Constitutional Freedoms released its *2012 Campus Freedom Index*, a report that measures the state of free speech at Canadian public universities. Based on a much larger report, *The state of campus free speech in 2012*, the *Index* looks not only at what universities and student unions claim to be their policy on free speech, but on what they do in practice. Its purpose is to see to what extent universities and student unions support and protect free speech on campus. The *Index* assigns letter grades to 35 Canadian universities and student unions across the country. For a full report, see www.jccf.ca.

Examples: McGill University ordered a Jewish club to refrain from calling an event "Israel: A Party" (a lightly ironic play on "a Partheid"), because it offended the Israel Apartheid crowd; The University of Prince Edward Island banned an issue of *The Cadre* campus newspaper for containing images of the Prophet Mohammed; York University forced the cancellation of a speaking event with Middle East affairs commentator Daniel Pipes, by charging the student sponsors exorbitant security fees they could not afford; Simon Fraser University and the University of Calgary knowingly condoned the physical obstruction of pro-life displays on campus; The University of Ottawa threatened Ann Coulter with civil and criminal penalties if she expressed her views in what the university considered an unseemly way during an impending visit, then failed to provide adequate security for the event, facilitating disruptions that led to its cancellation; Carleton University had members of its pro-life club arrested, handcuffed and charged with "trespassing" for attempting to express their views on campus; Dalhousie University cancelled campus events scheduled for the "too controversial" Jared Taylor and British MP George Galloway.

One hugely influential "discipline" is desperately in need of pushback and I could easily spend an hour on this topic alone. And that is Women's Studies, a misnomer for Feminist Studies. Feminist Studies is not a discipline at all, of course. It is a pseudo-discipline. A pseudo-discipline is one that has no basis in direct observation (Astronomy is a discipline; astrology is not; Female Studies would submit the female sex to objective study; instead it "studies" gender, which is not a phenomenon but a theoretical invention.) Pseudo-disciplines exist to promote the interests of a belief system, or to exalt one group at the expense of another or others.

The Nazi universities instituted pseudo-disciplines of racial studies for the purpose of giving credibility through bogus "scholarship" to the canard that Jews were racially inferior to Aryans. Today Women's Studies, a pseudo-discipline par excellence, gives bogus credibility to women's superiority over men. That is a harsh comparison, not meant to suggest the end result of Women's Studies will mean the extermination of men – although to be sure some extreme feminists have called for exactly that prescription without censure from their colleagues – or that in general feminists hold men in contempt. I think it is fair to say, however, that while not all feminists are man-hating, feminism demands that all feminists be man-blaming.

Women's Studies began in support groups, not in the observation of evidence or from objective curiosity. Its purpose is to support political advocacy and to recruit foot soldiers in what Italian Marxist Antonio Gramsci called "the long march through the institutions."

The march through the institutions has been accomplished. Feminists dominate the teaching, social work and legal professions at the policy-making levels. Politicians hang on every word uttered by their respective parties' women's committees, and the recommendations made in their "pink books." Family court judges are trained by feminist psychologists and sociologues.

The media take as gospel the often-bogus statistics and data culled through selection bias and bad methodology (like opinion polls) issued from women's shelters and social service agencies, all branch offices of Women's Studies. All law enforcement policy with regard to domestic violence in particular is presently based entirely on feminist perspectives and feminism-generated data, much of it demonstrably misleading. A great deal of injustice against boys and men is perpetuated by this legalized imbalance, and combating these injustices has become a cornerstone of my professional inventory.

Feminism has permeated all the cultural disciplines (literature, fine arts, Whiteness Studies) and social sciences, and is even trying hard to get a toehold in the hard sciences.

We were made rather brutally aware of a feminist's idea of "gender justice" when Larry Summers, president of Harvard University, spoke a truth concerning the relative statistical abilities of men and women in the sciences. Summers holds the distinction of being the only university president forced to resign for speaking the truth, and since it was an inadmissible hypothesis, a truth connected to difference between the sexes, it was feminists who "mobbed" him and forced their colleagues to fall into line. Psychologists who knew he was right sat on their hands and let it happen.

Feminism dominates some branches of law, and even the teaching of law. Robert Martin, professor emeritus of the University of Western Ontario law faculty, where he taught constitutional law from 1975-2005, and author of *The Most Dangerous Branch: How the Supreme Court has Undermined our Law and our Democracy*, sees feminism behind the move in the 1970s away from teaching law as a coherent and articulated body of doctrine to be mastered and assimilated, and the study of law as though it were a social science.

Feminism's insistence that all institutions, relations, ideas and precepts are tainted by patriarchy and cry out to be eliminated produced an all-out war on legal education. Martin sees a vast literature of ideology masquerading as scholarship as the result, with lawyers more interested in manipulating the law for political causes than understanding and applying the law as written.

As a case in point he notes the famous "sock puppets" of Osgoode Law School who made complaints to more than one Human Rights Commission against *Macleans* Magazine and Mark Steyn for the "Islamophobic" content of Steyn's articles. They complained when the Ontario Human Rights Commission did not take their complaint because it "lacked jurisdiction," calling that a technicality. But lack of jurisdiction is far more than a technicality, which as law students they should understand and respect. Martin says he once taught a course in Media Law, which was mainly about freedom of expression. He reports: "Students were hostile to freedom of expression."

It has been 20 years since the term "political correctness" entered the popular vocabulary in its contemporary "multiculturalist" guise. The brilliant journalist Mark Steyn calls "political correctness" a "refusal of reality, a refusal to call things by their real name," hence the propagation of a lie.

I do not envy your generation. Many of you – "you" in the sense of the university population – are choosing to just "get through" your time on campus by walking close to the wall and saying and writing what it is clear professors want to hear. That is an intellectual loss, because such submission not only prevents the acquisition of the ability to think critically, it erodes the desire to.

Others, alienated by the prevailing orthodoxies, feel marginalized and uncomfortable. They are learning, but defensively, often in isolation, and that is not good either. So great is the ratio of liberals to conservatives on campus that the academy is now considered a liberal career, just as nursing is considered a woman's career.

Ironically, the marginalization of conservatism in the universities has produced a counter-counter revolution amongst conservative thinkers. Conservative thinkers in the fields of history, economics and sociology, knowing they have no future for their research on campus, have been migrating to think tanks, supported by private individuals and companies. This is something Adam Daifallah predicted and urged on in his 2005 book written with Tasha Kheiriddin, *Rescuing Canada's Right*.

Look at the recent crop of new conservative Canadian policy advocacy groups: The MacDonald-Laurier, the Frontier Centre, The Institute for Marriage and the Family, all having sprung up in the last five years. This is good and bad news. The bad news is that they are doing research that can't be done at the universities; the good news is that it is getting done by first-class thinkers and writers, and their reports and recommendations are making their way into the public forum. The conservative forum, Civitas, to which Adam and I belong, is also a reaction to the paucity of fresh intellectual air on campus.

Abraham Lincoln said: "The philosophy of the schoolroom in one generation will be the philosophy of government in the next." The university is therefore our most important cultural institution, and preserving its credibility and excellence – in this case rescuing it from its present lack of credibility and excellence – our highest civic duty.

Those of us privileged to have studied when the torch flamed brightly were naïve to assume the torch was inextinguishable. No flame is proof against a lack of oxygen. I hope many of you will be the breath of fresh air our campuses need.

"But if I am only for myself, what am I?"

This essay was delivered as the endowed Hill lecture for Cardus, a think tank dedicated to the renewal of North American social architecture, on October 15, 2012.

In *On Liberty*, the Ur-text for many free speech libertarians, John Stuart Mill argues that the demands of liberty and authority will always struggle, because the one cannot exist without the other. And so "some rules of conduct, therefore, must be imposed – by law in the first place, and by opinion on many things which are not fit subjects for the operation of law."

Many of Mill's devotees would be surprised to learn how much weight he gave to social opprobrium in matters that cause "offence" to the public.

In tyrannies and fundamentalist enclaves, one's social role is prescribed, and one's individuality scanted. But we who live in free societies that emphasize individual human rights must constantly negotiate the boundaries between our individual rights, our interest group rights and our civic obligations to the communities in which we live.

Such boundaries constitute the essence of the often-quoted dictum of rabbinic sage Hillel: "If I am not for myself, who will be? But if I am only for myself, what am I? And if not now, when?" I also drew inspiration for this evening's talk from one of Hillel's lesser-known dicta: "Do not separate yourself from the community." A cryptic sentiment whose wise sum is a great deal more than its few parts.

The main body of my address will focus on examples of subjects I have written on because my interest was aroused by their common theme: the disturbing effects on communities when interest groups are "for themselves alone" and who do "separate themselves from the community."

My first example deals with the issue of public safety in the context of a new journalistic interest: pit bulls and policy-making around dangerous dogs. I was first drawn to the subject by an article in *City Journal* magazine about pit bulls I read a few years ago. I was struck by the author's opening anecdote, in which he describes a takeover of the park near his young family's then Bronx home by thuggish young men and the menacing pit bulls they were training to fight. Nobody would go near the park when the pit bulls were there. The police were afraid to challenge their truculent owners. Seniors cowered when they passed. A climate of fear prevailed.

A rash of unsettling incidents, including maulings of other dogs, convinced the author this was no place for a growing family, and they decamped from the area. He writes: "We had learned that intimidating dogs can impair a neighborhood's quality of life and *give the sense that no one is in charge* every bit as much as drug dealing, prostitution, or aggressive panhandling."

That sentence, and that phrase, *the sense that no one is in charge,* got my full attention and activated my journalistic "spidey sense."

The author moved away from that area as his fortunes improved. But I thought about all the people who weren't in a position to move away, and how their community, formerly poor but dignified and with a common social environment in which residents could mix freely and contentedly, had been blighted, and its residents really almost terrorized by these dogs.

It stayed with me. I am troubled by what I have now learned is an international, escalating anti-social attraction amongst deracinated and often fatherless youth to fighting dogs as compensation for their multiple insecurities and grievances. Islamists in Europe march through the streets with pit bulls in spite of the Islamic precept against dogs' ritual impurity, and in Turkey a friend witnessed a grand parade of "anti-speciesism" activists who took over the streets for a demonstration, claiming to be promoting rights for all animals, but in fact most of them, he observed, walking with pit bulls straining at their leashes. Invariably such pit bull owners take pleasure in the shrinking away of intimidated bystanders.

The "right" of people to own dangerous dogs should not be privileged over the right of a community to enjoy its resources without fear. But there is a very powerful, well-funded and organized advocacy group for pit bulls that has been quite influential in preventing or repealing dangerous dog legislation by using the language of human rights – "discrimination," "racism" and "genocide" – applied to dogs.

It was when I was researching material for a long essay I was writing on the pit bull advocacy movement – the final essay of this collection – that I began to think about how we educated, civilized people take our orderly environments for granted. In good neighbourhoods and communities, where people have internalized the social contract, you don't need someone to be "in charge" most of the time.

I was set thinking about how easily a community's quality of life can be eroded by the intrusion of a new, aggressive and anti-social element that imposes itself on the community without regard for the community's holistic health. Looking back over my most impassioned writing, I saw that much of it has been sparked by ideological or cultural trends that begin with "rights" and end with erosion of civic confidence in the common social environment.

Spontaneous social reciprocity depends on civic trust between fellow citizens. If left to their own devices, communities in free societies evolve organically. Normal people want to get along with each other. It doesn't serve anyone's interests to be at odds with one's neighbour.

Everyone knows the expression, "Good fences make good neighbours." We want to interact with others, but we feel somewhat naked without social boundaries. We don't want our fences so high we can't see and talk over them. But we don't want them so low we become anxious about our security.

Erosion of civic trust can take many forms. I'm going to illustrate some of them with a few issues I've tackled in my columns. Their common pattern is a problematic cultural trend that either breaks down the natural fences we need between us, or else builds its own fence too high to see over, and creates a general sense of insecurity – physical, psychological or moral – that we feel in our public spaces and our dealings with others.

I most recently addressed that question head on in a recent column on Quebec and the changing social climate in Montreal. Linguistic tensions had been dormant for some years. But in the recent election campaign Pauline Marois, leader of the Parti Québécois, behind in the polls, played the anti-English card.

She started throwing up trial balloons about people running for public office having to be able to write in French as well as speak it, and French becoming the language of "common use," effectively saying it wasn't enough for anglophones to speak French at work or to civil servants, now they should speak it to each other socially as well in order to ensure the health of the French language in Montreal. She is now talking about reducing the time spent teaching English in school. We also hear talk of English being taught like any other "*langue étrangère*" (foreign language).

Everyone understands the implication of these shots across the bow. Mme Marois is saying that language is a zero-sum game: that every time someone speaks English in public, it diminishes the French language. Her attitude filtered into the populace and ratcheted up hostility to the English language. She deliberately heightened the fence between those who speak French and English as their language of daily use. Outside the fence is to be beyond a social Pale.

So much so that there were troubling incidents that had my social alarm bells ringing. Shortly after the election a transport employee put up a sign on his subway collection booth that "here things are done in French" and refused to speak English to a woman making inquiries. Nothing in his contract prevents him from speaking English. His antagonism was a trickledown effect of scapegoat politics that gives licence to xenophobic impulses. On two occasions, someone overhearing two anglophones conversing in public actually assaulted one of them, specifically giving as a reason the offensiveness of hearing English spoken in their presence.[1]

I wrote, "I actually can't think of any time before Marois' election campaign where, as in these two cases, private citizen A has criminally assaulted citizen B for speaking English to citizen C. The scenario suggests that English is not only an unwelcome language, but that it is some kind of virus, that can not only infect a person who is obliged to speak it, but can spread through the air to bystanders."

I had a lot of feedback from that column, in which many anglophones expressed agreement with my concluding expression of insecurity in a city where one normally feels safe. It is that easy to poison the social air we breathe.

The troubling thing is how easily we accept new conditions in which we are the ones to adjust our expectations, even if the demands made are undemocratic or based in myth. For English is in fact an official language in Quebec, by virtue of Section 133 of the BNA Act and the federal Official Languages Act.

When the PQ came to power in 1976, Bill 1, the Charter of the French language, was its first priority. Camille Laurin persuaded the Cabinet to declare French the only official language of the National Assembly and the courts, even though all knew this was unconstitutional. The Supreme Court struck that down in 1979 in Quebec (*Attorney General v. Blaikie*). Yet most people continue to believe the myth that French is the only official language of Quebec.

Ethnic nationalism is one trigger of civic distrust. Religion is another sensitive area where individual rights and communal health are often at odds, and where in my columns I have defended the right of a community to express its concern for its health without being labelled phobic.

For example, in July 2007 I wrote a column about a group of Hasidim – ultra-religious Jews, the men easily identifiable by their black fedoras and coats and side curls – who had purchased a former hotel in St. Adolphe-d'Howard for their community's summer use. St. Adolphe is a beautiful little lakeside town in the Laurentian mountains, and the hotel had been for sale for some time. The town was happy it had been bought, but conflicted over the new social dynamic it symbolized.

I took my lead from a *National Post* headline, "Town Uneasy about Jews' Resort Purchase." In it the town manager was quoted by a reporter to whom the manager had confided anxiety about a group "that might not integrate into the Saint-Adolphe community with the result that the property would be ghettoized." Naturally the remark was interpreted by many people as anti-Semitic code for "we don't want Jews here," especially considering the Laurentian hotel trade's ignominious and well-publicized past in refusing custom to Jews.

But even though occasional acts of anti-Semitic vandalism or graffiti do occur in Laurentian towns, the era of official, institutionalized anti-Semitism in that area is not only over, it is over in a big way. Traverse the Laurentians today, and you would be hard-pressed to find a community or town or resort that is not in large part supported economically and culturally by Jewish vacation-home owners, Jewish camps and Jewish skiers, including many Orthodox Jews (who often are, but should not be, confused with Hasidim, as sociologically they are entirely disparate entities, and indistinguishable from others apart from a small knit *yarmulke*).

Indeed, mainstream Jews are arguably the single most integrated anglophone group in the tourist-friendly towns of Saint-Sauveur, Sainte-Adele and Sainte-Agathe. I did not believe for a minute that the town of St. Adolphe was anti-Semitic. The townspeople were uncomfortable with the too-high social fence the purchase represented.

It is important to understand that Hasidic Jews do not interact socially with anyone else, not even with other Jews. When Hasidim settle *en masse* in city neighbourhoods, they have virtually no social contact outside their group. They deal in business with their own kinsmen, their children attend their own schools. They are a closed community within the larger community. This is not socially healthy. They separate themselves from the larger community. They are "only for themselves."

In the countryside, Hasidic enclaves are almost hermetically sealed social ghettos, from which small towns derive modest economic benefit, and almost no civic interaction, apart from politicking for group benefits, services and accommodations, reasonable and otherwise. Hasidim are not bad people. They're law-abiding and peaceful. But in their neighbourhoods, if you should happen to stray into them, they look right through you, as if you didn't exist.

In other words, near-zero social reciprocity: mostly take, little give. Which is why in Israel, the growing Haredim population – close siblings to Hasidim and the same for the purposes of this talk – has become a critical social problem that has led to disturbing acts of violence.

So it was hypocritical to label St. Adolphans anti-Semitic, as many pundits reflexively did. If Hasidim moved en bloc to my neighbourhood of Westmount in Montreal, I would have the exact same concerns as the people in St. Adolphe did. Does that make me, a mainstream Jew, anti-Semitic? To many it did, so schooled are they in the dogmas of multiculturalism, which allow for no discourse suggesting that minority cultures have responsibilities as well as rights.

I had a lot of blowback from that column. I was accused of wanting to take away the Hasidim's "right" to settle wherever they wanted. But I did not say it wasn't their right. It is their right. But that is where most of us are trained to stop thinking. If something is a right in law, that is the end of the discussion. It should not be the end. I only said it was normal for the townspeople to worry about the impact of such an inorganically imported swell to their tiny population, and they had the right according to natural law to defend the health of their community's social ecology without being accused of anti-Semitism.

I am an equal opportunity critic of fundamentalist religions, and so I move on to another religion and a not unrelated problem. Namely, Islam, and the problem of the niqab – or face cover in general. This is one issue I have columnized on frequently.

Most pundits who support the right of women to wear the niqab, and who see no social threat to it – and that means all liberal and libertarian ones, including my own editorial board at the *Post* – continue to understand the niqab as a) a religious obligation and b) as an article of clothing. They are wrong on both counts.

The niqab is a regional custom, not a religious obligation, as numerous Islamic authorities remind us, and frequently proscribed in Islamic countries. It is a custom often understood as an obligation, but that should not be our problem. We are not ourselves obliged to countenance practices that contradict principles we are pledged to uphold.

It is also not an article of clothing any more than a shroud is. The niqab is cloth draped over clothing. The niqab is not "worn," but "borne." This is an important distinction. This full-body mask must be understood as an apparatus whose sole function is to disguise a woman's femalehood and to anonymize her humanity. But again, even if it is understood merely as an aid to sexual modesty, that motive should not trump our natural abhorrence of the masked face (where there is no rational reason for it, such as protection against infection or cold).

Even those who support women's right to wear face cover disapprove of the reasons for it. But they believe it is niqab'd women's right anyway. My objections spring from my view that the harm done to society by this face cover trumps the individual's right to hide herself from public view. I wouldn't support a full ban as in France, but a partial ban. Yes in private life, but No when giving or receiving tax-funded services: courts, hospitals, schools, licence bureaus, voting booths, etc.

What do I mean by the "harm done to society"? Here I fall back on Mill's words: "some rules of conduct, therefore, must be imposed – by law in the first place, and by opinion on many things which are not fit subjects for the operation of law." I interpret this to mean community standards of decency. And I find the niqab to be indecent.

Everyone used to know what the word "decency" meant, but nowadays it conveys a certain old-fashioned prudishness that is out of step with today's unfettered candour and nonjudgmentalism in exploring and celebrating sexuality in all its various manifestations.[2]

The only problem with that assumption is human nature. Decency codes in dress and behaviour are a universal phenomenon, even if different cultures have disparate notions of what constitutes modesty. Decency is the invisible fence that permits transient social reciprocity between the sexes without anxiety over potential sexual aggression.

In our culture, we think of indecency in a unilateral way. We think of it as too little body coverage, or too explicitly-sexual behaviour. Everyone understands why we don't allow public nudity or overt sexual display in the common environment, except in specific, "safe" situations such as Pride parades.

In the last few years, since I have been exposed to the sight of women in full cover walking in my own neighborhood – not many, but it didn't take many to stimulate interrogation of my reflexive discomfort in their presence – I have come to the conclusion that indecency is not a one-way street, but a phenomenon that occurs at both ends of a spectrum.

On one end of the spectrum is public nakedness. It's forbidden, as I noted – here and everywhere. (In San Francisco's gay Castro area, where nudity has been allowed for a few years, a ban is now being imposed. The permissiveness eventually became untenable, as any realistic observer could have predicted.) There are nudists for whom nakedness is a philosophical imperative, but they have always been, and will always be, a quirky fringe group at the margins of society. They compliantly confine themselves to designated zones because they understand it is unreasonable for them to impose their nakedness on the vast majority who find it intolerable.

For the same reason, there is no need to tell people they may wear bikinis on a beach, but not in a courthouse or house of worship. Everyone is well aware of the rising stringency of propriety codes according to the degree of gravitas conferred by the setting or institution.

Moving to the opposite side of the spectrum, we find that the psychological discomfort we feel in seeing too much body exposure is similar to what we feel in too little exposure: that is, in the presence of someone with the face fully covered as a matter of course when in public.

Masks fascinate us for a reason. To wear a mask is to disappear socially. Encountering masked faces is alarming. That is why we like costume parties. Socializing masked with those we trust, with everyone complicit in the dehumanizing and discomfiting game, is a safe way to simulate a situation we would otherwise find frightening.

Covering the face in public as a norm is therefore a form of social aggression, and we are justified in feeling discomfort. We cannot see the women behind the mask, but they can see us. We can smile at them, but they cannot smile back. We cannot see their mouths, so there is no incentive to speak. They are separated from the community. They are for themselves alone.

On the naked end of the decency spectrum, there is too much intimacy for comfort; on the fully covered end there is too much mystery for comfort. Too little coverage provokes disgust; too much coverage provokes anxiety. Nakedness projects the uncomfortable image of the human being as an animal; full coverage evokes the image of the human being as an object. Doubtless people in places where the covered face is the norm get used to it. But only because they have internalized the idea that a woman is not a full human being.

That is why most people intuitively adjust their clothing to the middle of the decency spectrum to meet the psychological needs of their fellows – and to have their own met in return.

It is no use pretending fully covered women do no harm to the social fabric. They arouse internal disturbance: a mixture of pity, guilt, fear (of the men who

94

own them), and resentment, the last because in any encounter with them we feel shunned, just as we feel invisible amongst Hasidic Jews. Thus any Westerner privileged to live according to the value of gender equality, as most of us do, who says that the sight of a woman in full coverage neither upsets nor offends him or her is either lying or has no heart.[c]

Well, no talk about rules of conduct that are not fit subjects for the operation of law, but must be imposed by opinion would be complete without a discussion of sex and community standards. Which brings me to my final examples.

A few months ago, Ottawa's Museum of Science and technology opened their *Sex: A Tell-All Exhibition*.

As anyone familiar with our culture's obsession with unfettered sexual freedoms could have predicted, when controversy about the edginess of parts of the exhibition arose, the issue was framed by liberal commentators as a battle between the crabbed impulses of censorial puritans and the enlightened progressivism of disinterested pedagogues.

That's just nonsense. The exhibition crosses the boundary between decency and indecency. This is the other end of the decency spectrum I spoke of. Both ends of the spectrum are obsessed with sex. When a fear of unregulated sex overrides all other aspects of religious life, the religion turns cultish and separates from the community. When a fear of *repression* of sexuality overrides all other aspects of secular life, it turns pagan and co-opts the community.

Consider the most controversial element of the *Sex: A Tell-All Exhibition*: animations of a male and a female masturbating (later removed in response to public protest). The stated rationale, that this was in some way educational, is simply risible. Through the ages, a great deal of wicked ingenuity has been pressed into the service of *hiding* knowledge about masturbation from children's behaviours – but nobody has yet succeeded.

But for the sake of argument, let us assume children do need to be taught about masturbation. What principles should guide our choice of materials and context for such teaching, if we are truly thinking of imparting knowledge for its own sake? We would have to begin with the recognition that human beings are the only creatures for whom shame, guilt and modesty (especially in girls) are instinctive. We are also the only creatures who assign certain behaviours to the realm of the private, and certain to the realm of the public.

Is it not obvious that there is therefore a huge qualitative difference between learning about such intimate behaviour from a book or a single trusted adult in private as opposed to seeing graphic material in the company of strangers?

It's disturbing that educators seem to have lost their ability to distinguish between the private and the public. Private sexual activities exposed to the public gaze have *de facto* left the arena of education and entered the realm of voyeurism. Consider who will be attracted to such an exhibition. Consider the adult who not only takes pleasure in watching masturbation depicted on a screen, but even keener pleasure in standing beside real young people in order to observe them watching this video.

Does one need a degree in curatorship to understand that such an exhibit is pandering to highly questionable elements of human nature, and to people in their thrall, the kind of people we are normally at excruciating pains to protect our children from?

The exhibition was ideologically tainted in other ways. One exhibit on unplanned pregnancy and what to do about it urged swift abortion and no other option. And yet, I am sure the creative drivers of this exhibition would never agree to, let alone conceive of, an abortion "tell-all" exhibition, even though that is a subject on which near-total ignorance reigns. Indeed, when pro-life activists on campus attempt to educate people in exactly the same spirit of graphic depiction that the liberal ideologues welcomed in their sex exhibition, they are usually censored and shut down.

I have the same objection to elements in the sex-ed programs targeted at quite young children. I believe it is ethically wrong, and psychologically invasive, to burden children prematurely with unsolicited information regarding their sexuality that should be acquired at a time when sexuality is pertinent to their lives.

I am therefore troubled by educators' determination, in the interest of inculcating social approbation for atypical forms of sexuality that only manifest in puberty, of "answering" sexual questions that have not been asked. You cannot explain homosexuality to a child without also talking about sexual desire. There is no way around it. I hasten to add that I have no problem with adolescents being taught about human sexual desire – heterosexual and homosexual – in non-judgmental, informative ways (I do not share the opinion of many social conservatives that homosexuality is either inherently evil or a voluntary choice in most cases), but only at the age when they are fully receptive to understanding and processing what they are learning.

But children in the latency period of childhood don't want to know about sexual desire; they are biologically *programmed* not to want that knowledge yet. The latency period is their protective fence between a time to learn about the world beyond the self and the inwardness that comes with sexual awareness. Too-early sexualisation of children's minds for ideological ends is an aggressive act, laced in my opinion with a touch of prurience, and can be a harmful one.

Many parents – and not all of them practising Christians or even especially religious – want their children to associate sexuality with morality. They prefer that children learn about sexuality when they have the cognitive maturity to appreciate the humanizing benefits of modesty, high selectivity, self-discipline and deferral of gratification. And they feel perfectly competent to teach those values themselves. That is, or should be, their right.

It is well understood that even benign intimate physical touching of young children is off limits to anyone but a child's parents or their proxies. Too early sex education is the intimate touching of a child's mind, and should also be off limits to anyone without the express permission of the child's natural protectors.

I found it troubling that the sex exhibit had already travelled to two other Canadian cities for sojourns of many weeks, which means that hundreds or thousands of Canadian children were exposed to the imagery I spoke of, yet until it arrived in Ottawa, nobody raised any public alarm bells.

That tells me something. Not that Canadians have completely given up on standards of decency, but that they self-censor themselves from speaking up about those standards, or from speaking up about their discomfort with 7-year olds learning about sexual diversity out of fear of ridicule, or fear of accusations of homophobia or some other politically incorrect thought crime. Just as the English have grown fearful of speaking up for their rights in Quebec. Or practically anyone expressing their disgust with niqabs out of fear of being labelled racist.

Blessed are those who can look at their communities, and say with the psalmist, "Behold, how good and how pleasant it is for brethren to dwell together in unity!" All people of good will and sound moral principles yearn for communities that work to everyone's benefit, and where social reciprocity is so instinctive, nobody has to be "in charge."

But good communities are not given to us. We who care the most for their health must work for them the hardest. For if we are not for ourselves and our principles, who will be for us? If we do not speak out for those rights that are not covered in law, when our neighbours build their fences too high for our comfort, or too low for our and our children's sense of security, who will speak for us? And if not now, as it is happening, when?

97

Family Court's War Against Fathers

A talk delivered to the Men's Centre at the University of Toronto, March 1, 2012.

B oys and men are disadvantaged in many ways in these misandric times. But there is one area that causes more existential anguish for men and for children than any other – namely the family law system – and that is my subject this evening.

By coincidence, on the morning I was setting out the materials I wanted to incorporate into my talk, I happened to be reading the Arts section of the *National Post*, and my eye was caught by the title of film reviewer Chris Knight's column, "Oscar Bait: Do good dads go unrewarded?" He begins:

"When Oscar winners take to the podium, they thank their agents, stylists, directors, gods and Harvey Weinstein. Seldom does Dad get a shout-out, except as half of 'my parents.' This year, however, nominees should thank their paternal stars. Fully 60% of the hopefuls for best actor and best supporting actor were cast as father figures par excellence."

Then he names some father-centred movies this year, amongst them *The Descendants, Moneyball,* and *A Better Life.* Knight notices two oddities about the films I've mentioned. One is that "these men's wives are dead, comatose, divorced or otherwise out of the picture." The other is that good dads are often nominated for Academy Awards but seldom win. The last "great dad" to win an Oscar was Robert Benigni in *Life is Beautiful,* and his was a role performed in such extreme circumstances that he can hardly be said to be representative of fatherhood.

Chris doesn't go on to speculate about the reasons for the missing mothers. I think I could have enlightened him there. There is an unspoken Hollywood rule that fathers cannot be portrayed as exceptional parents when there is a mom around. Nobody competes with mom as the more necessary parent. Dads can only be accorded attention and respect when they are in the situation of a "coping" parent.

That is, if the mother is absent, the father may step in and take over her role, after he has learned how, of course. In most cases good-dad roles portray a father who is not naturally nurturing, and who only learns how to nurture when tutored by the mom, or when extraordinary circumstances force him into that role.

In other words, where there are two parents on the scene, the mother has to shine. If she doesn't shine, then the father has to be equally or more flawed (In the 2009 film *Precious*, for example, the mother is so awful you think nobody could be worse. Turns out the father is long gone and the stepfather is much, much worse.) But if she dies or leaves the scene, then the father is allowed to shine, because in effect he has become the surrogate mother.

A few excellent films that follow this rule have dealt with the iniquities of the family law system. My *National Post* colleague, columnist George Jonas once said that you know the family is in trouble when a whole branch of the law is devoted to it. How right he was, and these films show us why.

In 2003 Pierce Brosnan produced and starred in a moving film, *Evelyn*, based on the true story of Irishman Desmond Doyle who fought the Irish government and the Catholic Church to overturn an outdated custody law and recover his three children after his wife abandoned the family.

In the 1979 movie *Kramer vs. Kramer*, the archetype of this genre, a New York mother, bored with child care, bolts to Los Angeles "to find herself," leaving her husband suddenly in sole charge of their little son.

The heart of the movie is the riveting evolution of a patriarchy-era father – career-obsessed, domestically disengaged – into a New Man: putting career ambitions second to his child's needs, parenting clumsily and frantically at first, but eventually with tender efficiency.

Not without realistic missteps and emotional pain along the way, they form a loving bond. The child is happy. Nevertheless, when the mother swoops back into town 18 months later and sues for custody, a patriarchy-era court ignores the dad's obviously superior moral claim – and the child's wishes – awarding the mom custody on the basis of her sex.

As many New Men are shocked to learn, all the midnight feedings, bedtime stories and soothing Band-Aid applications to scraped knees count for nothing against morally indefensible gender bias in family court: In most litigated custody cases, the mother gains sole custody.

Thus, with mom-friendly courts always the trump card up a mother's sleeve, even the best of fathers in all custody negotiations must depend on the mother's good will, rather than justice, for anything approaching equal access to his children.

In 1997, when the current Divorce Act came into effect, a special joint committee was convened to make recommendations on child custody and access. After 55 hearings and more than a year of study, the 48 recommendations of the 1998 report, *For the Sake of the Children*, converged on one theme: The sole-custody adversarial system, as it pertains to the majority of custody and access disputes, denies children and non-custodial parents basic human rights, and puts children's psychological and emotional health at risk.

The report recommended the "non-rebuttable presumption" of equal parenting (in the absence of abuse) as both fair to parents and best for children. But it was ignored by the then-Liberal government and fell into a political black hole. Where still it languishes under a majority Conservative government, whose platform has long contained that very plank.

We know what Canadians think on this issue: Polls show that 80% of Canadians support equal parenting. And the social science is airtight on the importance of fathers and mothers in the whole range of life experience as children grow older.

University of British Columbia sociology professor Edward Kruk, Canada's foremost expert on custody, has for many years been writing papers on the results of a wealth of peer-reviewed data to support the superior effects of "shared parental responsibility." Yet, as he observes, judges in family courts tend to perpetuate old stereotypes, ignoring evidence in cases where the father is provably the more responsible caregiver, or presuming fathers only seek sole custody to evade financial responsibility.

Under mounting critical scrutiny in recent years, the judiciary's lack of expertise in determining the "best interests of the child" has become increasingly apparent. As a result, a new parental "responsibility-to-needs" discourse has emerged in the socio-legal realm.

A child's needs cannot be optimally met by a single parent, however loving. Kruk's findings show that a child must spend at least 40% of his time with a parent to establish and maintain a beneficial attachment.

Kramer vs. Kramer ended happily, with the mother's recognition that fairness to the child required voluntary relinquishment of her legal entitlement. Unfortunately, Hollywood is not running the divorce industry in Canada. In real life, mothers are rarely so selfless; court-battle endings are rarely so happy for fathers and children.

From the day I ventured into this almost-orphan topic, journalistically speaking, I started receiving narratives from disenfranchised dads, detailing and often documenting their Kafkaesque adventures in family court and the despair they felt in being forcefully separated from their children. Their stories were heartbreaking. I have a fat file of them at home. It would be hard to choose one over another as an example of how irrational and destructive family court can be. But again, coincidentally when I was working up my notes for this talk, I received a short, succinct personal account from a father that is such a perfect vehicle for our theme tonight that, with permission from its author, Chris Walker, who is here with us tonight, I am sharing it with you.

Chris wrote this in response to a recent column:

> Hi Barbara;
>
> I very much enjoyed your article.
>
> I am that father you are talking about.
>
> I have 4 court orders to help save my children from their mother's emotional abuse and alienation.
>
> She at one point asked for $200,000 and my entire monthly salary. With that, she would let me see the kids. (I could live at my mom's for free, she said.)
>
> A respected counsellor assessed the family and made a recommendation to remove the children from their mom's custody.
>
> The judges so far have failed to take a stand. The scope of what she has done is too vast for a simple 2 hour motion.
>
> The CAS are "waiting to see what the courts do."
>
> Judges will not fine her, and they will not put her in jail. They tell me that at trial I can get custody to help reverse this tragedy, but I can't get on the trial docket till October.
>
> My children are 13, 12 and 10.
>
> Brazil recently made the act of [parental] alienation a criminal offense with enforcement.
>
> I can tell you the presumption of shared parenting only works on mothers who are afraid of the consequences ....
>
> In Canada there are no consequences and my EX is proof.
>
> I stood in front of 2 judges and listened to them tell me they could not enforce their own orders to help the kids.

They explained clearly that fines and jail would not stop her. So they made a new order for her……. which she broke 7 days later.

They did suggest that perhaps I should stop trying to see my kids.That maybe when there are older (18-20) they would see what their mother has done to them.

They would then "come around" and the mother would then be abandoned.

I drove 6 hours last month to see my daughters skate for 3 minutes.

My Ex hid them in the competitors' locker room so that I could not speak to them.

I haven't seen my son in 2 months. So I can tell you from experience that the $100,000 I spent in legal fees does nothing without enforcement.

My stories fill three boxes of affidavits, which I hope will convince the trial judge to give me custody and order her into care so that she can be involved in their lives without hurting them.

I have spoken to every expert I can get my hands on and the consensus is that trial is all that is left (something I will now have to do as my own lawyer).

The other area that is a concern is my children's ages. If I am successful at trial there is still a chance my children will run back to their mother. My EX has informed the children, that 'even if Daddy gets custody, you can run away and live with Mommy.'

In fact, [even] if I have sole custody, she can still continue what she is doing. I was so shocked I went to the local OPP detachment and asked about enforcement.

Sure enough the OPP confirmed, if a 12 year old can prove he is sheltered, fed and going to school, there is nothing a parent can do, even with sole custody.

So I am committed to fight the fight as hard as I can and hope for the best outcome for my kids.

* * *

This is by no means the worst case I have read, but I was not looking for the worst case. I was looking for a "normal" case, if one can use such a word in this context.

Every single professional in this case – judge, CAS officials, police – think that what they are doing reflects the "best interests of the children" and strangely, the "best interests" coincide with the best interests of a mother who has exhibited clear signs of immaturity at best, unfitness to parent at worst. How is that possible when it is so clear that the best interests of Chris' children are not being served at all?

Let's take a look at the system. But before I begin, I want to make a general stipulation. Neither sex has a monopoly on moral innocence. Both men and women have the capacity and the free will to act with honour and good will, or dishonour and bad will, in stressful situations.

But when a man or woman's most cherished relationships are at stake, and when the fate of those relationships are in the hands of strangers sitting in judgment, it strains the bounds of human nature for either a mother or a father to resist the temptations of an unlevel playing field that tilts in her or his direction. In family court the playing field is badly tilted towards women. If they take advantage of that fact, it doesn't mean that women are intrinsically worse than men; it means they are human. There was a time when courts tilted the other way, which didn't make men villains, just human as well.

Justice is supposed to be gender-neutral, but gender is still the single biggest predictor of who gets sole custody in disputes, and even though fatherhood has changed a lot since 1970, the statistics for sole custody have not. The statistic of 90% is often attached to contested custody suits resulting in maternal custody. That statistic is a combination of "sole custody" – over 80% of rulings – and the misleading "joint custody with primary residence" to the mother; in both cases the mother has sole control over what happens to the child. Ontario actuary Brian Jenkins, who has made a specialty of statistics around custody issues, tells me: "Personally, I think that 90% is actually a bit low for effective maternal custody as the judges do as they please and please is almost always against paternal parents."

For some years now we have understood the mantra "the best interests of the child" to be the guiding criterion for custody outcomes, and presumably the judges who effect these gender-skewed scenarios believe they are abiding by that guideline. But since there is no actual definition for "best interests," it all comes down to a judge's "weighing" of the situation. As noted in an earlier essay, for example, Supreme Court Justice Rosalie Abella considers the happiness of the residential parent, usually the mother, to be the litmus test for the child's best interests.

But how do judges "weigh" narratives from two people they don't know and a situation that can't be understood in any depth, and that is absorbed through competing accounts? We treat judges with reverence; we take for granted that judges are the most educated and the most intelligent citizens amongst us. Educated in the law, yes. But are they really the wisest amongst us?

What is the purpose of any court, and for what are courts devised? In every kind of court but family, judges decide or guide others to decide what is to be the consequence of harms and wrongs that were done in the past. Only in family court do we have a system where no harms have been done in the past – or none that have been the state's business – and where circumstances will be continually changing in the future, but where judges get to decide where harm *may* happen and judge accordingly. As if they were gods and could predict the future, not mere men and women with knowledge of a set of laws, knowledge that has no bearing on their real subject, family dynamics and natural parental rights (which are not enshrined in our Charter but should be).

Family court deals with complex, emotion-drenched, existential issues. Decisions made in family court have life-altering, and even life-or-death implications for everyone involved. You would think that the judges in this court would be handpicked for their knowledge of human nature, for their emotional intelligence, for their previous studies in psychology or criminology or ethics or philosophy or even cultural anthropology.

You would be wrong. Very few judges have such an educational background, and many judges are emotionally illiterate personally. Most have taken undergrad courses in history or political science or economics. Some students go into law school direct from CEGEP (an acronym for the post-secondary pre-university collegiate institute unique to Quebec). They complete a three-year program in law and graduate as generalists.

Their knowledge of social science and epidemiology is meagre to marginal. They have no idea of the statistics accompanying fatherlessness. They haven't read the academic literature on domestic violence. They don't know the statistics on child abuse by women, higher than for men in all areas except sexual abuse, or the disproportionately high figures associated with sexual abuse of children by the post-separation live-in boyfriends of mothers with sole custody.

As a few recent cases have demonstrated, judges are starting to have, slowly, an understanding of the horrific scourge of Parental Alienation Syndrome[4], but most still have no idea the damage is wrought by the alienating parent – man or woman, but, given the statistical liklihood of mothers having sole custody, more by women. They haven't wilfully ignored evidence; they haven't been made aware of it.

The result is that judges are just as likely to defer to social theories based in gender ideology as anyone else in society. They are no more likely to know the difference between fringe ideas and sound social science than any third year student on campus. Let's not forget that in the 1990s, judges embraced the now-discredited theories of false memory syndrome as enthusiastically as the ideology-marinated psychologists who propounded it, and as a result many lives of adults falsely accused of sex abuse by indoctrinated former children in their care, were ruined.

But that is not to say that judges are not trained at *all* before they preside in family court. They do take a short backgrounder case prepared for them by the National Institute of Justice (NIJ). The NIJ is an insular organization whose board of directors is composed entirely of judges and law professors. The program taken by the judges provides a "focus on three major components of judicial education: substantive law, skills training and social context issues."

Social context issues. These are the three scariest words many unlucky Canadian fathers will ever hear. One of the reasons they're scary is that the words are nebulous, and we don't know what these judges are learning in the program. The NIJ will not release details of the courses they give – not even to lawyers, let alone the press or ordinary citizens.

But we do know some of the people who are teaching these courses – and as well those who should be, but aren't asked to teach them. Some of the social context teachers are the most doctrinaire ideologues in the business, so it is not a stretch to call the courses indoctrination rather than education.

My friend Grant Brown, a former family law lawyer in Alberta, trained in philosophy and now retired from law because he couldn't stomach the gender bias in the system and the injustices his male clients were subjected to, once wryly commented to me, "feminists believe men and women are absolutely equal, except in those areas where women are superior." It is to Grant's eloquent writings on the family law system that I owe a great deal of my education on the subject.

And one of the areas in which feminists consider women to be superior is parenting. Grant ascribes gender-biased judgements to two different sources. One is the chivalric attitude we saw in the movie *Kramer vs Kramer.* You see this white-knight-to-the-rescue syndrome in aging judges who got their law before the colonization of law schools by feminism. They see parenting in the old paradigm of the provider father and the nurturing domestic mother. They see women as vulnerable and in need of their protection.

On the other hand you have the younger judges schooled in feminist rubrics. In this paradigm, women must have choices they didn't used to have – work, mothering, a combination, whatever. They must not be "controlled" by men, who all, according to feminist belief, would control women if they could. In any case the result is the same: women's "rights" to their children are deferred to by those trained in "social context issues."

Let's take a little tour of the "social context" in gender rights that our cultural and political elites consider normative:

- Women have the right to conceive a baby through fraud, by telling men they are using contraceptives. An unwilling father has no right to refuse to support that baby for the next 18 years, whereas a woman who doesn't want a baby can hand it over to the state with no financial responsibility whatsoever; conversely a baby wanted by a father can be arbitrarily aborted by its mother or, as we saw in the case of Hendricks vs Swan in Saskatchewan, given away to adoptive strangers because the strangers had more money than the father;

- Women have the right to damage unborn children through substance abuse or knowing exposure to HIV with no penalty, while a man is held criminally responsible for any damage to a fetus during an act of domestic violence;

- Women who are charged with criminal abuse of children, including murder, are protected by privacy laws, supposedly to protect the child from embarrassment or suffering; while "deadbeat dads" who don't or can't pay child support are exposed to public view on the Internet, which one might assume would cause pain to a child too;

- Men who refuse to or cannot pay their child support can have their passports taken away (which are rarely suspended even after serious crimes, and is a breach of the mobility rights enshrined in our Charter, considered a fundamental right of citizenship), their houses and computers searched without warrant, and – even though Debtors Prison was abolished in 1868 as inconsistent with our values – can be imprisoned for periods longer than those meted out to a cocaine dealer (as I noted in an earlier essay, cocaine dealers and deadbeat dads both receive sentences of 30 days; but cocaine dealers routinely get out before the end of their sentence, while deadbeat dads don't);

- but women who deny fathers court-access to their children are rarely penalized in any way, let alone jailed.

This last imbalance really sticks in the craw of anyone who believes justice should be blind. As Judge Jack Watson of Alberta's Court of Appeal commented on a case of denied access: "It's not my job to punish mothers." Actually Judge Watson, if it isn't your job, whose is it? And if not delinquent mothers, why do you consider it your job to punish delinquent fathers when they can't or won't pay child support? All of life is transactional. A father paying child support has fulfilled his obligation, and is surely entitled to time with his children.

And yet Judge Watson, who claims it is not his job to punish mothers, has a whole section of family law to back up such a punishment. Alberta's Family Law Act, section 40 gives judges the power to order compensatory time for missed access; posting of a security against further delinquency; reimbursement for expenses undertaken in the effort to see the child; imprisonment for up to 90 days; and anything else the court deems appropriate.

But this is one *quid pro quo* our family court judges fail to respect. It is no coincidence that Chris Walker's judge thought it made sense for Chris to give up seeing his children and hope that they would "come around" when they were adults, as if the loss of six or seven or eight years of fathering one's own flesh and blood were a mere inconvenience, and of no special significance.

Where do these ideas come from? They don't come from International law, that's for sure. Article 16(3) of the Universal Declaration of Human Rights states: "The family is the natural and fundamental group unit of society and is entitled to protection by society and the state." But in this country the courts are the "ultimate legal guardians." We speak of courts "giving" custody. Custody battles in family court are not about giving a child to one parent. That parent already has the child. No, the court is about "taking away" children from another parent. The words we use are important.

The ideas come from a belief system – not evidence – that assumes a mother's presence is more important to a child than a father's, and that a child needs mothering more than fathering. In reality, it is only in early infanthood that a mother's presence may be understood to be crucial. The problem in family court is that judges often retain anachronous chivalric feelings about the mother-baby bond. They give great weight to the status quo, not recognizing that children can form flexible habits very quickly and easily, and that children's needs change as they grow. Their need for a father is far more important than the need for one bedroom rather than two.

The optimum situation for children is always to have near-equal access to both their parents. If individual couples, for practical or other reasons, agree that the children are best off with their mother – or their father – for most of the time, they should have the right to negotiate their own arrangement. Most fathers want equal parenting. The few I know who seek sole custody have fears for their child's safety. I am sure there are exceptions. But ordinary women should not be blamed for their tendency to want sole custody. They have been assured by so many educators and child-care professionals and judges that it is not harmful to a child to be separated from their father that they find sole parenthood reasonable.

The easiest way to establish a status quo of sole custody is to remove the other parent from the home by legal means for a period of months or a year. One

Alberta judge told my friend Grant Brown that she reckoned 80% of charges of domestic violence or sex abuse of children of fathers during custody battles are false allegations.

These allegations do instantly remove the father from the scene, but they do not go to criminal court where proofs would be demanded. They simply set up delays that are on the resident parent's side, and by the time they are demonstrated to be false allegations, the damage is done, and the alleger is usually not punished. Conversely, allegations of real abuse of the children by fathers against mothers are rarely taken seriously. As a result many innocent children have died because the Children's Aid Society (CAS), so frequently ready to believe the worst of a father, refused to believe that a mother could be a danger to her children.

As one of many examples I could cite, the name Elaine Campione may ring a bell. Elaine Campione drowned her two little girls, Sophia and Serena in a bathtub. The CAS was well aware of Elaine Campione's quixotic, actually alarming history. They knew that Campione had demonstrated many signs of psychosis, that she had been hospitalized in psychiatric wards, believed people were out to kill her and kidnap her children, and had exhibited such bizarre and/or negligent behaviours toward her girls that mother-substitutes, including her own mother, had to be constantly parachuted into her household if it was to function at all.

Yet the CAS decided the mother was the "safe parent" because of the wife's unsubstantiated allegations of domestic violence against her husband. Mr. Campione fought like a tiger and indebted himself trying to wrest control of the children from a woman he knew to be unstable and a potential risk to them, but nobody listened to him.

Why? Because when fathers kill, they are not assigned any motivation but their own evil impulses. When mothers kill, everyone in the system kicks into denial mode, and assumes the fault has to lie elsewhere – anywhere, as long as the woman doesn't have to take responsibility for her actions, and can be offered sympathy. When fathers show disturbing tendencies, the system acts, or tries to. When mothers show disturbing behaviour, the system protects the victimizer.

Just the other day, I received an email from a distraught father, who has tried to extricate his daughter from an unhealthy situation, but abetted by social services, the situation persists. The father appends a handwritten letter he received from his desperately missed 11-yr old daughter in which she pleads to join him, writing, "I hate staying in this house [with her mother and stepfather] because I'm scared. I don't know why but I feel like I don't want to live anymore." One can only pray this girl doesn't end up as another example of 'too little, too late.'

It is now settled sociological science that fatherlessness is the single greatest predictor for negative social outcomes like drug use, promiscuity, school dropout and gang membership. There are more than four million single fathers in North America. That's a pretty big control group. If mothers really are more important than fathers, then by now we should be aware of studies or some reliable evidence that motherlessness is a predictor for worse outcomes than fatherlessness. Since such evidence would bolster feminist arguments for privileging mothers in custody disputes, I think we would be aware of it if it were out there. But whatever literature I have seen on the subject tells me that single fathers do as well or better at parenting than single mothers.

On to support payment. Judges may be indifferent to fathers access to children but they are frequently, irrationally obsessed with maintaining the children's lifestyle through support payments that may have no relevance to the father's current ability to pay. Their willed blindness to reality can have dire results.

Take the case of Darren White of Prince George, B.C. He was ordered to pay $1,071 child maintenance plus $1000 spousal support per month on a gross disability income of $2,200 (stress leave – he was a train engineer). He was already under an order to pay $439 per month child support for his eldest child in another province. In other words his support orders equalled 114% of his gross income. The judge chose to believe that White was not paying the $439 and that he would "soon" be back at work. Since his ex-wife was also a train engineer, it was a puzzlement as to why she needed spousal support. But never mind. The judge ordered him out of the family home, adding the cost of new lodgings to his burden. So Darrin went into the woods and hung himself.

Variations on this story fill the literature on the injustices of family court. Interestingly Stats Canada does not keep separate tabs on these suicides, nor does the FRO. What we do know is that 70% of male suicides in Canada are "relationship" related, and that custody suits cause huge flare-ups in the suicide rate for men. Since suicide rates for mothers in custody disputes do not budge, it seems logical to conclude that custody outcomes do not cause despair in women and do cause despair in men. Surely here is a situation that begs for further research. If women's suicide rates tripled or quadrupled during custody disputes, would the research not already be in progress?

Spousal and child support guidelines and their failures are a huge topic in themselves. I have no time to get into them, but I will just say that guidelines, which took the place of individual case assessments some years ago, have not reduced child poverty and equalized household standards of living as they were meant to. Judges have discretion to up support payments but they almost never lower them. In other words the state was counting on fathers to end the "feminization of poverty."

The guidelines don't take into account a father's obligations to a second family or other burdens of a second residence. Within three years of separation, a third of dads and a quarter of moms have new partners, half of which include other children. By nine years after separation, 40% of both dads and mums have second families. Real life isn't like theory. In any case the scheme hasn't worked. The rate of low-income children remains the same as it was seven years before the guidelines were initiated and seven years after they were in place.

As for the Family Responsibility Office (FRO), as it is called in Ontario or Maintenance Enforcement Program (MEP) in other provinces, and its evils, that too is a subject in itself, and one I think best handled by professionals who work within the system. Suffice to say that a model of equal parenting would be the most intelligent way to achieve compliance from both parties and a more equitable financial burden for each parent.

I will end with a quote from Erin Pizzey, the courageous founder of the Women's Shelter movement who was "disappeared" from the movement by feminists when she dared to speak the truth about spousal violence being bilateral. At a 2008 conference on domestic violence in Sacramento, where she was the keynote speaker, Pizzey told her standing-room-only audience that for gender politics "Canada is the scariest country on the planet." Scary to men who suffer because of it, certainly, but apparently not to most other Canadians, who remain curiously indifferent to the demonstrable misandry permeating the institutions that define and shape our culture.

Anti-Israel Bias on Global Campuses

I delivered this talk to the annual meeting of SAFS – the Society for the Advancement of Freedom in Scholarship –in London, Ontario on May 11, 2009.

The Society for Academic Freedom in Scholarship would not exist, and I wouldn't have been invited to speak today, if it were not a given amongst us that academia is in crisis, and that weekly, daily, hourly, all of us continue to witness signs, large and small, that the profanation of once-vaunted academic ideals runs amok in our nation's classrooms.

A young woman at one of our major universities sent me an e-mail not long ago with a personal anecdote that brings together many of the individual threads that constitute the problem's messy tangle. She wrote:

> *My political science professor, Dr X, decided to screen the movie today in class entitled "Loose Change." This movie is about 9/11 being an American conspiracy. He gave a pre-amble to the film speaking about how this is his opinion and how we need to question everything (i.e. question the U.S. government). Now in class before he screened the movie I asked him if he had ever looked at the other side of it and watched movies or read books/articles about it and he said no. (I guess that goes to show that he is not really well-informed). And then he went on to say that the Americans are trying to take over the world and how there is evidence to support that and how it's a bad thing. Well anyways, after the movie I spoke to him privately and told him how disgusted I was that he would show that movie in class, as a professor should teach objectively and not*

try to brainwash his students into believing his opinions. I told him how that shows no academic integrity and his entire semester-long course has been devoted to preaching his opinions (i.e. anti-Americanism and anti-Israel when he said Israel is a criminal state and such). He replied by saying that his views are what he wants to teach and I have no right to dictate his course. He also said that we clearly have opposing views as to what the purpose of university is. He thought it was a great idea to teach his beliefs because then after he does so, students can decide for themselves. Ya Right!

It's all here: education as a conduit for personal ego and ideological purposes, disdain for facts and evidence, indifference to objectivity and balance, contempt for students' intellectual rights, and of course tediously reflexive hostility to America and Israel. Most of all, it is the siren call of the conspiracy theory, true scholarship's bane, as the simple answer to the world's evils that we doubtless all find particularly troubling.

For the conspiracy theory is the engine driving all academic ideologies, notably Marxism and Feminism, and woe betide those targeted as obstacles to the ideology's progress to its utopian end, for it always ends badly for them. More often than not in history, that target has been the Jews: as a religion, as a race and now as a nation.

For anything approaching the virulence of anti-Israel bias on campus today, you have to look back to the universities in Germany of the thirties. Despite their long tradition of rigorous scholarship and intellectual vitality, academics in the arts and in science faculties lent themselves to the manufacture of propaganda under the guise of scholarship. The words "academic freedom" became a shibboleth for the falsification and distortion of knowledge in the service of a wicked ideology.

They put a respectable "scientific" face on evils to come. In his book *Studying the Jew: Scholarly Anti-Semitism in Nazi Germany* History professor Alan E. Steinweis sizes up German academics who demonized Jews: "With some exceptions [they] were not intellectual frauds or Nazi party hacks...They were dishonest scholars, but scholars nonetheless. Their careers and their work violated the presumption that the scholar has a responsibility to use knowledge honestly and for positive ends. In the final analysis, the great failing of Nazi anti-Semitic scholars was more ethical than intellectual."

Apart from the somewhat reassuring fact that Nazi-era academics were guided and cheered on by their governments, and today's academics are opposed by theirs, at least in the West, although not necessarily or much longer in some cases, I do not feel that I am being sensationalist in saying that this quotation speaks directly to the demonization process of Israel today.

Academics of the thirties were complicit in the attempted eradication of a people; academics today are complicit in the hoped-for eradication of the country that is the homeland of that people. Whether it all ends in concentration camps or a self-righteous vote at the UN, the willing executioners of academia who propagated the lies then and propagate them now sport the same ugly moral stain.

As in the universities then, the so-called scholarship supportive of their theses are rooted in irrationality, contradiction, outright falsehoods, selection bias, double standards, conspiracy-theorist level obsessiveness and – most insidiously – the Rumpelstiltskin temptation: the magical thinking that presumes you can spin the mouldy straw of mendacity and scapegoatism into the gold of political and social justice.

For a graphic example of the syndrome at its most pathological, it is worth revisiting the breathtaking candour of professor Michael Neumann of Trent University, who famously blogged: "[My aim is to] help the Palestinians [and] I am not interested in the truth, or justice, or understanding, or anything else, except so far as it serves that purpose...If an effective strategy means that some truths about the Jews don't come to light, I don't care. If an effective strategy means encouraging reasonable anti-Semitism, or reasonable hostility to Jews, I also don't care. If it means encouraging vicious racist anti-Semitism, or the destruction of the state of Israel, I still don't care."

As bad as was Neumann's infantile joy in fouling his academic nest, worse in what it signifies was the reaction of Trent president Bonnie Paterson, whose brush-off to criticism included: "the free expression of ideas in university [is] essential to our teaching."

What a perversion of the great ideal of free exchange of ideas, when permission for the dissemination of lies and incitement to hatred of an identifiable group of citizens – and one only; try to substitute any other community in that statement; you can't – can be considered "essential" to teaching.

Neumann's explicitness is shocking, his candour is revelatory. He has lost his capacity for scholarly shame, but he only expresses what many activists feel. More important, his president's support is revelatory of pusillanimity at the top and therefore of a systemic rot that runs unchecked in academia.

Anti-Israel bias on campus is not haphazard, it is structural, purposeful and professionally organized by well-funded ideologues with the specific goal of Israel's extermination as a Jewish homeland. Former Soviet "refusenik" and Israeli politician Natan Sharansky speaks of the three D's that distinguish the anti-Semitic critic from the mere critic of this or that Israeli policy:

Demonization – Israel is inherently and holistically evil with no redeemable features, an impossibility absent bias. To demonstrate to what a near-parodically corrupt degree determined Israel demonizers will go, here is a pinch-me example from Israel itself, where many of the world's most virulently Israel-hating academics freely ply their self-hating wares.

A sociology Master's thesis carried out at Hebrew University posed the question: How is it that, contrary to the accepted practice of other occupation armies, the IDF does not rape Palestinian women? Ignoring the obvious answers: that the IDF code of ethics is higher than that of other occupation forces or that Jewish men are raised with higher moral standards than those of many of their neighbour cultures, the researcher determined that the failure to rape was attributable to the soldiers' dehumanization of Palestinian women: "Consequently, a sexual act cannot be carried out with someone that is perceived as less than human." She concludes that Israeli soldiers' failure to rape is in fact a kind of psychological rape. This is the very essence of demonization: heads we win, tails you lose.

Not only was the thesis accepted, the student was awarded a prize by her department and later another prize by the university. And that tells you pretty well everything you have to know about the Alice-in-Wonderland state of affairs in the human sciences at liberal universities in Israel. As the old saying goes, the Jews are like everyone else, only more so.

Double Standards: No other country in the world is held up to the standards Israel is expected to observe. Tamils and Sikhs and Muslims can wreak carnage in the thousands on their own or other peoples, and it goes unnoticed. Let a sparrow fall by Israeli defence force hands, and the campuses and campus-trained media erupt in savage indignation.

Particularly anguishing to objective scholars is the Orwellian inversion of words and meanings, words like "apartheid," "colonialization," (what empire did Israel represent after all? Jewish settlers were fleeing their former homes) "genocide," "Nazi," and so forth, meaningless in the face of actual evidence, deliberately employed to incite hate.

Finally there is the third D – **Delegitimization**: entrenching the idea that Israel has no right to exist, a notion unheard of in 2500 years (since Carthage).

Demonization has been accomplished. Apart from North America, the world hates Israel and in the last European poll something like 70% of respondents – up many points from a few years ago – considers Israel the world's greatest evil and obstacle to peace.

Anti-Semitism is promulgated by three currents: the extreme right, the extreme left and Islamism. Only the two latter groups can be found on campus, and although a minority, in alliance are vocal enough and politically tactical enough to intimidate opposition. Middle Eastern Studies departments are a source of special concern, a veritable Augean stables of brazen, all-consuming Israel hatred.

Columbia University's Middle Eastern Studies department was the worst of the worst until the film *Columbia Unbecoming*, made on a shoestring budget, cast such a lurid public light on the malignancy of the bias that the university was forced to take action.

Anti-Israel bias in academia can take many forms – calls for boycotts or divestment, shunning of Israeli publications, pressuring governments to stop funding Israeli research, etc – and we've seen examples of them all in one university or another.

American universities have been more likely to call for disinvestment, British university union leaders, amongst whom the boycott movement started in 2002, are very keen on boycotting everything and everybody who comes from Israel. So far they have come tantalizingly close, but resolution stayed firm at the government level, and the boycotts were stymied for legal reasons. But the votes have been very close, and one day they will probably succeed. British academics seem to be the most ruthless of a bad bunch.

Hostility directed at Jews is such a commonplace on campus in Britain that this past February there was virtually no media coverage when the Stop the war Coalition prevented the deputy commander of Israel's (first) Gaza operation from speaking at London's Hillel House, when a crowd of about 70 students attempted to storm the building.

After the Gaza ceasefire was declared, anti-Israel sit-ins were organized at 17 university campuses, some of them leading to criminal damages. A series of demands, such as scholarships for Palestinian students, fund-raising for Gaza and amnesty for the protesters, and many more, were met by many of the universities; only a few – Manchester metropolitan, Birmingham, Nottingham, Leeds and Cambridge – resisted the blackmail. At Oxford a University Reader reportedly told a meeting that "within five years, Oxford will be a Jew-free zone."[5]

In 2006, when some UK universities pushed for a boycott of Israeli academics, almost all the major university presidents in North America came out with strong statements against an Israel boycott. In Britain only three of 105 universities issued a denunciatory statement.

The same year a British All-Party Parliamentary Group Against Anti-Semitism was struck, whose report concluded that there was indeed a singling out of Jewish students for negative treatment (some faculty members refer to Jews as "the Zionists among us") and that "calls to boycott contact with academics working in Israel are an assault on academic freedom and intellectual exchange."

Anti-Semitism is far more prevalent in Britain and Europe for historical reasons than here, while the Muslim populations are more numerous and more disaffected. Anti-Semitic incidents abound and the mood is tense for everyone, not just students.

In North America anti-Semitism remains generally taboo. Our communities are far larger and more organized than in Europe. In the 18-35 age group, about 15-20% of students graduating from top universities here are Jewish, a critical mass, and even then the majority remain passive in the face of aggressive hostility and classroom bias. Nevertheless, the sheer numbers give rise to minorities within willing to push back and raise media awareness of the problems, which in turn generates pressures on the university administration from the general community to clean up their act, at least cosmetically.

In Europe about 1-2% of the students in that age group are Jewish, perhaps 200,000 in all of Europe, and they are scattered, not clustered, as they are here. They have almost no campus infrastructure, like Hillel, to support them, and their community leaders – there are perhaps 50 professionals in all of Europe – keep a low profile. Under such circumstances, it is extremely difficult to counter the received wisdom of Israel's illegitimacy and the big lie of Israel's original sin.

France has always had problems coming to terms with its history of anti-Semitism. Philosopher Bernard-Henri Levy says that "The French university is the only major institution that has not repented its mistakes under the Vichy regime." A pro-Israel Jewish activist, writing in Le Figaro, observed, "On some university campuses, like Nanterre, Villetaneuse and Jussieue, the climate has become very difficult for Jews...We hear 'Death to the Jews' during demonstration [for] the Palestinian cause."

Ireland and Sweden are probably the countries that most frequently raise their voices against Israel. In September 2006, 60 Irish academics published a letter in the *Irish Times* calling for a moratorium on European grants to Israeli academic institutions.

In Russia and the former Soviet countries, anti-Zionism and open anti-Semitism are deemed acceptable across all academic disciplines. Ukraine is a particular concern. MAUP – the Interregional Academy of Personnel Management – organizes anti-Zionist and anti-Semitic conferences. In November 2005, MAUP's president, Georgy Tschokin, issued a statement of solidarity with Iranian President Ahmadinejad's threat to destroy Israel. Infamous racist David Duke was awarded a Phd at MAUP for his hate-imbued thesis on Zionism.

In Spain, the main problems with Israel in the universities are in the international relations departments. There are only two universities there that treat

Israel with respect and are not reflexively anti-American: a small private college in Madrid and the University of Navarra.

As to the state of scholarly integrity on the Israel file in the Arab countries: I can't help thinking of the anecdote about Chaim Weizmann arriving in Jerusalem in 1918 and being handed a typewritten copy of the *Protocols of the elders of Zion* by the British commander, General Sir Wyndham Deeds, who allegedly told Weizmann, "You had better read all this with care. It is going to cause you a great deal of trouble in the future."

And so it came to pass. According to Manfred Gerstenfeld, author of *Academics against Israel and the Jews (2007)*, from which many of the facts in this essay were taken, *The Protocols* are taught as fact in some Arab universities. Holocaust denial and historical fabrications run rampant everywhere in the Arab academic world. Here is a typical statement from Dr Ahmad Abu Halabiyah, rector of advanced studies at the Islamic University:

"The Jews are the Jews...They do not have any moderates or advocates of peace. They are all liars. They must be butchered and must be killed...It is forbidden to have mercy on them...Any place that you meet them, kill them."

Strangely nobody in the west is calling for a boycott of his university or any others in the Middle East where this declaration would feel right at home. Of course it isn't strange at all. Willed blindness to the vicious anti-Semitism of the Arab world, including academia, merely confirms the double standards where Israel is concerned, and the soft bigotry of low expectations that characterizes leftwing intellectuals.

I could go on and on with bad news, but I'd like to spend my remaining time on the good news. For although it took an unconscionably long time for Israeli academics to even notice, let alone react aggressively to the creeping menace, in the last few years, exasperation with Israel Apartheid Week and the boycott initiatives has aroused a panoply of official and unofficial initiatives to take back the campus.

I could give an entire talk on the positive effect Alan Dershowitz has single-handedly brought to the issue, first with his 2003 book, *The Case for Israel*, and lately with the film version, which I highly recommend and which will make excellent classroom fodder for those wiling to use it. But he has been effective as well with his threats of lawsuits against those academic institutions who try to boycott Israeli universities and academics: "Any moral person who is aware of the true facts would not sign a petition singling out Israel for divestiture. There is no third alternative."

But the discrete achievements of "star" performers from outside the university is of less interest to SAFS members than what can be done inside, for systemic change will depend on the persistence of stakeholders. So let me describe a case study where a terrible situation was somewhat reversed by legitimate means that can serve as a model for others.

The School of Oriental and African Studies in London is perhaps the worst of British anti-Zionist universities. Journalist Melanie Phillips, author of the 2007 book *Londonistan*, wryly glosses the acronym SOAS as the "School of Orchestrated Anti-Semitism."

SOAS programs anti-Semitic events, films and lectures in a steady stream. Their "Palestine Society" held a long monopoly on anti-Israel discourse because no Jewish society had existed on campus for 30 years.

In 2004 Gavin Gross, a postgraduate student at the time, reconstituted the SOAS Jewish Society. In February 2005 for the first time ever, an Israeli diplomat was invited to speak. In an echo of Montreal's 2002 Concordia University fiasco, when Benjamin Netanyahu was prevented from speaking by rioting anti-Israel activists, the event was almost scuttled when a fire alarm was deliberately set off as the assembly gathered and doors were smashed. But unlike at Concordia, where Netanyahu did not speak, the event was reconvened the same evening because unlike at Concordia, the administration did not cave in to its anti-Israel Student Union or to fear. He and the diplomat spoke to a standing-room-only crowd. Melanie Phillips wrote about it, calling the evening "a candle for freedom."

Eight months later another Israeli lecturer came, but this time there was no disruption, the Student Union cooperated and rational discussion took place. Since then, more pro-Israel events, including Israeli films, and documentaries on subjects like the 1972 Olympic Munich massacre, have been held, which have mostly been attended by non-Jews: European, Asian and Arab students and faculty.

A gratifying symbolic peak was arrived at when Alan Dershowitz spoke at SOAS, his title: "Zionism is not racism: The Case for Israel." Two hundred people were turned away from a packed hall. He spoke only for 30 minutes, then took Q and A for 90, limiting questions to critics of Israel. Afterward many attendees thanked the Jewish Society, noting that these events were the first time they had ever heard the other side of the story.

Thomas More once said, "if you cannot have the best society, at least we must try to prevent the worst." If educated Canadians truly wanted the best kind of society, they would demand better from their universities, for academia is the training ground of society's political and cultural leadership. We would know if they wanted better universities, because if they did, the membership of SAFS would number in the tens of thousands.

So we must realistically aim for prevention of the worst in our universities.

One group I would single out for praise in this regard, because it works from inside the universities, is Scholars for Peace in the Middle East (SPME). Begun as a minor listserver, SPME now comprises over 20,000 scholars at more than 1500 institutions.

The boycott push in 2007 was a spur to SPME's network expansion in Britain, France, Germany, Austria, Australia, Italy and parts of the Middle East, Asia and Latin America.

SPME's members include: faculty members, Rhodes scholars, 33 Nobel laureates, as well as 58 college and university presidents. Their newest or developing branches are at: Columbia, Stanford, University of California at Santa Cruz, University of California at Irvine (two of the worst for anti-Israel activism), at Davis and at LA, at State University of New York at Buffalo, Rutgers, MIT, CalTech and Canada's McGill University.

I myself sit on the academic advisory board of the Canadian Institute for Jewish research (CIJR), an independent research and advocacy group now in its 21st year that brings objective analysis of Israel and Middle-east related issues quickly and directly to the public via a daily electronic briefing and other widely-read publications.

CIJR's year-long Student Israel Advocacy Program is an innovative vehicle for educating Jewish students on the Middle East and coaching them in strategies for dealing with the mendacity and intimidation tactics of the anti-Israel militants.

It begins with the Jews, but it never ends with the Jews. Our universities are sick. Rouged-over anti-Semitism is the most serious presenting symptom of the disease. SAFS offers an antibiotic. Now all we need is the patient's cooperation. Thank you for this opportunity to speak about a problem that troubles me personally, and one that should trouble anyone who cares about the health of the most important cultural institution in any free society.

How to Read and Why, by Harold Bloom: A Book Review

I reviewed this book during Jewish Book Month at the Jewish Public Library in Montreal in 2005.

The title of this latest of many books of literary criticism by Harold Bloom is rich in multiple ironies. The 'How To Read' part conjures up those tall, shiny-faced paperbacks available in hardware store racks with titles like "How to Grow Tomatoes on your Balcony" or "How to Drywall like a Professional." One might reasonably infer from this part of the title that the contents will include a guaranteed step-by-step route to critical expertise for the average reader. It is anything but. The second part of the title "And Why" reflects a more significant and profoundly sad irony. That people must be given a reason, be persuaded to read in our era, aptly dubbed "the society of the spectacle," is for those of us who read as naturally as we breathe a sobering and unsettling reality.

And yet, when I read film critic and best-selling author David Denby's remark, "In America a grown man or woman reading at home during the day is not a person to be taken seriously," I found myself in intuitive agreement. Who among even the most educated people we know is acknowledged to have "a reading life," apart from the monthly book club, newspapers and those organs for professional development – magazines, journals and the like – which keep us 'in the loop' and tenuously abreast of the myriad tributaries to the informational flood. Today's unusual rage for the adventures of Harry Potter notwithstanding, most young people are in thrall to the endless bombardment of films, MTV and other electronic distractions, which elude the attempts of parents and educators, however ardent, to lobby for the hopelessly slow, solitary and quiet pleasures of reading.

Harold Bloom's quarrel in *How to Read and Why*, though, is not with the competing claims for attention from the world of consumerism and entertainment. *How to Read and Why* is rather a grinding indictment of the culture wars of the last 30 years, whose effect on literature has been to undermine the Great Canon of Western literature. The Great Canon comprises the prose and poetry studied by all of us who graduated before the tumultuous counter-culture that erupted in the late 1960s. The humanist school of criticism which guided our studies was supplanted by what Harold Bloom calls the "School of Resentment," the literary wing of today's "culture of complaint" (a phrase coined by Robert Hughes in his eponymous book).

How to read and Why occupies the same pew as recent books by other similarly motivated thinkers in a rising counterweight to the ideologues of the academic left who have dominated the critical environment, taken over the English departments of most western universities, and produced a generation of students for whom the *pleasure* of reading has been replaced by the *politics* of reading.

Here are a few other writers in this save-the-western-canon trend:

1. Italo Calvino: *Why Read The Classics?*

2. Martin Seymour-Smith: *The 100 Most Influential Books Ever Written.*

3. Harold Bloom: *The Western Canon: The Books and School of the Ages.*

4. David Denby: *Great Books: My Adventures with Homer, Rousseau, Woolf, and other Indestructible Writers of the Western World* (cited by Kirkus Review as "one of very few truly good books on the culture wars").

5. Dale Salawek: *A Passion for Books* (collection of different authors) of which one reviewer could have been speaking of Bloom when he wrote: "what does give this collection an extra sad edge is the feeling that the end of the printed word may well be nigh, which is why we have the worshippers singing their anthems louder while the pagans mill outside."

6. Robert Alter: *The Pleasures of Reading in an Ideological Age.* This is a personal favourite, the one you may find yourself reading for its cool and elegantly informative persuasions as an antidote to Bloom's too-passionate jeremiads.

7. Allan Bloom: *The Closing of the American Mind* (decline of the humanities).

These writers share a common idea: that books should be read for the aesthetic pleasure and mental enlargement they bring, and they also share a common belief: that literary greatness can be objectively assessed, and that the canon is worthy of preservation and distinction because of the influence that great writers have had on shaping our culture.

To begin, then, with the other, implied, 'Why' of the title: Why are Harold Bloom and these other defenders of the humanist tradition so angry?

To answer that question we must go back in time more than a century, well before the concept of writing instructional guidebooks to the study of literature for the general public was even a gleam in the eye of any English professor: before, indeed, there was such a thing as an English professor.

Historically speaking, English Literature as a formal discipline is a relative newcomer to the university syllabus. In his inaugural lecture about a 100 years ago, George Gordon, one of Oxford University's first such professors, had this to say: "England is sick, and…English literature must save it. The Churches… having failed, and social remedies being slow, English literature has a triple function: still, I suppose, to delight and instruct us [as Aristotle prescribes] but also, and above all, to save our souls and heal the state."

The entrenchment of English Literature as a course of study, then, was a consequence of the perceived failure of Christianity. It was hoped that the reading of great literary works – the Canon – would provide the moral basis for industrial-scientific culture that the Church could no longer supply with credibility.

In a parallel way in the United States, the core curricula that once flourished in many American universities, now obligatory only at a few, such as Columbia University's Literary Humanities and Contemporary Civilization program, were intended to enshrine the literature of Christian Europe for the benefit of the huge influx of Eastern European immigrants (mostly Jews and Italians) who needed to be assimilated into the larger culture.

Of course literature could never fulfill the huge ambition outlined by Professor Gordon. The poetry of Goethe on the bookshelves of Nazi warlords didn't crimp their evil impulses, and English professors are not especially celebrated for their kind and morally superior characters.

With its failure to deliver the goods, so to speak, the Canon came under attack from a variety of moral and ideological standpoints. Nowadays a humanities student can graduate without ever having studied Shakespeare or Jane Austen. Literary studies have become loosely cultural and leftist, with a heavy accent on Marxist, gender and ethnic studies.

To illustrate, here is a sample from a huge smorgasbord of course offerings currently available at American universities, compiled by the Young America Foundation in its study, "Comedy and Tragedy: College Course Descriptions and What they tell us about Higher Education Today":

1. **Harvard**: *Feminist Biblical Interpretation*: "the significance of Feminist Hermeneutics for contemporary theological reflection and education for ministry";

2. **Carnegie Mellon**: *Sex and Death* ("this course will address the question of whether we need to liberate death now that we have figured sex out");

3. **Bowdoin University**: *Music and Gender*: "The main question addressed in this course: Is Beethoven's ninth symphony a marvel of abstract architecture, culminating in a gender-free paean to human solidarity, or does it model the question of rape?"

4. **University of Texas**: *Race and Sport in African American Life*: "The class will explore how sports have been used to justify and promote antiquated, eugenic, and ultimately racist notions of blackness.";

5. **University of Virginia**: in a course on Marxism, the description declares that Marx's work "is the standard against which all subsequent social thought must be judged."

It would be hard to find a university today whose faculty has not been torn apart over the question of the Western Canon – that is to say, those persisting subjects of literary history, criticism and scholarship that in common practice stand for the twin pillars of Graeco-Roman literature and philosophy, and Judaeo-Christian culture as reflected in the typical European – derived syllabus that used to be the standard fare of university courses.

But in the last thirty years a thorough "interrogation" (to use a favourite postmodern term) of our cultural heritage has scattered such received wisdom to the four winds. In our post-Holocaust, post-colonial age that heritage, rather than a symbol of pride, is seen by many as elitist, the agent of suffering and ruination to the disempowered and disenfranchised peoples of the world. American "hegemony" (another favourite) in technology, consumerism and the media has lit a fire of self-loathing in the academic left. The so-called "great" works of the Canon have become the whipping boy, the stand-in for tools of centuries of oppression.

The main argument of the academic left is that the construction of a monolithic cultural identity has marginalized and ignored minority cultures. Terry Eagleton, Marxist and professor of English at Oxford, summarizes the debate in this way:

> *Is there a Canon of great books? What is a masterpiece? Who decides what the great books are? ...Do colleges and universities have an obligation to expose undergraduate students to some of the great works of Western civilization...? Do we also have an obligation to expose students to the work of other cultures and of the historically dispossessed within our own society?*

Or, as one Afro-American student at Columbia put it: "Why is Mozart better than some African drummer?" She professed that listening to Mozart was for her a "re-enslavement" even though she was generations away from any such reality.

You may discount the words of a young student. But what about Toni Morrison, Pulitzer prize- winning feminist Marxist ethnocentrist African-American novelist? She claims that African-Americans should not have to study Moby Dick because – I am not making this up – "the insane whiteness" of the whale "indicates exclusion of African-Americans from Melville's overt vision…"

The greatest blow to the Canon was Academe's embrace of the concept of Relativism as opposed to pre-postmodernist Essentialism or Foundationalism, the belief that there are absolute and universal standards for assessment and judgment. For relativists, all truths are a function of perspective. All truth is socially assigned or "constructed". There are no absolute truths – only "your" truth and "my" truth, black truth and white truth, female and male truth.

There is no "right" and "wrong", because that would be elevating a "local construction" (western humanism) to a universal principle. Another student at Columbia declares, for example, "If a culture believes in ritual sacrifice, then it is all right within that culture to sacrifice people."

If there are no absolutes, then, there can be no idea of the aesthetic. Shakespeare has no more "value" than subway graffiti. They are both "texts". And here is the final irony of Bloom's title. To a student of Discourse Studies (the new name for Literature) a critical book by Bloom called "How to Read" has no more intrinsic literary value than "How to Drywall." As the essayist Annie Dillard puts it, literature used to be "a great widening stream" with fixed landmarks offering an accumulation of wisdom; now it is "a land of unlinked lakes seen from the air."

As for culture, it would seem that only minority cultures, that is to say the *victims* of western culture – women, gays, aboriginals, people of colour – can have anything relevant or worthwhile to say. Western culture, because it is powerful, is not "innocent." As Robert Hughes dryly comments on the postmodern line of reasoning from the Left, "Oppression is what we do in the West. What they do in the Middle East is 'their culture.'"

With the ascent of Deconstruction as the fashionable critical approach to literature, students were taught that the author was "dead" as a concept, and that all 'texts' (no longer 'novels' or 'short stories') were to be dissected, interrogated for ideological content and exposed for the vehicles of hegemonic discourse they were, the very opposite of reading for the pleasures of the text.

Writer and critic Alison Lurie writes: "The term deconstruction implies that the text has been put together like a building or a piece of machinery, and that it is in need of being taken apart, not so much in order to repair it as to demonstrate underlying inadequacies, false assumptions and inherent contradictions…it is a kind of guided rape."

For traditionalists like Bloom, such a cold and adversarial posture to reading is anathema. In his book *The Western Canon*, to which *How to Read and Why* is something of an appendage, he argues for the aesthetic value of canonical literature. Mustering all the force of his enormous authority in his field – two long-term professorships (NYU and Yale), a sterling roster of original books – together with a passion and missionary zeal reminiscent of the biblical prophets, Bloom argues for the superior aesthetic qualities embodied in the Canon.

He brushes aside the suggestion that the Western Canon is just another form of western imperialism. Aesthetics are everything to him. Morality and ideology have no place in literature, and the relativization of beauty is loathsome. For him, and many others, canonical works live because they have earned their honours; they have a vitality that sustains their presence in the cultural memory.

He says:

> If we read the western canon in order to form our social, political or personal moral values, I firmly believe we will become monsters of selfishness and exploitation…All that the Western Canon can bring one is the proper use of one's own solitude, that solitude whose final form is one's confrontation with one's own mortality.

This sentiment is repeated in *How to Read and Why* in a slightly different way: "the pleasures of reading are selfish rather than social." "Ultimately we read… in order to strengthen the self and learn its authentic interests." Reading is "the search for a difficult pleasure." And the words most quoted by reviewers: reading is "the most healing of pleasures."

All this has been by way of seeming preamble, but it is offered as a means of showing respect to an old soldier's deep anger at seeing his country's flag trampled in the mud. This is a book where the 'back story' hovers over every line, and where the motivation for writing is as much what the book is about as the book itself. Now let us turn to the "How To Read" part.

Most reviewers have been kind to *How to Read and Why*, just as admired older actors often win an Academy Award for their latest performance as a way of rewarding many previous achievements over a lifetime. The fact is, the title of the book is misleading. Those readers hoping for a structured approach on how to read literature deeply will be disappointed. Unlike less flamboyant but more accessible writers like Robert Alter, for example, Bloom does not really address strategies for analyzing and assessing works of art.

The book is divided into conventional categories: poetry, short stories, plays, and novels with summary observations in between. The fact that there is no bibliography is your first clue that this is not a 'serious' book in the academic sense. What you will be reading is a very interesting and eloquent portrait of Harold Bloom's loves, hates, prejudices, opinions, and insights. You are neither invited nor encouraged to compare what he says with the views of other scholars.

It isn't to say that you won't be engrossed and entertained; it isn't to say that you won't learn anything. There are a number of wonderful nuggets, original insights that will stay with me, and that I am grateful for. The trouble is that I had to scoop them up during the literary equivalent of running with the bulls in Pamplona.

To continue the metaphor, while reaching down for the nuggets I was continually being gored, and not very playfully, by Bloom's pet bull: his obsession with Shakespeare. Shakespeare is the greatest writer the world has ever known. But in Bloom's critical world Shakespeare is more than one standard by which others are judged; he is the only standard. This is no surprise: anyone who has read *Shakespeare: The Invention of the Human* is aware of Bloom's thesis that Shakespeare is a secular scripture from which we derive much of our language, our psychology and our mythology. According to Bloom, Shakespeare invented something that hadn't existed before. Bloom defines this as "personality," inwardness, what it means to be human.

If Shakespeare's drama is a secular bible, Bloom is its high priest. What is disconcerting is the zero sum game he plays. He persuades us that Shakespeare is great by attacking those who don't share his vision. Shakespeare fastens on character over plot and action. Therefore for Bloom only character matters in a literary work. Bloom's compulsion to denigrate those second-raters – i.e. those who are not Shakespearean in their vision, even such heavyweights as John Webster and Ben Jonson – is irritating.

Bloom loves Checkhov because Checkhov is "more Shakespearean even than Turgenev." For Borges "Shakespeare is at once everyone and everybody." Tennyson's Ulysses has "Shakespearean vitalism." "…when [Hemingway] is most ambitious in his stories [he] is most Shakespearean."

When Bloom loves, he loves according to the Shakespearean quotient of the author: "Shakespeare and Dante," he says, "are at the center of the Canon because they excel all other writers in cognitive acuity, linguistic energy and power of invention. Beyond them [the Canon]…is what they absorbed and what absorbs them."

Well, this may or may not be true, but how is a reader to argue with such a statement? You must accept, when you read Bloom, that you are in his church.

When he reads the service, and delivers the sermon, you listen quietly, you believe or you leave.

Preachers in a bully pulpit bring down the word from on high, but they don't feel the need to give their reasons. In his section on short stories we are informed that O. Henry is "greatly preferable to the abominable Poe," but he doesn't say why Poe is "abominable." Not Shakespearean enough is my guess. Or he declares "we have no popular artists today". This is just untrue. What about Steven King for starters? Or Tom Wolfe?

As a reviewer of novels, I was naturally the most interested in what Bloom had to say in this area. Novels are the vehicles of choice for writers portraying people striving to grow and acquit themselves in society over extended periods of time. They are a kind of laboratory for the study of character in the making, and they bring us a little closer to an understanding of what I consider the thing most worth knowing: human nature.

I was happy to hear Ruth Wisse admit last week, in speaking of her new book, *The Modern Jewish Canon*, that she deliberately addressed novels as being the most interesting and representative of the ideas she was investigating. Novels are the acknowledged favourites of most critics and teachers for reading pleasure, but the approach to reading them is incredibly diverse.

"The main question as to a novel," wrote Sydney Smith, "is – did it amuse?" If Ruth Wisse believed that, she would have included Mordecai Richler in her canon, but for her a novel must have made a significant contribution to its own culture, and in saying significant she would mean a positive contribution, one that strengthens the culture in an original way. It is of course noteworthy that when Wisse speaks of a Jewish canon, she can do so in the pre-postmodern sense of the word, because while Jewish culture is extremely diverse, it is still organically centred in a shared history and commonly accepted myths.

Aristotle, the first literary critic, declared that literature must both "delight and instruct." Some critics lean more toward the "delight" side – the aesthetics of writing, like Bloom – while others take up the defense of the "instruct" mode – the "ideas" school of writing. Wisse, like the nineteenth century writers and critics, and like a personal favourite of mine amongst critics, George Orwell, insists that literature should leave a philosophic and moral residue, that it should connect or re-connect the reader with the world around him and remind him of his relations with other human beings in all their complexity. Both would be impatient with works that only seek to entertain, no matter how beguiling their artistry.

Wisse might agree with Desmond MacCarthy who once said: "It is the business of literature to turn facts into ideas." That is perhaps why Philip Roth and

Saul Bellow are in her Jewish canon but not mentioned at all in *How to Read and Why*.

Bloom, as we have already noted, has the opposing perspective, one that sees a literary work in relation to the individual divorced from a social context, assessing the success of the work in terms of its aesthetic and experiential impact. In his section on novels he says that he adores Cervantes who "seems to me Shakespeare's only possible rival in the imaginative literature of the past four centuries." And here we find one of the nuggets I spoke of before: in praising the complex and subtle friendship between Don Quixote and Sancho Panza, he notes that Shakespeare's women can maintain friendships but not his men, adding casually that everyone in Shakespeare has difficulty listening to each other, while conversation is the bedrock of Don Quixote and a vehicle for greater awareness. This is critical gold. So is his entire analysis of Dickens. He says that to read Dickens is "to read as if one could be a child again."

At the same time he makes flat statements of personal bias that will flabbergast the average reader, such as: "There is no more sympathetic character in modern fiction than [Hans] Castorp" (protagonist of Mann's Magic Mountain); or "Unless you are an ideologue or a puritanical moralist, you are likely to fall in love with Hamlet."

In re-reading this book and in taking specific notes on those authors Bloom likes particularly well, I began to see a pattern. Like Shakespeare Bloom enjoys characters who go to extremes – characters not unlike himself. He likes Stendhal who "celebrates desire that goes beyond all limits." He likes Dostoyevsky's *Crime and Punishment* because "it alters our consciousness." He loves Moby Dick – no one in American literature is more extreme than Captain Ahab – because Captain Ahab is "clearly a Shakespearean figure" and the "forerunner of all American questers" who "[established] a standard of defiance that no one in his wake has matched."

Faulkner's *As I Lay Dying*, which deals with "the horror of family and community" offers "the one value of stoic endurance." In Nathanael West's *Miss Lonelyhearts* he finds a "reality in America more grotesque than you can trump." Thomas Pynchon's *The Crying of Lot 49* is "apocalyptic."

But the lengthy analysis that best exposes Bloom's fascination with the pathological extreme is to be found in his enthusiastic recommendation of the novel *Blood Meridien* by Cormac McCarthy. This novel chronicles the true story of the Glanton gang, a murderous paramilitary force under joint orders by Texas and Mexico to massacre as many Indians as possible.

In his usual dogmatic way Bloom prefaces his remarks with the statement that "no other living novelist…has given us a book as strong and memorable as

131

Blood Meridien." He then goes on to say that the content of the novel is so violent and full of "overwhelming carnage" that he had to make three attempts before he could read it. He tells us that the story includes "continuous massacres and mutilations" and that the protagonist, Judge Holden, is "the most frightening figure in all of American literature." On the other hand its "high style is Shakespearean…"

Personally I find Bloom's fascination with extremism and defiance disturbing. Although his chapter on earlier novels includes Jane Austen and Thomas Mann and Henry James, all of whom put a microscope to the complexities of hyper-social behaviours, none of his recommendations for modern novels deals with protagonists acting within civilized or rational boundaries. All are severely marginalized or pathological figures. It is a truism that modern art's great subject is alienation – but there are degrees.

It is difficult to put a definitive label on a book as idiosyncratic as *How to Read and Why*. It is by turns rhapsodic, banal and erudite. Many good points are informative and accessible, others are made in language so jargon-ridden that it seems intended only for PhD candidates. Bloom tells the reader that poetry should always have a close reading, but does not tell us how to do it. The book supposedly targets the average reader, but Bloom speaks about works no average reader could possibly want to read. Keats' "La Belle Dame Sans Merci" and the long ballad "Tom O'Bedlam" are poor choices for showcasing the value of poetry, while Cormac MacCarthy, after Bloom's description of *Blood Meridien*, is permanently off my reading list.

Harold Bloom's accomplishments must be seen as cumulative to be appreciated. His greatest achievement has been in wrestling control of the Shakespeare agenda away from the sharks of Academe. Shakespeare has been the lightning rod, a focus for the culture wars from the beginning. As we know, Bloom is the alpha "bardolator": bardolators regard Shakespeare as the Perfect Master, and consider it the scholar's job to reveal his perfection. To the theorists Shakespeare was the Perfect Slave: a tool of the power elites of Elizabethan England.

An entire generation of academics has devoted itself to turning Shakespeare's works into exemplars of deconstruction, postmodern Marxism and postmodern Freudianism. Theorizing has replaced reading Shakespeare or even seeing his plays enacted! But, thanks to Harold Bloom, that tide has turned.

Last May the Shakespeare Scholars Convention was held in Montreal, and I would like to give the penultimate word to excerpts from a watershed paper delivered by Professor Linda Charnes from Indiana University. She identifies Bloom as "someone who comes from our ranks and has contemptuously risen above them and has written a best-selling and profitable book…"

...we'd better look very carefully not at what Bloom's doing, but what we're doing in the academy.

We all avow we speak for oppressed voices of class, race, gender, nationality; we don't 'interpret', we 'intervene', we don't 'analyze', we 'interrogate'...is this all we have to offer as critics?...it's time to get beyond the institutional debunking of the bourgeois autonomous or essentialist humanist self. The time to make a career beating that horse has passed."

...bashing the 'bourgeois subject' has to some extent calcified us into an elite corps of yuppie guerilla academics...if Bloom's right about anything it's this: the world doesn't give a fig for our critiques of its epistemology. Post-humanism may exist in the academy but it won't be found in the hearts and minds of the book-buying public. For at least in Bloom's zesty world there's some humour, some poignancy and some openly avowed love of art.

Harold Bloom is not a lovable critic, but he is an antidote to the study of literature that exists at the level of theory and concept. Literature gives us interesting characters living individual lives whose destinies resonate in us and perhaps change us. Successful literature both delights through plot and stylistic devices, and instructs, by giving us characters whose spiritual struggles extend beyond the page and symbolize the eternal strivings of all of us to be better people.

When I have read a great novel or a great short story or seen a great play I am a subtly different person from what I was before I started, and it seems to me that I understand a little more of the human condition than I did before. Bloom reinforces this feeling.

In articulating some of the enduring truths of great literature, and by demonstrating the continuing power of great writers to resist the theorizing barbarians at the gate, Bloom reminds us of why we are so attracted to literary study in the first place, and for that we must be grateful.

That being said, if you want to know more about "how to read and why," you really should read Robert Alter's *The Pleasure of Reading in an Ideological Age*. Alter delivers what Bloom promises.

Jews and Power, by Ruth Wisse:
A Book Review

I reviewed this book in March, 2008 at the Beth Tzedec Synagogue in Toronto.

Montreal's Jewish community is a very small world, especially for those involved in Jewish cultural life. I therefore was privileged to have established a friendly relationship with Ruth Wisse before she was lured away some 12 years ago to become a Professor of Yiddish Studies and of Comparative Literature at Harvard University.

In the years before that, Ruth taught at McGill University in the Jewish Studies Department she helped to found in the late 1960s. I was lucky enough to make the cut for a wildly popular course she taught in European and American Jewish Literature. Her course was always over-subscribed with eager students who never missed a single class. I still have all the notes I took over the course of the year, and refer to them frequently when I review Jewish authors.

I miss Ruth's presence in our city. Last May I saw her at a fund-raising dinner for *Commentary Magazine* in New York City, where she introduced the keynote speaker, Senator Joe Lieberman, who is also her *m'chitin,* as Lieberman's daughter is married to one of Ruth's sons. The dinner was attended by the *crème de la crème* of conservative American intellectuals, Jewish and otherwise: magazine and newspaper editors, think tank fellows, politicos and well-known academics.

It was rather fascinating to look around the room while Ruth was at the podium and note the attentiveness, the warmth and the enormous respect focused on this mild-mannered, graying little *bubbie,* who looks like Miss Marple, and speaks with the irony-tinged candour of a latter-day Tevye the Dairyman.

Ruth is nowhere near so humble as she looks, though. As she hits her stride, the quiet power of her words soon reveals the confident moral steel behind those bashful smiles and self-deprecating shrugs.

Ruth is more than the doyenne of conservative Jewish thinkers in the West, she is something of a prophet. She has rarely, if ever, been proved wrong in her political predictions where Israel is concerned.

Intellectual acuity, a vast referential knowledge of Jewish history and literature, and an unsparing eye for the timeless strengths and frailties of human nature often lead Ruth Wisse to conclusions that prove discomfiting to mainstream Jews. Let's see if they discomfit you, as we examine the question posed in the title of tonight's review: Why are Jews so dumb when it comes to handling political power?

Jews and Power roams across Jewish history from the kingdom of David to the beginning of the Second Intifada. The book doesn't deal with Jews' actual power – Israel is militarily mighty for its size, and Jews in the West have influence – but rather with the ambiguity at the heart of Jews' relationship to political power.

Wisse's perspective has already stirred up vigorous discussion within and beyond the Jewish world. Those of you who have read it, I hope will find stimulation tonight for further reflection, and those who haven't, I hope to pique your curiosity enough to want to read it.

Jews are, on the average, more intellectually accomplished than other people. That's not an opinion, that's actually proven scientific fact. There are today 2.1 billion Christians in the world, 1.3 billion Muslims and almost a billion Hindus. Jews? Maybe 14 million. Yet they make their mark on the world in absurdly disproportionate numbers.

Almost a quarter of Nobel prizes have been won by Jews. They publish oceans of words annually. They advise presidents. They teach, they research, they editorialize, they judge, they heal, they notarize, they invent world-changing technology, they save people taxes. They don't control the banks, as their enemies claim, but they do run Hollywood, for what that has been worth politically to Jews – not much, in fact.

Israel, with less than 1/1000th of the world's population, has more business start-ups than any country in the world after the U.S. It is ranked second in venture capitalist funds. It is third in companies listed on the Nasdaq after the U.S. and Canada. It has the highest percentage of engineers at 135/10,000. The U.S. is next with 85/10,000.

So we're smart at lots of things. Yet we are dumb when it comes to politics. In the Diaspora we vote for the wrong leaders, insist against all evidence that our enemies are rational people with whom a dialogue is possible, and meekly hand over endowments to the institutions that teach our children that Israel is the world's greatest obstacle to peace.

In Israel Jews make stupid deals with their enemies, (the dumbest of which – Oslo – was the inspiration for this book, Wisse says). They cling to a form of government that allows extremists on both sides to paralyze decision-making. They spend a fortune on archeological digs and a pittance on leadership-training for Israel advocacy in the Diaspora.

The best and the brightest in Israel eschew politics because it is difficult to remain a politician of integrity and honour there. (As Natan Sharansky famously remarked, "Unlike most Israeli politicians, I served in prison *before* I was elected.") The best and the brightest are critics of those in power.

Both in Israel and the Diaspora we are so eager to be fair to our enemies we are unfair to ourselves. Our anti-Semitism watchdogs anguish over neo-Nazi graffiti, but remain *shtumm* on the hate speech – real hate speech of the "Jews are apes and pigs" variety – that spews forth from certain mosques. Our community's leaders in the Diaspora take university presidents to lunch to gently discuss campus anti-Zionism like reasonable people, while rabid anti-Semites take over our campuses during Israeli Apartheid Week and pound away at the Big Lie of Israel's moral illegitimacy.

Israel is surrounded by 22 tribal-based Arab countries, all of whom consider Israel a cancer in their midst which they are honour-bound to destroy or vanquish. Arab-financed *madrassas* all over the world teach their children that it is Jews who are the world's cancer as well. We saw the fruits of this teaching just last December in Mumbai, where the members of a Chabad centre were brutally massacred by jihadists with no political, territorial or historical connection to Israel, for no other reason than to terrorize Jews everywhere.

There are 495 million Europeans. Of them only 15-20 million are Muslim. Yet that 3% of the European population accounts for 50% of anti-Semitic acts there. North America is presently the last bastion of widespread friendliness to Israel on the planet. For how long will that friendliness last?

In *Jews and Power*, Ruth Wisse poses and answers the question: Why is our political condition so exceptional?

Her answer begins with the destruction of the first temple in 586 B.C.E. Following the normal way of defeated tribes, the Jews should have assimilated. Instead, they maintained their autonomy by adopting a unique relationship with the political powers that dominated them.

Wisse says that ancient Jews compartmentalized their allegiances. To their earthly masters they demonstrated outward meekness and compliance, but

137

internally they did not define themselves as slaves. They answered to a higher power.

Interpreting their defeat as a sign of God's displeasure, they determined to satisfy God's demands and show that they were worthy of his favour. In this way they banalized their temporal submission, refused to accept the judgment of their enemies as arbiters of their fate, and kept the flame of peoplehood alive.

The defining event for our ancestors was the destruction of the second temple by the Romans in 70 A.D. Up until then the Jews had been a martial people, and focused on statehood. By the time the temple burned at the end of a four-year siege, the city was surrounded by the bodies of 10,000 crucified Jews. That was the first defeat in a series of Jewish rebellions against the Roman Empire that finally ended in 135 A.D., resulting in a Jewish Diaspora that lasted nearly 2,000 years.

Exile and mourning the loss of Jewish sovereignty thenceforth became a central motif of Jewish peoplehood. Jews were now vulnerable, conscious of their loss of sovereignty and this time wary of regaining political power. The gap in attitudes that opened in 70 A.D. "cuts like a chasm between the before and after," says Wisse.

Jewish culture turned introspective, focusing on moral power rather than the strength that comes from an army and institutions of central authority. While in exile the Jews grew comfortable with submission. The great scholar and ethicist Maimonides said in 1172: "We have acquiesced, both old and young, to inure ourselves to humiliation."

Jews threw their efforts into perfecting the art of accommodation to local conditions, learning many languages, and developing the skills that made them useful to their political masters. They became a "middleman minority," like the Chinese in Malaysia, the Armenians in the Ottoman Empire and the Ibos in Nigeria. As these middlemen are more educated and skilled than the majority population, as they lend and charge interest, barter rather than produce necessities, they are resented – or worse – by the majority.

As the saying goes, the Jews are like everyone else, only more so. In addition to their economic role, and unlike other minorities, Jews served their host populations in the realm of culture. Also unlike other minorities, they did not assimilate after a few generations.

"Proving oneself to rulers was the precondition of exile." To rulers Jews had value: They didn't make trouble, they were good for the economy and their loyalty could be counted on, because they had no internal means of protecting whatever rights and freedoms they were allotted at the ruler's pleasure.

"Jews had to win toleration through exemplary behaviour and proofs of service," Wisse writes. Life was precarious for Jews, and unpredictable under both Christian and Islamic rulers. But it worked on the whole, because Jews continued to set their valuation of themselves according to what they believed God expected of them, not the valuation set on them by the cultures they lived in.

The Enlightenment was supposed to put an end to the ghettoization and low status of Jews. In 1791 France's Decree of Emancipation gave Jews full citizenship for the first time in history. Jews were ecstatic. They plunged into the professions, the culture and the economy with all the zeal, ambition and canniness we are familiar with in our North American story, an adventure that ended well for us.

Wisse believes (somewhat controversially) that Jewish education should concentrate far more on the Enlightenment than on the Holocaust, which occupies a disproportionate of educational and cultural programming in our community. For The Holocaust, Wisse explained once in a lecture, "only" affected Jews. The Enlightenment affected *Judaism*.

Up to the Enlightenment the Jews had been a tolerated collective with no entrenched rights, but united under God and one or more versions of Orthodoxy. The Enlightenment made individuals out of collectivists. As fully equal citizens of their host nations, Jews were free to decide what form their Jewish identity would take. It was the Enlightenment that made secular Judaism the driving engine of Jewish destiny. It was Jewish secularism that gave rise to the Zionist movement.

The Enlightenment failed Jews. Now, as citizens, it wasn't the rulers Jews had to please, it was voters. And here Wisse provides an interesting insight. It was a lot easier to impress one czar or king or caliph with Jewish utility, much easier to placate, to flatter, to enrich one than to convince many.

That the Enlightenment and full civic equality was not going to be the salvation it promised was soon made clear. In 1840, an Italian monk and his servant disappeared from their Damascus cloister, never to be found. Soon an anti-Semitic blood libel made the rounds. A Jew was arrested and tortured. He "confessed" to the kidnapping and murder of the missing men by innocent community leaders, some of whom died in prison, others of whom converted to Christianity. There were riots against Jews all over the region.

All the major powers got involved in the "Damascus Affair." The press in France took the side of the libelists. Jews were shocked when France sided with Syria for its own political reasons. Suddenly they were vulnerable again.

Wisse concludes: "Jews failed to appreciate that the replacement of a single autocratic ruler by an elected assembly had potentially reduced rather than increased their political influence...The same politicians they tried to enlist in their defence could also sacrifice their interests to far larger competing constituencies...Seen from this angle, the Damascus affair was a template for the anti-Semitic movement that arose thirty-five years later." [Update: These very words could have been written today with regard to the so-called "Arab Spring." Proof again of Wisse's prescience.]

When seeking to explain their bad fortunes, *hoi polloi* are easily aroused to scapegoatism. The Jews were now subject to mob volatility in a way they hadn't been before when under a decent ruler's protection. One word sums up what happened when Jews became "normal" citizens: Dreyfus. Dreyfus was the Jewish 9/11.

Dreyfus was proof that democracy is no match for a cultural zeitgeist. Jews had now more reason than ever to fear for their security. Conspiracy theories erupted. Jews were denounced as the enemy within. To the left they were bloodsucking capitalists, to the right they were rootless cosmopolitans without allegiance to the state.

Attempts by Jewish leaders to accommodate and ingratiate themselves were perceived as part of the conspiracy. Jews' singularity had become a terrible handicap at the very moment of their supposed normalization. The Enlightenment was ironically the necessary prelude to the Jews' greatest tragedy.

The Jews tried to defend themselves against these accusations, but they followed a now familiar template of ingratiation rather than counterattack, because counterattack is the touchstone of people who desire and expect to gain political power (something to think about when we compare the aggressive self-promotion of many Muslim immigrants to our own non-proselytizing, self-effacing stance. While Islam has known periods of political passivity, its defining philosophy is expansionism and even triumphalism with regard to other religions and cultures. With no line separating mosque and state, and never having suffered *dhimmitude* – second class status – in their own lands, Muslims do not share the accommodationist instincts of Jews.)

In an interesting footnote to this phenomenon, I met (on another topic) with a sociologist at York University, Rob Kenedy, who told me about a research paper he is writing, for which he was interviewing French Jews who have come to Canada in the last few years. He said the recurrent theme in these discussions was the wonderment the French Jews expressed at the very idea of feeling they "had" to leave France.

One of his subjects, a second generation Tunisian Jew, said his family had come to France to escape Arab persecution. They were now astonished to find themselves in flight once again, this time from a democratic country that was supposed to offer permanent security. Citizenship had not translated into acceptance. As he noted, "We are Jews first" in France. He does not feel that way in Canada, I am happy to report.

Wisse tells us that the Jews only sought political power as a last resort, when it became clear that neither assimilation, conversion, socialism or hyper-patriotism could assuage the militant rise of anti-Semitism. The establishment of the state of Israel in the same decade as the Holocaust, and the reclamation of Hebrew as a national language is an extraordinary historical achievement.

But now what? The Jews have a state. They have political power. But what do they do with it? They go on acting exactly as if they did not have political power. They continue in the same habits: being useful, peaceful and naively expecting that the people in the region they have come to live amongst will be grateful for the skills and culture they can offer. (One reviewer of this book, Yale University professor David Gelernter, rather cleverly remarked that the early Zionists' big mistake in their approach to the Arabs was to offer them help, which stung their pride. They would have done better, as most immigrants do in the normal course of things, to ask for help.) They had no political smarts.

Ben Gurion, Israel's founding president, worried about this tendency. He said: "We did not disappear from the face of the earth as other nations did, but we failed to remain independent in our homeland; we failed to save our state. This time our task is not to maintain a state, but to build it; this constitutes a much more political skill, and I do not see that we know it."

Mere hostility to the early Zionists soon became an organized movement, as Arab leaders took their cues from the Nazi leaders, whose exterminationist policies they sought to emulate.

Arab anti-Zionism, Wisse says, is more lethal than European anti-Semitism. For in Europe, each nation-state had its own flavour of anti-Semitism and acted independently with regard to its own Jews. Hitler didn't call for a pan-European anti-Semitism; he had his own plan.

But anti-Zionism is different. Anti-Zionism is the unifying glue for the entire Arab, and most of the Muslim, world, which cannot find any other basis for inter-tribal cooperation. The Arab demonization of the Jews has been hugely successful, but Israel has been strangely passive in its own defence.

Wisse suggests this is because Jews are so hungry for acceptance and so used to the accommodationist paradigm that they are not motivated to strike back with denunciations of the Arab world. As always they think that by accommodating, they will win acceptance.

The Jewish impulse to accommodate, an ancient practice, ironically dovetails with the entire West's postmodern trend to self-criticism on a self-defeating scale. The U.S. and other liberal democracies feel morally accountable for their "sins" of imperialism, colonialism, slavery, residential schools, cultural hegemony, you name it. Unfortunately Israel has more at stake than the other nations of the West. Huge countries like Canada and the United States with no border enemies can accommodate a fairly high rate of internal disaffection without self-destructing. Israel cannot.

No Jewish act of accommodation could have solved the German problem with the Jews and no Israeli act of accommodation will solve the Arabs' problem with the Jews.

The Arabs and the Jews come from radically different traditions. The Jews subscribe to a culture of accountability. As westerners of largely European descent, they share in that civilization's penchant for self-criticism. Most Islam-dominated societies subscribe to the politics of conquest – and all tribal societies, like the Arabs, are mired in a culture of honour, shame and blame.

Those who think accommodation will win Jews acceptance in the Arab world are delusional. Oslo was their accommodationist delusion made manifest. What country in the history of the world, Wisse wonders, has ever armed its enemy in the expectation of security?

The one advantage Israel enjoys politically over the Arabs is that the West needs her. Israel is valuable as an ally in the war on terror. "We are all Jews now," said James Woolsey, former director of the CIA after 9/11. "We should all reflect upon the historic reality that when anti-Semitism raises its head, the rest of us...will be the next targets."

Other nations know they are depending on Israel to man the front lines in a long war. Wisse says: "For the first time, the ability of Jews to withstand their assailants affects the security of other nations as much as their own. Jews always believed they were meant to help repair the world, but now that belief has turned into plain political fact, albeit in the form they least expected and least desired."

But liberal Jews in the West are still playing the old game, the politics of complementarity, "whereby Jews tried to win protection by proving their value."

What does proving one's value mean today in the West? For secular Jews it means a redefinition of Judaism as liberalism. Except for the Orthodox, every branch of religious Judaism has struggled to fit the square pegs of feminism and post-nationalism into the round holes of Torah and our particularistic national destiny.

It means accepting the valuation of the political Left, now almost wholly subsumed by the Islamist agenda, that Israel is the most dangerous country in the world, and a racist nation. It means acquiescing to the fiction that the Palestinians are a uniquely displaced ethnic group, simply because they did not follow the traditional model of absorption into their ethnically appropriate adjacent lands, as for example 20 million Pakistani and Korean displaced populations did after their civil wars.

It means a complicity with the odious apartheid narrative which dares to point a moralizing finger at Israel, home to a million Arab citizens with full civil rights, when through a systematic process of ethnic cleansing of 900,00 Jews (now three million if you count their descendants, as the Palestinians count theirs), Arab lands became proudly *judenrein*.

In short, it means acquiescence to the canard of a moral equivalence between the Israel and the Arab nations. As Pultizer prize-winning journalist George Will once said: "It is not that Israel is being provocative, but that Israel's being is provocative." When Arab aggression ends, there will be peace. When Israeli defence against Arab aggression ends, there will be no Israel.

Perhaps you've heard the poet Robert Frost's humorous but not inaccurate definition of a liberal as one who "is too broad-minded to take his own side in a quarrel." Many people say – I have always reflexively said – that Jews who allow Judaism and Israel to serve as scapegoats for liberal frustrations that the world won't bend to their utopian ideals – and you know who these Jews are: they are all too vociferous on our campuses, some of which are now war zones for Jews, and in the media – I have always said these are self-hating Jews.

Ruth Wisse set me straight on that. No, she said in a recent talk in Montreal, these Jews are not at all self-hating. If anything, they are overloaded with unearned self-esteem. They love themselves for their vaunted so-called objectivity, their tolerance, their ability to self-criticize.[f] No, it is not themselves they hate, it is the demands being Jewish imposes on them they hate. They are hostile to those who put them in the awkward position of having to choose between their precious liberalism and their people.

We see this at election time. Stephen Harper is a staunch friend to Israel. He was the first to repudiate the Durban conference as a hatefest Canada wants no part in. He refused to allow Israel to be singled out for censure by the Francphonie. He supported Israel's right to defend her interests in the 2006 war with Hezbollah. He refuses to truckle to UN pressures to demonize Israel.

Yet many Jews don't vote for him because he is "scary," which usually translates into the accusation that he takes a less than wholehearted personal view of unlimited abortion and gay marriage. Defending Israel is not "progressive" enough for Jews. They don't judge liberalism by how well it adheres to Judaism; they judge Judaism by how well it adheres to liberalism.

In choosing Obama, which Jews did in overwhelming numbers, whose middle eastern policy is likely to mimic Jimmy Carter's as opposed to the staunchly Israel-defending McCain, Jews here made it clear that in a showdown between political smarts on Israel's behalf and liberalism, liberalism wins. Even if McCain wasn't problematic for other reasons, and I agree he was, it wouldn't have mattered. Jews didn't vote for Ronald Reagan either. [Update: they also didn't vote for Romney either in 2012 in significant numbers.]

If Israel's existence enrages Arabs and the Left, it is because they blame Jews for their own dysfunctionality. The Nazis came to power by deflecting the public's focus from their own problematic nature by focusing on their victims' right to exist. It is the same today.

Jews must recognize and embrace the idea that the court of public opinion – whether run by Rome, other religions, absolute rulers, France's "democratic" courts, Adolf Hitler, Karl Marx, the UN, the Cairo Conference or Jimmy Carter – has never offered Jews or Israel equality under the "law", whatever that has meant in its day. Jews became used to being the defendant.

We must stop thinking of ourselves as defendants, Wisse insists. Israel's right to exist must not be up for discussion. In any fair court, either of law or opinion, which we have yet to see where Jewish interests are concerned, Israel would be recognized as the plaintiff.

In her conclusion Wisse quotes the French intellectual, Jean-François Revel, who during the Cold War feared that a combination of forces determined to vanquish democracy would overwhelm those forces bent on preserving it. Democracy's strengths are high moral standards and a willingness to criticize itself, which contain the seeds of its own destruction.

In his book, *How Democracies Perish*, Revel said:

"Democracy tends to ignore, even deny, threats to its existence because it loathes doing what is needed to counter them. It awakens only when the danger becomes deadly, imminent, evident. By then, either there is too little time for it to save itself, or the price of survival has become crushingly high."

Wisse says she writes to give young Jews backbone in defending Israel's right to fulfil its historic destiny as "a nation like the others." The relentless drumbeat of anti-Zionism they are surrounded by, with Jewish and Israeli activists in full-throated cry in the vanguard, has sapped their will and their confidence. How ironic it is, she notes, that from 1948 to 1967, it was Israel that exported confidence to the Jews of the world. Since then, it has been the task of the Diaspora to export confidence to Israel.

As Wisse concluded in a recent *Commentary Magazine* article, "Forgetting Zion:"

Distance from the battlefield, and well-protected freedoms allow American Jews to make the case for Israel more forcefully than Israelis can make it for themselves. We (I include myself) are blessed with advantages greater than any Diaspora community has ever enjoyed, hence charged with greater responsibility than any Diaspora community has ever borne. History will ask only one question of our generation, and the next one and the one after that: did you secure the state of Israel? Woe to an American Jewry that does not ensure a rousing reply in the affirmative.

Our dogs, Ourselves:
The mysterious and disturbing world
of pit bull advocacy

"Yeah, but this is a different breed...the power that comes behind bull dog, pit bull, presa canario, the fighting breed – they have an extra boost, they can go into a zone, they don't feel the pain anymore. He is using the bulldog in him, which is way too powerful... So if you are trying to create submission in a fighting breed, it's not going to happen. They would rather die than surrender... If you add pain, it only infuriates them...to them pain is that adrenaline rush, they are looking forward to that, they are addicted to it...That's why they are such great fighters....Especially with fighting breeds, you're going to have these explosions over and over because there's no limits in their brain." – Cesar Millan, celebrated dog trainer and pit bull fan, in Episode 4, Season 3 of his TV series, The Dog Whisperer.

"These dogs aren't killers because they have the wrong owners, rather they attract the wrong owners because they are killers." – Semyonova, Alexandra, The 100 Silliest Things People Say About Dogs. England: Hastings Press; 2009. P. 127.

"If the pit bull is the only dog you can love, then you are not really a dog lover." – From an e-mail to me; I suspect the writer was quoting from another source.

Introduction

What are the signs of a failing culture? That's what veteran British novelist Martin Amis sets out to explore in his 2012 novel, Lionel Asbo: State of England.

147

The eponymous protagonist's surname, Asbo, is an acronym for Anti-Social Behavioural Ordinance (a project, now defunct, devised by Tony Blair's government to register official disapproval for social rudeness). Lionel is about as dysfunctional a human being as one can find in the West: a ruthless thug and a social bottom feeder.

The plot gets under way when, while locked up for his role in a wedding riot, Lionel learns he has won a lottery jackpot. Money doesn't change the "lotto lout," as he is dubbed, except now Asbo can afford expensive booze and women instead of cheap or none. But it does change his relationship to the world. For he was a nobody before the lottery win, and suddenly he is a Somebody. The tabloids now follow him around, chronicling his every sleazy move for a hungry public. Lionel finds he quite likes being famous. Indeed, he revels in it.

It isn't Lionel in himself that interests Amis. It is England's culture, now in a perilous state of decline. In an interview,[7] Amis notes that Asbo represents an era that began roughly between 1977 and 1981. He says that was the point at which two emergent cultural themes – fame for its own sake and terrorism – took a seductive hold on the popular imagination.

"In England," says Amis, "and perhaps Europe, fame is the new religion...it's reached a point where not being famous is seen as a kind of deprivation; it's seen as a kind of a civil right."

In Lionel's newly famous state, his own socially disordered, crudely anti-intellectual instincts converge with the just as crudely anti-intellectual, equally socially disordered world of the tabloid press, which caters to mass voyeurism. Of the tabloids: "It's a desire for self-righteousness run amok." Amis adds, "It's great fun being self-righteous...[I]n fact, it's a real high...and that should never be under-estimated."

One of Lionel's charmless habits is to feed Tabasco sauce and beer to his dogs ("the tools of me trade" – his trade being terrorization in the service of debt collection). His dogs are pit bulls. Well, of course. Because pit bulls are only favoured by the criminal classes, right?

Yes and no.

Pit bulls are certainly the dogs of choice for the Lionel Asbos of the world they so resemble, but – coincidentally or not, for about the last 30 years – they have also become the dog of choice for hundreds of thousands of other people. Many of them are the kindest, most compassionate people you'd ever hope to meet. For every Lionel Asbo pit bull, there's a pit bull owned or admired by people at the most "civilized" end of the social spectrum: academics, medical professionals and moral authorities in the animal welfare industry.

What is it about pit bulls that makes for such strange bedfellows?

Pit bulls? In my wildest dreams...

Until a few years ago, it never occurred to me that dogs would become a subject for serious professional attention. My views on the treatment of all animals are mainstream. I naturally believe it's unacceptable to cause animals needless pain; I believe animal abuse is usually a sign of pathology; I hate blood sports; I admire principle-based vegetarianism, but haven't the discipline to adopt it myself. Nothing controversial there.

I like dogs. I had a number of them growing up, our children grew up with them and we still have one. We favour Labrador Retrievers, which makes us the most conventional (breed) dog owners in North America, and statistically the least likely to have to worry about our dog harming another animal or human.

Before we made Labs our dog of choice, we looked up breed characteristics and consulted knowledgeable people. We naturally wanted to know if our dog would be compatible with our lifestyle. We didn't want a high-strung or nervous dog, as we had small children. We didn't want nuisance traits like constant barking, because we pride ourselves on our neighbourliness. We didn't want a dog that couldn't be happy unless it was constantly exercised. But as I say, until a few years ago, "canine correctness," as I have come to think of it, wasn't on my radar screen.

That all changed when, a few years ago, I read an enlightening article in *City Journal* magazine[8] by one of its editors, Brian C. Anderson, about the public safety hazard pit bulls represented. I'd had no idea how popular these dogs had become, and also no idea the civic damage their very presence in numbers could inflict on the social environment.

Aside from the mass of objective data Anderson adduced, I was struck by his opening anecdote, in which he describes a takeover of the park near his young family's now-former Bronx home by thuggish young men and the menacing pit bulls they were training to fight. Nobody would go near the park when the pit bulls were there. The police were afraid to challenge their truculent owners. Seniors cowered when they passed. A climate of fear prevailed.

A rash of unsettling incidents, including maulings of other dogs, convinced Anderson this was no place for a growing family, and they decamped from the area. He writes: "We had learned that intimidating dogs can impair a neighborhood's quality of life and *give the sense that no one is in charge* every bit as much as drug dealing, prostitution, or aggressive panhandling." (my emphasis)

149

That sentence got my full attention and activated my journalistic "spidey sense." My most impassioned writing has always been sparked by cultural trends that begin with "rights" and end with erosion of civic harmony in the common social environment. I had an immediate intuition that pit bulls[9] and their owners might fit that paradigm.

Anderson is like me – and, I assume – you, Reader. He is highly educated. His sojourn in that seedy area of the Bronx was voluntary and meant to be transitional to a better neighbourhood as his fortunes inevitably improved. I am sure that after they settled into a "normal" neighbourhood, his family never felt menaced by pit bulls again.

Because nice, civic-minded folks like us don't want to own pit bulls. We associate pit bulls, subliminally or consciously – and quite properly, if too narrowly – with blood sport, and with low-status, dysfunctional people like Lionel Asbo.

Andersen's story stayed with me. I thought about all the people who weren't in a position to move from the area, and how their lives had been blighted, really almost terrorized one might say, by these dogs.

I realized pit bulls often came up in news items as having attacked someone or mauled other animals. But I couldn't remember any opinion columns in the mainstream press arguing they were a public health or safety issue, as opposed to issues like drugs and prostitution that are constantly chewed over by pundits on both sides of the debate.

On the contrary, now that I was on the alert for commentary, the few articles or columns about pit bulls I saw in the newspapers that I read regularly seemed to be skewed to defence of pit bulls as a misunderstood and maligned breed. And when pit bull depredations turned up in news items, there was a tendency to downplay or sometimes even suppress the culprit's breed.[10]

None of them addressed the cold hard genetic and statistics-based realities about this and other genetically-related fighting dogs, alarming facts that after a spate of highly-motivated research I was now in possession of.

As I got deeper into the subject, I realized that I was seeing something new in the history of human-animal relations. Over the centuries there have been many people who have agitated for the more humane treatment of animals. In our own era we have seen a whole movement that militates not only for animal welfare – i.e. the humane treatment of animals whose destinies we control – but for distinct animal *rights*, including, according to such hard-line groups as People for the Ethical Treatment of Animals – the right not to be eaten by humans. The common goal of all the various groups is the alleviation of animal suffering.

Amongst dog fanciers, there are those who love all dogs equally. And then there are those fixated on a particular breed. And here is where it got interesting for me.

The domestic dog, which evolved organically as a scavenger species (unlike the wolf, a hunter species that is, contrary to received wisdom, not the dog's direct forebear, but only distantly related to the dog[11]), has been around for thousands of years. Left to its own devices, a mutt will get along with other animals and people if its turf is respected. Unless it has been abused, mutts make fine, uncomplicated, low-risk companions, eager to socialize and resistant to aggression.

By contrast, systematically created breed lines, man-made constructs in eugenics, are a relatively recent phenomenon, the oldest of them only going back a few centuries.

Every breed is created and their stereotype refined for a specific reason. Border collies tend to herd, pointers tend to point, greyhounds tend to race, and retrievers tend to swim and fetch: Whether for work or recreation requirements, dog breeds exist for a practical human reason.

In canine terms, humans are all mutts. If we were bred as dog breeds are, some of us would be giant-headed intellectuals with pipestem arms and legs, some would be pea-brained warriors with massive chests and limbs, and others would be dazzlingly beautiful but unable to complete a simple task.

About 200 years ago, people with a taste for vicarious violence began to breed dogs that could fight bears and bulls in a pit. They produced the English Bull Terrier. Then they decided it would be fun to watch dogs tear each other apart, and they bred the English Staffordshire Terrier, also known as the American Staffordshire (colloquially AmStaff, a name invented to deflect negative reactions to the words "pit bull," even though genetically it is the exact same dog).[12]

The pit bull demonstrates how breeding alters a dog's brain chemistry, especially the part that governs aggression and impulse control.[13]

Pit bulls do not socialize well with other dogs, because the socializing instinct has been bred out of them. Unlike mutts and other breeds, they do not look for ways to avoid aggression, because they are bred to take pleasure in aggression. They attack without warning. Their attacks, unlike those of other dogs, are sudden, random, unprovoked and violent.[14]

Apart from bull, bear and dog fighting, the pit bull's ancestors have been used to track down slaves, to bait and hunt dangerous wildlife or to act as butchers' dogs, whose job was to incapacitate movement in animals by clamping down on their noses while their throats were cut. In each case, "these ancestor dogs

151

[were] bred to expand the human capacity for inflicting suffering on other animals, including the dogs themselves."[15]

This last eloquently rendered point bears repeating and elaboration. The pit bull cluster of dogs is the only canine type in the world that has, *and has always had*, animal and human suffering as its sole *raison d'être*. And *therefore* you would think that people who are drawn to them above all other 400-plus breeds – apart from those naïve souls who have been duped, and plenty have – would consider themselves *morally bound* to interrogate their motives for their attraction to this canine anomaly.

But here is the mystery this essay seeks to explain. There are the thugs like Lionel Asbo and professional dog fighting men, who make no bones about why they love pit bulls – that is, who will happily regale you with tales of how murderously competent their pit bull is at tearing other pit bulls limb from limb and scaring the pants off people. We get that.

But then there are hundreds of thousands of seemingly ordinary people, their numbers growing daily, who often are, and sometimes are not, themselves aware of the facts around pit bulls, but who vigorously throw themselves into public campaigns to disseminate lies in order to launder the pit bull's well-deserved reputation for aggression.

In other words, this is the first time in the history of human-animal relations that a movement – the pit bull advocacy movement (PBAM) – has formed, not to promote the well-known virtues of a beloved breed, but *to promote denial of a beloved breed's well-known vices*.

Because PBAM's organized campaign of truth suppression is facilitating increasing animal and human suffering on a growing scale; because PBAM's tactics of disinformation, harassment and intimidation have bamboozled the media, cowed dog-industry stakeholders and browbeaten public servants; and because I got sick and tired of getting hate mail comparing pit bulls to Holocaust victims and myself to the Nazis: I found myself consumed with the desire to uncover the cultural forces at work behind this phenomenon.

Martin Amis is on to something. Welcome to the strange and disturbing world of PBAM, where – as in the world of Lionel Asbo – extreme vanity, entitlement to fame, the drug of self-righteousness, and a fascination with unpredictable violence cloaked in moral rectitude are the anti-social norm.

The pit bull: From pariah to social-justice victim in 25 years

Eventually, as people became more enlightened about humane animal treatment, pit fighting was outlawed – in England in 1911 and America in the 1920s, with the exception of states where the Ku Klux Klan exerted legislative influence. Dog fighting was a significant source of revenue for the KKK. Actually, many nefarious trades were: moonshining, prostitution, cockfighting and any protection racket that could be enabled by crooked cops, sheriffs and judges.[16]

Even 25 years ago dog fighting was virtually unknown in inner American cities. Between Protestants' aversion to gambling, and the activism of revered writer Jack London,[17] who promoted the humane movement in the U.S., dog fighting was driven out of the respectable sporting press and society in general. Most U.S. animal control officers had rarely encountered fighting dogs.

But in the 1980s, as violence became a way of life in urban subcultures, dog fighting migrated via prison contact from white skinheads (the KKK's successors) to the black underclass. Amongst low-status black men engaged in gangs and crime, killer dogs became a kind of chic accessory – a novelty in self-ornamentation.

It began with medium-sized pit bulls, but demand grew for bigger dogs, and we're presently seeing "a kind of arms race going on [to see] who can breed and possess the biggest, most aggressive breed of dog."[18] We now see many more large fighting dogs like the Presa Canaria, the Dogo Argentino, the Fila Brasiliero, and the Boerbel. When you add their great body mass to their instinct for aggression, it is nigh impossible to restrain a determined attack.[19]

The distinctive feature of all these dogs is the "killing bite," which, unlike the transient "grabbing" bite of the German Shepherd or the "slashing" bite of the collie, is designed to inflict horrific damage. The killing bite seizes on a limb or a child's scalp or face and *does not let go*, while the teeth rend through the flesh and bone. You would not wish to see photographs of people (especially children) who have been subjected to a pit bull mauling. They are sickening.

As Dr. Patrick Byrnes of John Hopkins Medical Center says, regarding pit bull injuries he has treated, "I can't think of a single injury of this nature that was incurred by any other species other than a pit bull or a Rottweiler." (The Rottweiler is genetically kin to the pit bull.) Because of these dogs' uniquely damaging attack methods, Dr. Byrnes says surgeons have actually had to develop new techniques to try to mend them.[20]

His view is reinforced by that of Mark Wulkan, MD, surgeon at Children's Healthcare of Atlanta:

> *There is a difference with the pit bulls. In the last two years we've seen 56 dog injuries that were so severe the patient had to be admitted to the hospital, so this doesn't count just as just a little bite, and then goes to the emergency room. Of those 56, 21 were pit bulls. And then when we look at our data even further, of the kids that were most severely*

injured, those that were in the hospital for more than 8 days or had life threatening injuries, 100% of those were pit bulls.[21]

Add "gameness" to the pit bull's killing bite – high aggression levels and unstoppability in the fight to the death – and you have a weapon of terrible destruction. Precisely what dogfighters want and unashamedly seek out.

But breeders want to sell to everyone, so they don't advertise their wares with such transparency. "Breeders advertise in covert terms. They praise their dogs as guardians of home and hearth, wary of strangers, courageous, powerful – all of it secret language that indicates that the breed has been specifically bred for unbridled aggression."[22]

When aggression began to turn up in Golden Retrievers, their breed association took responsible stock of their lines, and paid for research[23] to identify the problem and try to breed it out. This may take a fair amount of time – many generations even.[24] The fighting dog breeders have no motivation to do any such thing. Why would they, when professional dogfighters will pay $1500 for a game puppy?

When the Disney movie *101 Dalmations* came out in 1961, all kinds of people rushed to buy Dalmations. The same when Taco Bell adopted the Chihuaha as its mascot in the 1980s – a rush on Chihuahas. Eventually the markets for these dogs were saturated, and the breeding operations adjusted to demand.

But with pit bulls, the demand never stops. Pit bulls with less than fullblown jihadist attack styles are used as bait dogs or killed without compunction by dogfighters. So to their other singularities, add the fact that there is no market correction for breeding of fighting dogs. Without Breed Specific Legislation (BSL), the numbers just keep growing.

But surely, one might logically ask, there should at least be a market correction amongst those who buy pit bulls as pets, once enough of them find out how unpredictable and dangerous they can be.

Ah, "finding out": There's the rub.

Market corrections can only occur in the light of objective information freely distributed. That is not the case with pit bulls. A disinformation campaign about pit bulls has been in progress for thirty years. Humane societies, having succumbed like other official bodies to PBAM pressure, push pit bulls as good companion animals in the same shameful way that cigarette companies once pushed tobacco as a benign, relaxing and even therapeutic product.[25]

Until recently, dogs that attacked human beings were automatically put down. Defending dogs that have bitten people is a relatively recent phenomenon. One of the first recorded cases in which animal advocates defended dogs who killed a human occurred during World War Two when defence plant worker Doretta Zinkes, 39, strolling near an Army transmitter station near Miami Springs, was set upon and mauled to death by nine pit bulls belonging to 43-year old Joe Munn of Hialeah. The dogs had already attacked people previously, and were condemned to die. But the local humane society received hundreds of calls begging that the lives of the dogs be spared.

Before Zinke's death, the last adult killing by dogs in the U.S. happened in 1937. Over the last decades, certain other breeds have killed children. But only Rottweilers even come close to the relatively stratospheric numbers of killings by pit bulls. Since 1982, pit bulls plus close mixes and Rottweilers have killed 219 and disfigured 1022 Americans and Canadians. All other breeds combined – that is, 95% of the dog population – have killed 106 people and disfigured 355. And yet PBAM's devotion to the breed seems to escalate in proportion to the damage they inflict.

PBAM's reach and strength has been immeasurably advanced in the last decade through social media and Internet chat rooms. These virtual clubhouses facilitate group solidarity and passion for the mission of reversing their breed's pejorative image. The sealed world in which pit bull activists immerse themselves reinforces an already cultish fervour, and provides staging grounds for "mobbing" of dissidents who dare to flout the reigning canine correctness around the pit bull's alleged victimhood.

As a journalist who attempts to inform the public of the truth about pit bulls, I can certainly attest to the vigour and singlemindedness of PBAM's rank and file in their determination to chill any discourse in the public forum that exposes pit bull myths. I have been called a racist, a bigot and an advocate for doing to pit bulls "what Hitler did to the Jews." PBAM activists have written to my editor accusing me of a lack of journalistic integrity. PBAM activists follow me on Twitter to monitor my tweets and swiftly react to any that "diss" pit bulls.

Other journalists confirm to me that they receive the same treatment when they step with "incorrect" attitudes into this peculiar social quagmire. But the persecution of journalists is merely the tip of an intimidation iceberg. Well under the public radar, PBAM has had great success in cowing an entire dog-related infrastructure.

Kennel clubs, humane societies, veterinarian associations, dog rescue groups, animal journals – all genuflect and declare allegiance to PBAM's party line: that all dogs bite, that no breed should be singled out for censure, that individual dogs should be considered innocent until proven guilty, that pit bulls present no greater inherent risk to other animals or people than any other breed.

Even though all these stakeholders know better, canine correctness demands that they play into what social psychologist Leon Festinger terms "dissonance reduction," in this case PBAM's rejection of evidence that upsets their deeply held convictions.

Through aggressive peddling in blogs[26] and bogus "official" websites"[27] of the Big Lie – that the pit bull is a reliable dog, much maligned by a few hysterical pit bull haters and a biased media – they have gulled a credulous mainstream press and millions of sentimental dog lovers.

PBAM activists are relentless in their harassment of dissidents.

Here's a good example.[28] In the U.S. there is a country-wide reading program called "Paws for Tales," in which volunteers bring their dogs to libraries so children can read to them. Pit bull owners decided this was a great way to "educate" kids about their beloved breed. But some libraries were already "educated" enough to know they were not comfortable hosting fighting dogs, and one library in the town of Burlingame, California banned pit bulls from their program.

Fervent pit bull activists Jim Gorant and Chris Cohen were offended by this ban, even though they had not been banned from another library they volunteered at. So they went to the Humane Society and the SPCA with the demand that the Burlingame library be excluded from the "Paws for Tales" program. When the Humane Society demurred at becoming involved, Cohen and Gorant threatened the town of Burlingame with a lawsuit. Concerned about their children's safety, and unwilling to be dragged into litigation, Burlingame pulled the plug on the program.

Gorant, like most of the pit bull advocates I hear from, equates his dogs with minorities like Native Americans and left-handed people, noting that no library would "discriminate"[29] against members of these groups. Such advocates call bans or exclusions of any kind "speciesism."

But such an equivalency is logically absurd, because as noted, dogs are a species, not breeds of dog. And you cannot "discriminate" against a creature that does not recognize itself as different from others of its species, or behave as if other members of its type are of special significance to him. Discrimination can only occur in the presence of two beings – the discriminator and the discriminated against – who are both cognizant of the injustice.

(A more logical comparison in this case would be humans who have been brainwashed since birth to believe people of another religion are infidels, unclean, or hateful beings and justifiable targets for violence, and whose presence triggers deep, irrational hostility. Would it not be reasonable to exclude such people as role models from a program in which children are being educated in the virtues of pluralism and tolerance?)

Cohen says: "Some may see [the closing-down of the program] as a loss to the children of the community. But I don't. If the person in charge is participating in discrimination, children should not be anywhere near that facility. There is too much hate in this world already; children do not need to learn it at the library."

Like the false mother in the biblical tale of Solomon, who would have the disputed baby cut in two rather than yield her claim, Cohen would rather the children had no reading program with any dogs if *his* dog – who has no knowledge of or understanding of or interest in the program – is not included. Cohen is emblematic of pit bull activists in that their protests are never about the dog; they are always about themselves. The extent of the narcissism and the sense of *entitlement* one is exposed to in this sub-culture is troubling indeed.

Statistics: All that matters

My primary source for statistics on pit bull and other dogs as a public safety risk is Merritt Clifton, an investigative reporter, humane-movement historian and watchdog of animal charities and animal lobby groups.[30] For four decades Clifton has been publishing reports about dog breeds and their relative risk to human and animal safety, with evidence culled from primary sources, such as the Centers for Disease Control, police reports, animal control centres, witness reports, victim accounts, hospital figures, humane shelter intake, re-homing and kill statistics, and the like.

Clifton is a statistics hound. His methodology and his data have never been publicly challenged.[31] He publishes a continually updated report on dog-bite related fatalities (DBRF), maimings and disfigurements. Using his reports and a few other useful sources, I have assembled the most relevant facts any intelligent observer must know before coming to an informed conclusion about pit bulls.[32]

As you read, please be aware that none of the following statistics or facts are ever cited by pit bull breed associations, by pit bull rescue groups, by humane shelters that aggressively "push" pit bulls on to ordinary pet-seeking citizens with no experience in handling high-risk dogs, or by kennel clubs in their literature. Indeed, when the American Kennel Club, describing pit bulls in its 1998 edition of the Complete Dog Book, included the words "not good with children," pressure from breeders persuaded them to drop the offending phrase.

ACKNOWLEDGEMENTS

Some statistics then:

- Americans keep 50% more pets than they did in 1986, and annual spending on vet care is four times what it was in 2001;

- By 1995, more than 70% of the dog population in the U.S. had been sterilized, but fewer than 25% of pit bulls and pit bull mixes had been sterilized;

- There are about 73 million dogs in the U.S. and about seven million in Canada. About three million are pit bulls (though fewer proportionately in Canada, where dog fighting is nowhere nearly as prevalent as in the U.S.; where several populous jurisdictions have instituted BSL; and where, for geo-cultural reasons, huskies are a trendier choice of pet);

- Dogs bite four to five million Americans every year;

- Serious injuries are up nearly 40% from 1986;

- Children are victims of 60% of bites and 80% of fatal attacks;

- Nearly half of all American children have been bitten by a dog by the age of twelve;

- Black children under the age of ten are more than three times as likely to be bitten by dogs – mainly pit bulls – as white children;

- Pit Bulls or crosses alone account for more than a third of DBRF;

- From 2005 to 2011, pit bulls have killed 128 Americans. Of these attacks, 51% (65) involved a family member and a household pit bull. In the first eight months of 2011, nearly half of those killed by a pit bull were their dog's owner;[33]

- Extrapolating from data published by the Centers for Disease Control, in a twenty-year study of people seeking attention for dog bites, a population of just over two million pit bulls in a total American dog population of 75 million dogs was responsible for 40% of bites in all years;

- Extrapolating further from statistics covering attacks on both humans and other animals, one out of eighteen pit bulls is involved in some kind of aggression against other animals or humans every year;

- Pit bulls have represented half the total actuarial risk for injury since 1982;

- Add in Rottweilers (systematically bred for the same hair-trigger impulses that distinguish pit bulls from normal breeds) and it is 75% of total actuarial risk;

- Each year, about one pit bull in 100,000 kills someone, compared with one non-pit bull in about 10 *million*;

- In the 30 year period from 1982 through 2012, pit bulls (and close pit bull mixes) accounted for at least 217 deaths in the US and Canada (three pit bull mix deaths in Canada, the pit bull factor being suppressed on supposedly credible pit bull sites);

- Pit bulls were responsible for 65 percent of all fatal dog attacks nationally in the U.S. in 2008. Someone in the United States is killed by a pit bull every 14 days. One body part is severed and lost in pit bull attacks every 5.4 days;[34]

- 33-45% of the U.S. pit bull population enters a humane shelter every year;

- 3.3% of dogs advertised online are pit bulls, but more than 16% of dogs adopted from animal shelters since 2007 have been pit bulls, which means that shelters are "pushing" pit bulls at five times the rate of pit bulls chosen when there is no influence exerted;

- About one pit bull in 30,000 adopted from a humane or rescue shelter kills or disfigures someone *after passing behavioural screening* (most pit bulls dumped in shelters are euthanized);

- Human damage by pit bulls is escalating with the dramatic growth of the pit bull population; nearly a *third* of all disfigurements in the past 30 years have occurred *in the last two years*. The year 2011 racked up the most since records started being maintained;

- Pit bulls are minimally *five times more likely to attack another animal or human than all other breeds combined*;

- Pit bulls are *six times more likely to kill their owners or family members than any other breed*;

- Yet there are more organizations focused on rescuing pit bulls than rescue and advocate for all other breeds combined;

- There has never been a time since 1851 when pit bulls did not account for more than half of all fatal dog attacks over any 10-year period even though until 30 years ago, pit bulls never amounted to even 1% of dogs in the U.S. and Canada.

What kind of people love pit bulls?

When I began writing columns advocating for legislation to curb further breeding of pit bulls (not for euthanasia of living dogs that had done no damage), adducing statistics like these above as evidence, I was stunned to receive hate mail in quantities and of a virulence I had never known before – and I have written many controversial columns on a variety of political and cultural topics.

Journalists know that any news story or column about animals in general elicits far more reaction in readers than just about any other topic except sports. But usually the response is generated by outrage against human abusers of animals. This hate mail was peculiar in that the anger was motivated by support for animal abusers of humans.

I knew that only a handful of the people who wrote to me had read my column, because actual readers respond immediately, while in this case the real avalanche of mail only started coming in a few days later. That meant the column was being systematically distributed to a network of activists in order to maximize the blowback.

Although many responders waved away my evidence as either false or irrelevant, not a single one proffered any countervailing data or statistics. They were not interested in statistics. They were interested in recounting narratives about their own good, sweet dogs that had never hurt a fly (yet). I would say 90% of my pro-pit bull respondents seemed earnestly to believe that assurance of their own dog's innocence would change my mind about pit bulls in general.

Occasionally, out of irritation, I would respond and ask, "So if I get e-mails from *two* people telling me that their pit bull attacked another animal or person, would you agree that you're wrong and that pit bulls really are a danger to society?" They didn't get my irony or its message that arguing from individual anecdote is meaningless in such a discussion.

Or when I was called a "racist," I would sometimes write back and say, "But I don't care who dogs mate with. You're the eugenicist who's hung up on breeding-line purity. Who's the Nazi here?" No reply.

I soon gave up attempts to engage in either irony or reason-based dialogues with them. To be fair, here and there I was able to have a civil conversation with respectful, well-educated people. But on the whole, I would have to rate my pit bull enthusiast respondents as quite lacking in critical thinking skills and in general of low intelligence.[35]

For example, out of curiosity I checked out one respondent on Facebook. He had accused me – in very bad grammar and spelling – of being a Nazi and wanting to start a "holocaust" against pit bulls. I very much doubt that he knows the meaning of either "Nazi" or "holocaust" – only that they represent the ultimate in hatred and victimization, and that was good enough for him.

His Facebook page sported a photo of a gun instead of himself. He had posted a maudlin account of his beloved gun collection, his social isolation and his pit bulls, the only friends who understood and loved him. It was very clear to me that he saw his own status as a social outcast reflected in these maligned animals, and it was also clear to me that he harboured fantasies of revenge against the world through violence, a fantasy he could easily project onto his dogs without guilt.

I suspected he was typical of a wide swath of the pit bull-loving subculture,[aj] and that there are a disproportionate number of pit bull owners with scarred psyches, and tendencies they are vaguely ashamed of, who find comfort in the love of an animal that is despised by society's "winners."

Actually my suspicion is borne out in research. In a 2006 peer-reviewed study published in the *Journal of Interpersonal Violence*, out of a sampling of 355 dog owners, all those who kept pit bulls had had some sort of brush with law enforcement. Lead study author Jaclyn Barnes of the Cincinnati Children's Hospital Medical Center writes: "Owners of vicious dogs who have been cited for failing to register a dog [or] failing to keep a dog confined on the premises...are more than nine times more likely to have been convicted for a crime involving children, three times more likely to have been convicted of domestic violence...and nearly eight times more likely to be charged with drug [crimes] than owners of low-risk licensed dogs."[37]

This study would seem to bolster the bromide, invariably trotted out following any publicized pit bull: "there are no bad breeds, just bad owners." But that statement implies that the owners are eliciting their dogs' bad behaviour. That is not the case. The dogs don't behave badly – although like all dogs they may behave worse – because they have the wrong owners. They attract the wrong owners because they behave badly.

Take for example, the case of Donna Tran of Calgary. In April 2012, her two pit bulls attacked Wendy Smith as she arrived at Tran's door. Smith, a stranger to Tran, was seriously mauled by Tran's dogs on her face – she almost lost her nose and required extensive reconstructive surgery – and thigh.[38]

Tran's case came to trial as I was putting the finishing touches to this essay. The judge upheld a previous ruling that the dogs had to be euthanized (why it wasn't immediately euthanized on principle shows how carefully the law now treads with dangerous dogs. The trial was a complete waste of taxpayer dollars even though the correct judgment was reached).

Notably, the judge affirmed that the pit bulls "grew up in a loving home." In other words, this was not a case of a "bad owner," not a case of dog abuse turned on a victim. This was a case of an unprovoked attack by supposedly well-socialized dogs. How could such dogs ever be trusted again? Reason says they can't. Emotional PBAM reflexes disagree.

A video embedded in the news shows a sobbing Tran leaving the courtroom. She is completely indifferent to the victim's horror story that has left Smith "scarred for life." A dog trainer (which is an amateur occupation anyone can claim for oneself, and not the same as an academically educated animal behaviour specialist) who had been flown in from Los Angeles – a colleague of Cesar Millan's – was not allowed to testify in court, but played on the heartstrings of the media, sadly alluding to the "deplorable" conditions of the dirty and unstimulating conditions in which the dogs were held ("no toys," "no bones"!). What she did not mention was that the dogs had behaved so aggressively during their custody that no safe human contact was possible, they could be allowed no toys, and their cages couldn't easily be cleaned.

The dog trainer complained about the "blood from [the pit bulls'] ears and mouths on the kennel walls," but where did that blood come from? Was it their own, from fighting during impoundment (which pit bulls in shelter often do if you house them together, even if they've lived together all their lives, and even if they are opposite sex)? As likely as not.

The prosecutor expressed regret that any dogs have to be euthanized, but "at the end of the day, public safety is our number one concern." Very sensible. But Tran does not care about public safety. She is not giving up yet, not "until all legal avenues have been explored." That could mean more wasted taxpayer dollars as she fights for her murderous dogs' lives through the Court of Appeal.

And here's the kicker that only appears at the end of the news story. Tran and other family members are also facing 19 drug charges in connection with a "massive" cocaine operation.

Lessons to take away: pit bulls attract narcissistic scofflaws. And PBAM militants couldn't care less about the moral character of the people they align themselves with, or the damage the dogs they are defending have done. It is all, and only, about the pit bull's life and well-being.

One more thing. Tran is pregnant. You can be sure that if she does not end up in prison, she will acquire one or more new pit bulls to replace the ones that are (hopefully) euthanized. And her child will be crawling around them under her benign gaze. Not a happy image.

Dog behaviourist Alexandra Semyonova divides civilian (i.e. not professional dog men) fighting-dog owners into three broad categories.[39]

In the first are grown men who suffer from feelings of personal inadequacy. They swagger and act the tough guy outwardly. They will impose their dog on you "because they feel the world owes them recognition." They bring their dogs to parks and enjoy seeing other dog owners shrinking from their dog. They are cowardly when their dog attacks another dog, because they have no idea how to handle them.

If you call the police, they target you for "terrorizing" attention the next time. In The Hague, where Semyonova lives and used to take her dogs out for free runs in the city's extensive wooded areas, such thugs have made that freedom impossible. She is constantly on guard, with her dogs always leashed.[40]

Second are adolescent males, many of them fatherless, seeking to form a masculine identity. They idolize rappers and athletes who have adopted pit bulls as a fashion accessory. "He sees the macho rapper on television, accompanied by the aggressive dog, and he wants one too." Just like he wants those Nike sneakers. He won't leash the dog, because that's wussy. The dog is a toy. When it attacks another dog or person, he is stunned and uncomprehending of the damage being inflicted. He is scared to intervene, and often flees the scene. He takes no responsibility for it: "The dog did it, not me."

Third are those from whom I hear a lot in my column feedback, most of them women. Semyonova refers to them as the "Egotistical Innocents."

These are tender-hearted, nurturing people who are suckers for any story of victimization. "The Innocent doesn't understand what [the breeder advertisement euphemisms] 'fierce protector of home and hearth, averse to strangers' means." Innocents are often middle-class, otherwise ordinary people, sentimental to a fault, who become members of rescue organizations and humane societies. They're not tuned into people suffering, but avidly consume narratives of animal abuse.

All animals are innocent in these people's eyes. If their pit bull is cuddly and sweet to *them*, why then all pit bulls are good and pure. If they have attacked someone, then they were provoked in some way. For one example of many one can find along these lines, I read of a pit bull being walked along a sidewalk who attacked and mauled a child getting out of a car. In a statement to the police, the owner protested that the car door opening so unexpectedly had startled his dog. His words left no doubt as to his thought process: He was blaming the child for her injuries.

To this last category I would append a subcategory of people with hybristophiliac tendencies. Hybristophilia is a disorder, mostly affecting women who do not act out in violent ways themseves, but are attracted to violence in psychopathic men. Every serial killer in prison has his own little coterie of women who write love letters to him or even visit and fantasize a life together with him. They consider him misunderstood and only in want of the love of a compassionate and nurturing woman to bring out their inner goodness. In their minds, they are that woman. In fact, they find his violent history arousing. Pretending he is himself a victim is a way of laundering their own dark, but socially unacceptable urges.

In July, 2011, for instance, I wrote a column about psychopathy,[41] arising from headlines about Luke Magnotta, a Canadian psychopath who murdered and dismembered a young Chinese student, then mailed body parts around the country. I wrote: "There are websites in support of Magnotta, such as a Facebook group with almost 1,400 members. In another group, members seek information on how to write or visit Magnotta in his Quebec detention centre."

Are these people normal? Only in the sense that they are unlikely to commit crimes. But no, they are not normal in the sense of being psychologically healthy individuals. Such mental fellow travelling with the kind of psychopathic violence that horrifies psychologically healthy people is surely proof of some disorder or other. Which brings us to the bizarre story of a pit bull called Lennox.

Lennox the Irish martyr dog

Lennox of Belfast was a pit bull that was put down in July 2012 after a two-year international campaign to save him.

Lennox had been impounded due to neighbours' complaints about his dangerous behaviour. His guardian, Carolyn Barnes, testified that he had never actually bitten anyone because he was muzzled in public, but he had apparently lunged at several people, including animal control officer Alexandra Lightfoot when she responded to the complaints.

Lightfoot, a respected and credible veteran in her field, assessed Lennox as given to "hair-trigger re-directs," meaning a dog rapidly shifts attention from one potential target of an attack to another. The hair-trigger redirect is considered among the most dangerous behaviours that a dog can exhibit, because it is the prelude to rampage attacks with multiple victims.

In short, Lennox was, in the words of an expert hired by the Belfast Council "one of the most unpredictable and dangerous dogs he had come across."

But the feckless owner wouldn't give up. She insisted he was a pit bull-Labrador mix (amongst the most common and reflexive "redirects" of pit bull owners when trouble strikes), but was later forced to abandon that subterfuge when photos of the dog were made public in all his 100% pit bulliness.

The real facts didn't matter to PBAM. Lennox soon became a poster child for tragically maligned pit bulls everywhere. Many of my respondents referred to Lennox in the kind of emotive language one would normally reserve for Holocaust victims like Anne Frank.

Some 200,000 people signed a petition to save him. His Facebook page was "liked" by 110,000 people. A Twitter feed, @savelennox garnered 13,000 followers, a website and a blog in his honour. Animal Rights groups weighed in. Prominent politicians offered mindless Twitter support.[42] Belfast Council workers were harassed. Threatening letters, one drenched in gasoline, were put through the mail slots of two female dog wardens. Another staff member had her car tires slashed.

The Metropolitan Police dog handler who testified against Lennox was subjected to particular vilification. A U.S. dog "expert," ex-police officer Jim Crosby, challenged the officer's competence to judge Lennox's behaviour, even though the officer had 25 years experience in the police force dealing with dangerous dogs and advises the government's department on dangerous dogs.[43]

(Interestingly, Crosby had himself in the past told the truth about pit bulls on his own website: "When [pit bulls] fight, human intervention has selected for animals that do not turn off, and do not stop fighting until one, or both, are dead,"[44] but took those comments down under the new canine correctness rubric [but not before they were cached by observant readers].)

Psychopath Magnotta has 1400 Facebook supporters. Factually, that is unsettling. Statistically, it is of little sociological concern. Psychopath Lennox[45] had *hundreds of thousands* of supporters. This is mass hysteria of a strange and culturally significant kind, it seems to me.

Semyonova's classifications ring true for anyone who has multiple exposures to PBAM apologists, as I can now attest. For the Egotistical Innocent especially, there isn't a pit bull-initiated tragedy for which there is no exculpatory explanation, especially in the case of attacks on other animals. If they attack another dog in the park, or bite the head off a cat, or leap off a second-story balcony to attack a passing dog in the street, or invade a neighbour's home through a pet door to kill the family dachshund – well, dogs will be dogs.

And, they will insist, it could have been any other dog that did the same. Even though statistics do not bear them out. In their minds, statistics are merely a reflection of media bias. They believe the media only report attacks by pit bulls – that is, they actively suppress reports of attacks by other dogs. As if they could. The very idea flies in the face of reality. Serious bites are reported to police and hospitals, from which reporters take their news. They can't be fudged. If one reporter was biased enough to exclude other breeds, another reporter would include them and the biased reporter wouldn't last long in his job.

The only possible explanation is that pit bull attacks are indeed more newsworthy because they tend to be more serious. But the Innocents cannot be dissuaded from their victim narrative, which in truth borders on a conspiracy theory that the whole world is out to get their breed. No matter what evidence you point to, they will simply enlarge the scope of the conspiracy against them.

Reporters have it in for them. But what about the police reports? The police are in on it too. And the emergency room physicians?[46] Them too. It is quite hopeless to believe reason will win the day on this issue.

If you point to a story of a two-year old child having her scalp ripped off with her back turned to the dog, they will counter with tales of pit bulls who have been burned, drowned, lynched or endured some other suffering that trumps your story of the child.[47] They are impervious to logic and evidence, so cannot be engaged in fruitful discussion.

*   *   *

I have said that pit bull advocates (again, I refer to the Innocents, as the thug types feel no need to apologize for the vices they actively seek out) are not interested in facts. But they are deeply invested in exculpatory myths. From my avalanche of hate mail, I know exactly what those myths are, because every single one of them was repeated *ad nauseam*, and in exactly the same words and phrases, which told me that they were not ideas arrived at through independent study, but mantras absorbed by osmosis from PBAM.

Here the main ones are, with the facts appended:

Myth: *The pit bull has always been America's most popular dog.*

PBAM will point to the fact that the pit bull was used in military posters in World War One (as a symbol of grit and a country that would never back down in a fight – a legitimate use of the dog's profile) or to the popular silent film character Buster Brown, who kept a pit bull named Tige.

Fact:

Tige appeared in only four Buster Brown films, where his central role was... attacking another dog and two humans!

The pit bull was always known as a fighting dog and was never a conventional family pet. By searching the classified dogs-for-sale ads between 1900 to 1950 on NewspaperArchive.com, *Animal People News* editor Merritt Clifton discovered that huskies and St. Bernards were the most popular dogs of that period. Of the 34 breeds searched, pit bulls ranked 25th.

Perhaps an even more persuasive argument arises from the dog literature of the pre-canine correctness era.

In the early to mid 20th century, Albert Payson Terhune was America's most popular writer of dog stories, as well as a breeder of collies. His books sold in the millions. The most famous of them – *Lad: A Dog* – was a collection of stories, which appeared in 1919, based on the life adventures of his own favourite dog.

In the most heartbreaking story, Lad is almost killed by Rex, a pit bull-collie mix, and an anomaly in Terhune's collie-ruled domain. Here is Terhune's description of him:

"Rex [was] a giant, a freak...an accidental blending of two breeds which cannot blend...He was short-haired, fully two inches taller and ten pounds heavier than Lad, and had the bunch-muscled jaws of a killer. There was not an outlander dog for two miles in either direction that Rex had not at one time or another met and vanquished. The bull terrier strain...made its possessor a terrific fighter."

Lad and Rex meet in the woods. Suddenly "Rex went back, all at once, to primal instincts, a maniac rage mastered him...With not so much as a growl or warning, he launched himself upon Lad. Straight at the tired old dog's throat he flew....Rex's fearsome jaws – capable of cracking a beef bone as a man cracks a filbert – had found a vise-grip in the soft fur of [Lad's] throat." "It was a grip and a leverage that would have made the average opponent helpless." (Lad's thick ruff saves him from death, but he is horribly mauled.)

This following is instructive, because Terhune knew dogs, and he was completely unfettered by any sort of self-censorship that people today have internalized as necessary to avoid offending "minority" sensibilities:

"There are many forms of dogfight...But the deadliest of all canine conflicts is the 'murder-fight.' This is a struggle wherein one or both contestants have decided to give no quarter, where the victor will fight on until his antagonist is dead and will then tear his body to pieces. *It is a recognized form of canine mania.* And it was a murder-fight that Rex was waging, for he had gone *quite insane.*" (my emphasis)

Does this sound like a description of America's "most popular" pet?

Myth: *All dogs bite/and variation i): "Golden Retrievers bite just as much as pit bulls"; and variation ii) "My pit bull won't hurt you, but he may lick you to death."*

Fact:

Of course all dogs *can* bite, although most dogs won't bite if they can help it. But even when they do, they don't all bite in a way that causes concerning damage. When we speak of pit bull biting, we speak of damage magnitudes higher than the average dog bite.[av]

The "all dogs bite" mantra usually includes accounts of a Chihuahua whose bite required 50 stitches. This is known amongst anti-pit bull activists as "the Chihuahua diversion." Pit bull owners are so grateful to see bad damage done by any other type of dog, they seize on it like...well, like a dog on a bone!

When you get 50 e-mails with the exact wording, "My pit bull may lick you to death," [but will never bite you], you know you're dealing with Manchurian-Candidate fanaticism.

As for the playing of the "Golden Retriever" card – which to my amazement, was actually dealt me in a conversation with the media relations director of the Ontario Veterinarian Association – nobody will ever cite you a source for such a foolish charge.

In fact it is such a common cheap trick it has a name: "The Hannover Formula." The formula is a reflexive conflation of pit bulls with Golden Retrievers in order to launder the pit bull image. It is named for the Institute of Animal Welfare and Behavior of the University of Veterinary Medicine, Hannover, Germany, where the comparison was first made.

Myth: *There are no bad dogs, just bad owners.*

I wish I had a dollar for every time I had this response; I'd be rich.

Fact:

The baddest owners in the world can't make other dogs do what pit bulls do. They've tried. Dog men have done everything humanly possible to get other breeds to fight with the enthusiasm and pain-indifference and gameness of pit bulls and have failed. And the long, tragic litany of unprovoked attacks on "good" pit bull owners and their families by their own loved dogs is testimony to the fact that it is not about bad owners, it is about the breed.

Indeed that it is "about the breed" has been tested in law. On April 26, 2012 the Maryland Court of Appeals ruled, in *Tracy vs. Solesky*, that "When an attack involves pit bulls, it is no longer necessary to prove that the particular pit bull or pit bulls are dangerous." The ruling establishes landlord liability in a case when a dog known to be a pit bull or a pit bull cross escapes leased premises and causes damage.[49]

Myth: *Blame the deed, not the breed.*

Fact:

The demand that pit bulls be treated as "individuals" rather than members of a breed when an overwhelming number of them exhibit dangerous behaviour is absurd, especially since when they do something right – when they cuddle up, play nicely and show courage in a good cause – their fanciers are quick to claim these are breed characteristics.

The whole point of a breed line is to inculcate the same defining traits in every single dog produced. When an individual dog displays the traits for which he has been bred, it is ludicrous to insist that he be treated as truly individual human beings are under human law.

Paradoxically, our universities and our cultural elites are rabidly keen on defining human individuals by their collective ethnicity, gender and skin colour in assigning opportunities or exculpatory explanations for bad behaviour. (More on this later)

What a topsy-turvy world it is when identity studies theorists insist that culture is a human individual's defining characteristic, as if he were a line-bred dog, and dogs that attack are to be treated as human individuals born with a 'tabula rasa' brain and temperament, with constitutional rights to an unbiased trial, the jury being instructed to ignore any evidence linked to their breeding.

Myth: *Pit bulls rank high on the American Temperance Test.*

I received many e-mails boasting of the high marks pit bulls receive on this test.

Fact:

This is not a myth exactly, because pit bulls do rate high. But then so do most breeds. Passing the test is no indication of the breed's risk to animals and humans. To wit: The breed of dog with the overall *lowest* passing score was the Skye Terrier at 37.5%. Interestingly, this breed bites so rarely it doesn't even make the Clifton report's base statistical line on dog bites for inclusion.

The myth is that the test is any indicator of a dog's reliability in real life.

This test, which any dog can take, is a series of simulated situations designed to startle or unsettle a dog (an umbrella suddenly opens in front of him; a menacing-looking stranger crosses his path). The owner accompanies but may not gesture or speak to the dog. The test is neither scientific nor does it random-sample breeds. Participation is voluntary and selection bias is inherent.

The test rewards high confidence and penalizes shyness. The test is also invariable and therefore can be trained for (although only pit bull owners trade tips on their websites or seem to prepare for the test with long training periods, warning fellow owners not to enter their dogs if they have management problems. That is, only pit bull owners have a "political" agenda: they seek to keep the numbers high for the breed so they can be used as propaganda).

But most important, the test is *not performed in the presence of other dogs*, the true test of a dog's obedience and aggression tendency. The test is therefore not a reliable indicator of a dog's predictability in real-life situations.

Myth: *Pit bulls are used as therapy dogs.*

Fact:

The words "therapy dog" do not have any official meaning. Any dog can be called a therapy dog if he brings cheer into a life. I can call my dog a "therapy dog" because he makes me smile when he wags his tail. Yes, individual pit bulls are trained to provide services for their owners, and may be trained for work done on leashes or under a trainer's oversight. So do many other breeds.

Let's just say you won't see pit bulls leading the blind any time soon.

Myth: *Pit bulls take the rap for other breeds that look like them*

Fact:

It's a funny thing with pit bull lovers. When their breed does something heroic, like waking up the family and saving them from a fire, it's a pit bull, no question. When it does something bad, like mauling a child to death, they demand a DNA test and complain that animal control people can't tell a pit bull apart from other breed, as we saw in the case of Lennox, the martyr dog.

Or they say there is no such thing as a "pit bull," only fighting dogs, even though all their websites feature the words "pit bull."

The fact is that even if human error occasionally comes into play, as with all policing, animal control people are trained to recognize and do recognize pit bulls and their genetic siblings. Over 350 municipalities are currently protected with BSL. Most of these ordinances include language that defines pit bulls, and many of these have withstood court challenges.

Myth: *The pit bulls rescued from disgraced football player Michael Vick's dogfighting operation (the "Vicktory dogs") were all successfully rehabilitated and re-homed.*

Fact:

The ASPCA, Best Friends Animal Society and other organizations did not euthanize 47 of the 51 pit bull terriers found in Vick's kennels. But most of them were only puppies or slightly older. They were not elite fighting dogs or even close to it. The one true fighting dog rescued was euthanized.

The ASPCA and Best Friends collected $1 million from Vick as part of a court settlement. Much of it was applied to finding extraordinarily dedicated owners for the rescued dogs. None of the dogs were re-homed with average people as average companion pets.

More than 80% of the animal shelters in the U.S. have less funding per year for all of their programs combined than was invested in the Vick dogs, considered by PBAM worth the investment because ensuring their successful rehab was propaganda gold.[50]

Myth: *The pit bull is so good with children it used to be used as a "Nanny Dog".*

Countless respondents reiterated the myth that the pit bull was so beloved in England and America and so gentle with children that people actually left their babies alone with them. (The question as to who would be so stupid as to leave their children to be babysat by any dog whatsoever, let alone a pit bull, is never raised.)

Fact:

In over 77,000 Google hits for "nanny dog," one is led to 120 sites dedicated to the Staffordshire Bull Terrier (a.k.a pit bull) that include the following passage in support of the nanny-dog myth:

"These dogs were renowned for their courage and tenacity and despite their ferocity in the pit were excellent companions and good with children. In fact it was not unknown for an injured dog to be transported home in a pram with the baby!"[51]

There is no basis in any archive, no matter how far back you go, for this statement, whether you are looking for material on the American Pit Bull Terrier or the American Staffordshire Terrier. Archive searches of British, American and Canadian newspapers back to the eighteenth century do not reveal a single mention of "nanny dog" with reference to any breed of dog.

The myth originates with a woman called Lillian Rant, President of and magazine editor for the Staffordshire Bull Terrier Club of America, on the eve of the "Staffie's" entry into the American Kennel Club. She wanted to polish up the dog's brutish image (Bullseye, the odious Bill Sykes' dog in *Oliver Twist*, was a Staffie). And ...she just made it up! This was 1971, when there were only 99 registered Staffies in the U.S. and dog fighting was not on the public radar screen.

The next mention of the "nanny dog" appears in 1987 in a *Toronto Star* article entitled, "Move to outlaw pit bulls under study in several cities." Toronto-area breeder Kathy Thomas, president of the Staffordshire Bull Terrier Association, and mother of two children, acknowledged that most of the breed were engaged in ripping each other's throats out – by now dog fighting had made its modern presence well known – but she personally only sold her puppies as pets. She was quoted as saying that her eight Staffies were "wonderful with children. In England our Staffies were called the nanny-dog because they were gentle with kids."

But the myth only became the meme it is today in 1991 when Lillian Rant, the myth's founder, published *Staffordshire Bull Terrier: Owners' Companion*, in which she reiterates three times the "nursemaid" fabrication, asserting, "He has a great affection for children, having earned the title 'nursemaid dog' many years ago." That would be 20 years ago when Ms Rant invented the myth in the first place.

Myth: *Helen Keller owned a pit bull.*

Fact: Helen Keller owned a Boston Terrier. One can find numerous photos of her with her Boston Terrier on the Internet. Readers insist that she also owned a pit bull, but so far nobody has provided me with any evidence of it.

Why aren't there more attacks by pit bulls?

By now, you should be wondering: If there are millions of pit bulls, and they are such a disproportionately dangerous breed, and the disproportion is due to inherent traits, why, in terms of actual *numbers*, however dreadful the damage, are there so relatively few deaths and maulings?

Good question.

For starters, most pit bull damage is done to other animals, and the public rarely hears about that. You may not consider the death or savaging of another animal a big deal, but if it were your dog or cat, I assure you, you would.

Next, pit bull owners lie to themselves about attacks on animals, rationalizing that it is part of "nature, red in tooth and claw," so it doesn't count as worthy of comment when responding to queries about their dogs' temperament. But other dogs do not rip other animals apart as a matter of course.

Pit bull owners often don't report bites if they don't actually have to go to the hospital, because they're in denial or embarrassed about them.[52] When the dogs become a more serious problem, they dump them. Remember those stats about a third of all pit bulls ending up in humane shelters? And that today *close to a million pit bulls* are euthanized every year? That adds up to a lot of problem pit bulls.

Pit bull devotees lie to themselves, and they lie to others. (There are Internet message boards, I am told by reliable witnesses, where pit bull owners encourage each other to lie to the public – and even to their friends and family.)

It's refreshing when the truth comes out. A chairwoman of the Dutch branch of the American Staffordshire breeders' club, for example, had always vouched for her breed's good temperament. Suddenly in 1999 she announced that she'd stopped breeding them. She was tired of the constant fighting amongst them, cleaning blood off her carpets, of being bitten herself, enduring her neighbours' wrath over their cats being killed and their dogs attacked.

Then there is the pit bull owners' "management" habits. Many pit bull owners keep upping the ante on the precautions they take to ensure the dogs don't do harm, without even being conscious of the fact they are taking precautions no other breed owners need to.

For a good example of this willed denial, here is the experience of the world's *best* pit bull owner, "Julia Templeton," my pseudonym for a woman who at one time allowed her name to be used publicly, but no longer does, because she is tired of being harassed by PBAM.

In a long letter to the administration of the SPCA chapter from which she had adopted the dog, Ms. Templeton chronicled her experiences with Bella, a rescue pit bull she had been encouraged to adopt. The letter explained why she was giving the dog back.

She does not name the chapter, but it could have been any of hundreds, as most of them take the same caninely correct attitude to pit bulls. The letter is a salutary warning about the danger of rescuing a pit bull, all of which have been – or are supposed to have been – deemed rehabitable by a shelter assessment team. Obviously those not deemed rehabitable are put down.

Bella was a young AmStaff Terrier in January 2010 when she was adopted into the Templeton family of three children and another mixed-breed dog. Ms. Templeton had done extensive research on pit bulls and "their specific needs." Bella was in "lockdown mode" – i.e. crated virtually all the time – for a month as per the humane shelter's advice (what other breed needs such meticulous separation from other animals and people in order to adjust?).

Ms Templeton gave Bella every opportunity to accustom herself to her new home and family. She handfed her, lavished her with love, desensitized her to every possible sight and noise she could think of. She could have saved herself the trouble, as she would learn.

The letter goes on for pages and pages and pages, describing every single strategy and tactic poor Ms. Templeton could think of to ensure Bella grew happy and confident. Very few people would have put in the time and energy of this determined and conscientious lady.

But Bella could not be made trustworthy. She was aggressive and needed to be crated all the time she was not in adults' direct oversight. Even so, there were "incidents" with animals no amount of oversight could prevent. Ms. Templeton could see "that Bella was getting dangerously close to a serious occurrence of human aggression."

Sure enough, fortunately while leashed, Bella directed aggression at some passing children. Soon after, she attacked the family dog without warning, and both Ms. Templeton and her husband together could not pry her off before she did serious damage to the other dog. When Bella directed aggression at the husband, they finally asked their vet to euthanize the pit bull. Regrettably, the vet advised them to return the dog to the SPCA for assessment.

More assessment? But what was there to assess? Ms. Templeton was not a bad owner or even an ordinary owner. She had performed superhuman service in accommodating Bella's needs. She was the "good owner" par excellence. And still she could not succeed in making Bella into something she was not.

Ms. Templeton returned Bella with explanations to the shelter, assuming they would euthanize her. She never found out that the SPCA did not euthanize Bella, but advertised her for re-adoption without including Ms. Templeton's caveats.

The letter exemplified the "frog-in-cold-water" management escalation desperately kind people are willing to undertake in order to make a success of their pit bull guardianship, as well as the state of denial of pit bull reality they fall into in the process.

Sometimes they admit this, sometimes they don't. If they have more than one dog, and one (or more) is a pit bull, they do 'crate 'n rotate', or some other means to keep the dogs separated at all times. They put them into closed rooms when company comes. People who take their pit bull to community dog events are always fanatically on top of their pit bull to make sure it doesn't stray anywhere near another dog; even so, there are often scuffles, which remain minor only because there are so many people ready to intervene quickly.[53]

One pit bull owner I know of exercised the management technique of having her Golden Retriever put down because the pit bull kept trying to kill it. About a million pit bulls a year are subjected to the extraordinary management technique of being abandoned to a shelter.

In the majority of cases where pit bulls maul or kill a human, the owner says, "But it was never aggressive before!" This might sometimes actually be true.[54] But all too often, a little probing reveals that the dog has been involved in other aggression incidents that have gone unreported.

Sometimes pit bulls won't give their owners any trouble even without the management techniques. It's well known among dog fighting men that full-blown aggression can take until a pit bull's fifth year to emerge.

In fact, averaged out – some days none, some days many – at least one human is being seriously bitten by a pit bull every day in the US. We have no way of knowing how many attempted attacks are stopped before a pit bull gets its teeth in. No one is keeping track of how many other animals are seriously hurt by pit bulls daily (except for Semyonova's tracking in The Hague of a normal dog every other day, which figure only represents people who resisted police pressure not to report the incident, and also only includes attacks on dogs.)

Humane shelters: friend or enemy of pit bulls?[55]

Unlike other dogs, pit bulls typically have been through three homes: their birth home, their owner's home and then, the dog having exhibited troubling signs of aggression, to a third – that of a "fixer" of some kind – before arriving at a shelter. Without BSL, humane shelters are inundated with pit bulls.

In her 1984 book, *The Animal Shelter,* Patricia Curtis issued a prescient warning about a resurgence in dog fighting and the rise of a pit bull presence in animal shelters. In 1986, about 8.4 million dogs were killed in shelters. Of those, about 168,000 were pit bulls, representing 2% of the whole. By 1993, even though the total number of U.S. dogs in general killed in U.S. shelters annually had fallen 40%, the number of pit bulls killed more than doubled to almost 360,000 – 15% of the total. By 2003 they accounted for 50% of the dogs killed in shelters – about 900,000, and by 2010 60% – almost a million pit bulls killed annually.

Under the principled direction of then-attorney-general Michael Bryant, Ontario adopted a law in 2005 prohibiting possession or breeding of new pit bulls, with living pit bulls "grandfathered" and highly regulated. The Toronto Humane Society objected strenuously, complaining that the legislation would promote a pit bull holocaust. In spite of the burdens placed on them by pit bulls, ideology trumps realism. Other caninely correct humane societies toe the same party line.

But, as the numbers above indicate, it is the humane societies themselves that are effecting the "holocaust" by refusing to recognize that fighting dogs are being euthanized because of what they are – a breed that cannot co-exist in harmony with other animals and people. Ironically, it is the very people who insist they want pit bulls to be treated as innocent until proven guilty who are responsible for all these euthanasias, because people who are duped into adopting or buying pit bulls are voting with their feet.

The "humane community" finds itself in a cleft moral stick. They refuse to admit that pit bulls are intrinsically unsuitable as pets. But the present situation of escalating euthanasias and mounting insurance costs is untenable (the pit bulls in humane shelters are an elevated risk to staff and other animals in the shelter).

Since 2004, insurance premiums paid by major shelters in cities that have legislation to reduce pit bull numbers have declined by an average of 20%. But at the shelters that actively promote pit bulls, premiums have increased by an average of 33%.

Insurance premiums, based in actuarial numbers, obviously reflect true risks. And yet – stupidly! – Michigan and Pennsylvania have passed laws to prevent insurers from charging breed-specific premiums. Similar legislation is up for possible passage in more than twenty other states. Nothing could be more calculated to exacerbate the problem than repressing a market solution.

Does Breed Specific Legislation work?

Yes. The proof is in the pudding.

Cities like Denver, Miami, and Cincinnati ban pit bulls outright (as does the province of Ontario). Those cities haven't killed 1000 pit bulls *over an entire decade*, while U.S. cities with no BSL kill about 2000 pit bulls *every year*. Because of the Ontario ban in place since 2005, Ontario shelters now kill fewer pit bulls, serving a cumulative population of 13 million people, than the Detroit metropolitan area shelters do, serving a human population of only 1.2 million.

Many pit bull advocates seize on the fact that in terms of frequency, the actual number of dog bites in Ontario after the ban declined by only 4%. However, the point of the ban was to reduce fatalities and maimings, as well as to reduce shelter killings. These goals were achieved, and are achieved wherever breed-specific bans are implemented.

Moreover, where bans are in place, dog fighting dries up, and the canine victims of that odious sport – the starved, the endlessly chained, the bait dogs, the burned and lynched dogs – are spared an ugly fate.

For example, in Lancaster, a city in Southern California, a 2009 ban on pit bulls was adopted with the specific intent of preventing gang members from intimidating people with fighting dogs, and thereby creating the climate of fear that drove *City Journal* writer Brian Anderson out of his pit bull-infested neighbourhood. When the ordinance was passed, 1,138 pit bulls and Rottweilers were impounded and 362 were voluntarily surrendered.

In 2010, Lancaster Mayor R. Rex Parris announced, "A year ago, this city was overrun with individuals – namely, gang members – who routinely used pit bulls and other potentially vicious dogs as tools of intimidation and violence. These individuals delighted in the danger these animals posed to our residents, often walking them without leashes and allowing them to run rampant through our neighborhoods and parks. Today, more than 1,100 of these animals have been removed from our city, along with the fear they create. Lancaster is now a great deal safer because of it."[56]

Not coincidentally, according to the mayor, Lancaster's violent gang crime

– homicide, rape, robbery and aggravated assault – fell by 45%, and there was an overall gang crime decrease of 41%.

Nevertheless, in spite of such compelling evidence, the PBAM beat goes on. Humane shelters trot out all the myths I cited above. And one sees exactly the same obfuscations and glossings-over by breeders and kennel clubs[57] and even veterinarian associations.[58] All of these intervenors are commercially invested in the dog industry, so they are not disinterested witnesses.

Nevertheless, with support from these organizations, BSL repeal campaigns are fought tooth and nail in cities and counties where BSL has been in place for years and working well.[59]

In late October, 2012, Edmonton, Alberta's councillors voted to repeal their 25-year ban on pit bulls.

As I write in November, 2012, baseball player and pit bull owner Mark Buehrie, just traded from the Miami Marlins to the Toronto Blue Jays, has a sycophan-tic press, spouting the usual myths, commiserating with him over Ontario's pit bull ban. I would not be surprised if a similar BSL repeal campaign to the one that failed in Miami-Dade County (see footnote 59) were to spring up around Buehrie's quandary and succeed. After all, a private-member's bill to repeal Ontario's 2005 ban had already gathered bipartisan momentum before the House was prorogued when the premier stepped down in October.

One of my columns was prompted by a news report in the *Toronto Star* news-paper about an "underground railway" that was spiriting illegally bred pit bull puppies to Nova Scotia. The article was a completely unresearched infomercial for the pit bull lobby, repeating sentimental myths and misinformation that compelled a response.[60]

In that column I focused on what happens when a breed ban is lifted. I cit-ed the case of one of my most enlightening sources for this essay, Alexandra Semyonova, a highly-experienced behavioural biologist, and author of the in-valuable 2009 book I have cited throughout this essay, The *100 Silliest Things People Say About Dogs*.[61]

Semyonova worked for years at a humane shelter in the Netherlands. During their ban years, they took in four or five pit bulls annually (mostly collateral catch from drug raids). In 2008, the year of the ban lift, there were 180 pit bulls awaiting execution; all had hurt someone. Today, various dog shelters there are going bankrupt, because they can't handle the tsunami of dumped pit bulls.

As I wrote in my column,

> Pit bull advocates are passionate and verbally aggressive. When
> Semyonova spoke publicly about the inherent dangers of pit bulls, she

was smeared through a methodical intimidation campaign so virulent that the Dutch Ministry of Justice acknowledged it as a pattern clearly constituting organized crime. "If you speak out about pit bulls, you are on your own," Semyonova writes. She notes that confiscated pit bulls were never sent to their hometown shelters "in order to prevent the violent, histrionic break-in rescues that the pit bull lobby sometimes organized."

Semyonova's battle was fought in Europe. What about PBAM in North America? Not as violently aggressive, but it still requires significant political will to stand up to their strenuous lobbying efforts.

In his newly-published memoir, *28 Seconds*, former Ontario attorney-general Michael Bryant says he enacted his province's controversial 2005 pit bull ban on principle; he was confident it would pay off in improved public safety and dramatically fewer dog euthanasias (it did, as noted).

The ban was international news. Bryant was vilified, threatened with violence and compared to Hitler on Facebook. Bryant writes: "The decision actually changed my political life. For years afterwards ... the average person knew me as the guy who banned pit bulls." What buoyed his spirits was grass-roots support. A poll reported the pit bull ban was the most popular public event in Canada since Newfoundland premier Brian Tobin's public spat with foreign fishing trawlers.[62]

Intellectuals, multiculturalism and pit bull rebranding

My opinion of PBAM reached its nadir when I received an e-mail from a pit bull lover who wrote – more, she said, in sorrow for my obtuseness than anger – "First they came for the pit bulls. But I did not own a pit bull, so I said nothing. Then they came for the Rottwei..." – forgive me, I must stop here: this mawkish exercise in self-righteousness is too excruciatingly contemptible to repeat in full.

This girl was hopelessly muddled. Pastor Martin Niemöller's famous warning was a denunciation of the intellectuals who failed to speak out against the Nazis during their purges of Communists, trade unionists and Jews. In any objective parallel, the pit bulls and the Rottweilers and the other dogs my respondent referenced would be the equivalent of the *Nazis*, not their victims. Indeed, if only someone had "come for" these fighting dogs in 1939, the world would be a safer place today.

But we live in ironized times, and the moral inversion of historical evils is the cultural Zeitgeist's calling card. The Holocaust in particular, one of the few words that still signifies absolute evil, even trickling down into the pea-sized brain of the Lionel Asbos of the world, has become a handy trope for narcissistic grievance-collectors of every sort, all eager to displace Jews from suffering's moral high ground and claim it for their own – or their dog.

But, though Niemöller was an icon of moral clarity, he was also somewhat naïve. For intellectuals are rarely the moral Cassandras we would like them to be. *Au contraire.* They are historically more likely to be the source of inspiration for tyrannies than democracies; more likely to look with approval on blood running in the streets, if the ideas such mayhem serves meet with their approval, than to call for a halt to revolutionary chaos; and nowadays more likely to lend their moral authority to apologism for terrorism than to commiseration with the terrorized. Indeed the alliance of PhDs and terrorist "victims" is one of the most commented-on phenomena of our era.

Regrettably, you can almost never go wrong blaming a negative social phenomenon on an intellectual's Bad Idea, even if you don't know who he or she is. Trace a negative cultural phenomenon back far enough and there you will find a Theory about Social Justice, contemplating its navel in an attic, a sidewalk café, a beer hall or a campus lounge. The various utopias of which such intellectuals dream are, however, usually omelettes in whose making many many eggs may have, regrettably, to be smashed.

So the buck stops at the top, and in the case of PBAM, the top is the ideology factory: the academy. PBAM takes its vocabulary of "rights" and "racism" and "profiling" and "hate" and "discrimination" from the dogmas of multiculturalism, which is in its turn governed by the philosophy of moral relativism: the idea that there is no absolute truth, no absolute rights and wrongs, no objective morality. There are only your truths and my truths, your "narrative" and mine – all are of equal worth and dignity.

And so with cultures. We mustn't judge "the Other" in the light of our own values. Because there is no one culture that is better than another.

By logical extension, political correctness surrounding human multiculturalism transmogrified into canine correctness around "multicaninism," as I dubbed pit bull love in a recent column.[63] It seems to me that it is precisely *because* pit bulls display so many traits in common with terrorists that it is so easy for intellectuals to take their side when public wrath descends on them. Terrorism and victimhood are intertwined in politically correct thought.

But to show rather than tell just how bizarrely aligned pit bulls have become with identity politics, we turn to one Harlan Weaver, newly anointed "human-animals studies fellow" of the caninely correct Animals and Society Institute.

On his website, Mr. Weaver self-describes thus:

Harlan Weaver is a soon-to-be graduate of the History of Consciousness

Department at U.C. Santa Cruz. Harlan's dissertation, Thinking and Feeling with "Trans Affect," explores the role of feeling in both transgender experiences of embodiment epistemological practices. Harlan's new project comes out of ten years of pit bull advocacy (and love). In it, Harlan explores the ways that species, breed, race, gender, sexuality, class, ability, and nation are mutually shaped by relationships between humans and so-called dangerous dogs, 'pit bull-type' dogs in particular.

Sorry, I have no idea of what a "Department of Consciousness" might be, although I instinctively believe it is up to no intellectual good. And I also have no idea what Mr. Weaver means by "so-called dangerous" when he refers to the objectively very dangerous "pit bull type" dogs on whose behalf advocacy endowed him with so much wisdom about "race, gender, sexuality, class, ability, and nation."

And I especially have no idea how one arrives at "the role of feeling" in transgender "embodiment epistological practices." But it hardly matters, since whatever Mr. Weaver writes is going to be the same gobbledygook he has clearly been studying for many years, a set of linguistic semaphores understood only by other academics in his domain, rather like the higher frequencies dogs can hear but humans can't. We don't need to understand what Mr. Harlan is trying to say. The point is that pit bulls have now arrived in academia as a privileged minority group whose social victimhood is a given, never more to be interrogated by normative academic inquiry.[64]

We're beginning to close the cultural noose on this weird sub-culture. It is no coincidence that sympathy for pit bulls amongst the educated class surfaced at about the same time that the once-marginalized "sport" of dog fighting re-emerged in the black underclass (at the same time Martin Amis pinpoints the join between the craving for fame and the obsession with terrorism). For the pit bull, once a metaphor for terrorist oppression of blacks by white supremacists, was now a metaphor for black liberation and identity pride. And identity pride – in whatever form it takes – is a sacred ideal in politically correct circles.[65]

When the KKK and the equally racist and socially-disordered skinheads were dog fighting, intellectuals could freely call them out for the moral trash they were, and their dogs for the abused and abusing brutes they were. You can be sure that if pit bulls were still strongly identified with the white underclass of the southern U.S., you would not see educated people committed to their defence or advocacy.

But now they are largely seen as accessories to disaffected black men, who see no wrong in the extreme abuse of dogs and who enjoy blood sport. They simply cannot be condemned; that would be racist.

White intellectuals saw an opportunity here to (partially) expiate their guilt for their racializing history. Instead of scolding blacks for dog fighting, they sought first to understand them, and then to sympathize with them, and then to "disappear" the bad image of their agent of violence into the oubliette of historical revisionism.

Of course, such thinking illustrates the soft bigotry of low expectations that is the corrupt heart of multiculturalism. If intellectuals really considered black people to be "equal" to whites, they would have been revulsed by their involvement in dog fighting, just as all civilized people were revulsed by the KKK and the skinheads, and they would say so.[66]

(In reality, as any objective observer can see, blacks' appropriation of a racist KKK legacy is a betrayal of their own best interest and even what might be called a post-facto victory for the world's most vile racists.)[67]

But soft bigotry is built into the fabric of multitculturalism. So intellectuals had to validate this "cultural" expression in a way that they could justify to themselves.

No problem. Rhetorical legerdemain is the intellectual's gift. Moral inversion is his or her specialty. In their minds, without skipping a beat, the pit bull was now transformed from an ugly weapon of destruction into a fine animal: game, courageous, loyal, good, and true. And a victim of terrible prejudice! Just like black people!

For an illustration of how all these ideas became conflated in the academic world, ending up as jargon-infused propaganda for PBAM, we have only to turn to a doctoral sociology thesis that was submitted to the University of Southern California in 2007 by Theresa Allen. It's called "Petey and Chato[68]: The Pitbull's transition from mainstream to marginalized masculinity."

In her introduction, Allen lays out the ideologically braided schema I have been talking about: "Sociology has hardly considered non-human animals as subjects, especially as actors, significant in the network of relations of power and violence to oppression. Just as we understand certain populations as marginal due to their perceived status as 'other,' the pit bull, as a stigmatized breed belonging to a marginalized species, reflects a similar structure of power and oppression."

Allen's subjects are young, lower-status, mostly black men she met and interviewed at a downscale veterinary clinic, where their pit bulls were treated. Many of them are unemployed. Their pit bulls are important to them as symbols of masculinity. Allen comes to like them and sympathize with them and their dogs.

181

In AcademicSpeak, such sympathy emerges as: "The construction of the pit bull as vicious serves the dominant population by addressing a fear of the inner city male, racial minorities, whose favored method in achieving a macho presentation involves the subversion of mainstream values."

Unpacked, she is saying that we – you and I, educated Reader of the oppressor class – have deliberately "constructed" – just made up! – an image of the pit bull as vicious, simply because it is the dog of choice of racialized youth, and because their concept of masculinity doesn't match our own "mainstream" vision. According to Allen, this unfounded image allows us to marginalize young black men and continue to enjoy our hegemonic status.

If you favour BSL of pit bulls, Allen alleges, then what you are really in favour of is racism: "By framing the bull breed as a bloodthirsty predator, we justify its destruction in the same manner that we justify gang sweeps, stepped up penalties for gang membership and punishment based on one's physical likeness to the stereotypical 'gang member.'"

Removal of gangs as a nuisance abatement, *just like BSL bans*, works to "sanitize the public realm" of that which seems threatening. (Gangs are in fact threatening, but that is of no concern to Ms. Allen.) Here we see again the false, apples-and-oranges alignment of stereotyped human individuals with line-bred dogs.[69]

This thesis is juicy with pit bull mythology and pulpy with conspiracy-theorist accusations. Pit bulls are the result of "selective breeding as a very loyal and innocuous human companion," they are "especially tolerant of children," they were well-known as "nanny-dogs" and so forth. And of course the media is to blame for over blowing pit bull incidents in order to direct negative attention to "young, poor, urban males of a racial minority."

In an academic thesis about pit bulls and their image, one might think the doctoral candidate wouldn't be able to avoid data and statistics about pit bulls' actuarial risk to public safety. One would be wrong. Data and stats are old hat in the postmodern "constructionist" universe.[70]

No, in our brave new academic world, as Ms. Allen explains, "the way in which we understand the world is dependent on our culture and historical context. A social constructionist points to daily interaction between people as the basis for the creation of knowledge – shared versions of knowledge are constructed."

That is to say, "knowledge" is what I personally "know," and what you personally "know" – but most important of all for the purposes of this thesis, what young, underclass black men "know."

(What do these young men know? When she asked them why they chose a pit bull, almost all said they liked its "toughness" and that it was "intimidating." Amongst the names of the dogs were monikers like Tonka, Felony and War. These young men had no illusions about the true nature of pit bulls. But strangely Ms. Allen doesn't accuse them of "constructivism.")

Life is dangerous for young black men in their "oppositional space" and therefore dangerous for their pit bulls as well, we're told. One subject mentions that a friend's pit bull "was shot by the police." This fact is duly recorded by Ms. Allen with no context or explanation as to why the police shot the dog. The implication is that the dog must have been innocent, just as young black men shot by the police sometimes are. But pit bulls are never shot by police at random. Why was Ms. Allen so incurious about the nature of the incident?

I could go on and on – this thesis is a parodic goldmine for proof of the corruption in scientific rigour that has metastasized throughout the groves of academe – but here is the rebranding of the pit bull as a "threatening outsider" and victim in a nutshell: "his brute animality made him the perfect vehicle for the projection of fears about human savagery that had been displaced onto racial-minority males. This displacement has a long history in colonialism, when imperialists often perceived of indigenous peoples as beasts, having brute-like qualities."

Summary: Black people are good and they like pit bulls; therefore pit bulls are good. White people are imperialists and colonizers and racists; therefore whatever bad things white people say about pit bulls is racist. To exclude pit bulls from society is to exclude black people from society.

Now, like Harlan Weaver, Theresa Allen is a non-entity in the real world. There isn't an original idea in her thesis, just the same superannuated clichés and moral inversions you can find in every other sociology thesis these days. The objects of interrogation may change, but the ideological framework is identical. Of course no commonsensical reader in the general public would be taken in by Ms. Allen's thesis, if any such person were to actually stumble upon it.

Which brings me to full disclosure and an embarrassing admission. I myself once got gently sucked into the pit bull propaganda mill. But not via academic swill like the thesis above. Rather I fell hook, line and sinker for the blandishments of a brilliant writer – a Yale University academic, a poet and contributing editor to *Harper's Magazine,* no less – who happened also to be a brilliant con woman regarding pit bulls. And I am betting thousands upon thousands of other intelligent readers did too.

This snake-oil saleswoman wrote what I think must be the Ur-text of pit bull laundering. Her name is Vicki Hearne. The snake oil is contained in a best-selling book, *Adam's Task: Calling Animals by Name.*[71] An unusual woman, in that she was both an academic and trainer of dogs and horses, Hearne wrote with great eloquence and out of authentic passion for animals. I read the book when it was published in 1982, and found myself besotted with her prose and charmed by the originality and sophistication of her perspectives.

Hearne loved and admired pit bulls, and after I read her paean to them, I admired them too. Hearne's words are elegantly deployed, but as I discovered on my recent second, more critical reading, they are duplicitous. Let me count the ways in which she misleads and manipulates the reader.

The chapter begins with Hearne waving away "horror stories" of pit bulls who "maul" (her quotation marks), as if they were fairy stories, because "I have my real life in a world in which there are no horror stories about Bull Terriers."[72]

That's an artful construction. On first reading you see the words "real life" and "world" and your mind runs them together. You think she is referring to the "real world" when she says she has never heard horror stories of pit bulls. I believed her on first reading. On second it shocked me. Because, even though Ms. Hearne is dead and can't defend herself, I know today that was a lie. No dog trainer with a special interest in pit bulls could fail to have heard many horror stories.

But upon rereading the sentence a third time, I realized that's not what she said. She said, "I have *my* real life in *a world in which there are no horror stories.*" Of course. She lived in an academic dream palace, where the "world" is what you have theorized it to be. And in that world – remember sociologist Leon Festinger's "dissent reduction" – you get to order reality as you like.

Hearne goes on, disingenuously, to note that of course pit bulls bite (*as "all dogs do"*) and sure, if they bite you, "you sit up and take notice" – "take notice" a nice euphemism for the likelihood of a pint of blood lost and 60 stitches needed to close the wound.

As for their gameness in fighting, why that's not a bad thing at all, because there's nothing *personal* in it: "In a true fighting dog, there is no ill temper, nothing personal held against an opponent, no petty resentments of the sort found in the snappy, ignoble animals so beloved of people who want to kill pit bulls."[73]

Of course the fact that there is nothing personal about pit bull attacks – the fact that nobody understands the reason these ambulatory grenades pull their own pins – is the problem, but the silver-tongued Hearne neatly turns it to a virtue, and with a gratuitous fillip, manages to insult rational and civic-minded dog owners everywhere, not to mention their dogs.

The first time I read this chapter, I suspended judgment on dog fighting, as I knew little about it. Now that I do, I find there is something a little sickening about Hearne's admiration. She says, "No one wants [dog fights] especially..." yet a few lines later, she says, "but at the center of it there is nonetheless awe and admiration in the presence of a beautiful and nearly pure cynosure: when Bull Terriers fight, what we see approaches a Platonic form. We are compelled by dogs and dog fighting (whether or not we hate them) in roughly the way the tail of a dog is compelled by the dog to wag..."[74]

It is easy to get lulled into a stupor by the eloquence of Hearne's prose. The first time I read this sentence, I actually found myself falling under her spell and struggling to understand the beauty of dog fighting.

But once you shake off the verbal spangles, you realize she is supporting an odious blood sport that does terrible violence to the bodies of the animals involved and does terrible damage to the souls of the people who make it happen. There really is no possible moral defence for it.

Hearne peddles the usual myths (which I didn't know the first time around were myths) about the pit bull being unusually child-friendly and America's most popular dog, alluding as well to the 1914 poster by Wallace Robinson, in which the pit bull is front and centre, "with a gay twinkle in his eye and an American flag around his neck." The image, as I freely conceded earlier, of a dog that never backs down from a fight, was an appropriate one for wartime, because *under such circumstances alone*, the pit bull is a useful metaphor for a conflict in which one is obliged to fight to the death, to give no quarter, to vanquish utterly or be vanquished. Yes, when duking it out with al Qaeda, a pit bull might be a welcome comrade in arms.

But Hearne goes further. She says that the pit bull's image has become tarnished because America itself is tarnished; the pit bull is now considered a berserker because it represents "an America that has gone out of its mind and become in its own visions an unconscious parody of such Bull Terrier-like heroes as Huckleberry Finn."[75]

At the time of my first reading, I was unschooled in the cultural self-loathing in which almost all academics had been marinating since the 1960s counter-culture swept American campuses. What she was really saying didn't register. Now I got it. It isn't the pit bull that is bad. It is America itself. We weren't wrong about the twinkly-eyed pit bull; that poster image was correct. It turns out we were wrong about *America*. America, she is saying, sold us a bill of goods about how great a country it is. Now we (intellectuals) know that was a lie. America is a terrible country, no different than the Soviets (she does make that wicked equivalency). In fact, America is not *worthy* of being identified as a pit bull.

Hearne doesn't much care what happens to America. She's only sad that the good pit bull got sucked under by evil America's imperialistic rip tide. She says, "I sometimes think that the most patriotic thing a movie company could do right now would be to produce a film with a glorious and noble Pit Bull as its hero."[76] In what realistic way does Hearne imagine that the pit bull could be portrayed as more heroic than any other aggressively protective dog or even as *only* heroic at all?[77]

Hearne's defence of dog fighting is linguistic sleight of hand worth beholding. If dogs are equally matched, she believes, citing pit bull authority Richard Stratton,[78] it is no cruelty to let them do what they love to do. She says that with certain dogs, "not only is it not cruel to 'roll' them (give them real fighting, as opposed to mere scrapping experience), it is cruel to prevent them from fighting, in the way it is cruel to put birds in cages, or at least in cages that are too small for them...So it is possible for me to contemplate the possibility that allowing the right Pit Bulls, in the hands of the right people, to fight can be called kind because it answers to some energy essential to the creature, and I think of energy...as the need for heroism."[79]

Oops. That word "heroism" again, but now it is tied to dog fighting. So would her fantasized movie plot turn on dog fighting as a symbol of patriotism? The moral inversion is pretty breathtaking. One doesn't wish to over-use George Orwell's famous dictum, but sometimes nothing else will do: "One has to belong to the intelligentsia to believe things like that: no ordinary man could be such a fool."

In the end, she hedges: "I don't (can't bring myself to) advocate dog fighting. Nor can I bring myself to oppose it. I don't even know what a question about it would look like."[80] Perhaps it's all that oxygen-thin air up in the ivory towers of academia that stymied Hearne. Because most of us down below amongst the Great Unwashed have no trouble posing the question at all, namely: are you for the abuse of animals and the dehumanization of men or not?

When she isn't aglow over the beauty of dog fighting, Hearne is telling us stories about her pit bull Belle, the apotheosis of dog loyalty, dignity and intelligence. Belle is so "committed," so "aware."

What is comical in all the gushing over her dogs is the way she slips in the odd clue, the little caveat here and there in which the truth of the matter is exposed. At one point she says rather elliptically, "[pit bulls] are unresponsive to anything short of genuine training." Translation from Hearnese: *You'd better hope your pit bull wants to do what you'd like him to do, 'cuz hope is about all you've got if you're not a real trainer like me.*

A little further on, more transparently, "It is now time for me to say emphatically that my praise of this breed should not be construed as advice to rush out and get a Pit. They do like to fight other dogs, and they are in many ways a tremendous spiritual responsibility. If you're ready for it and can find a *real* dog trainer to help you figure out what you've gotten hold of, then go to it."[81]

Translation from Hearnese:

> *If you're determined to get a breed that will not socialize with other dogs, but is likely to try to tear them apart, which means forget about dog runs and other fun places most dogs and their owners like to congregate, and that you can't train yourself, so don't even bother trying, because it clearly needs very special handling, remember I didn't advise you to get it. Even though of course I have never heard of a "horror story" about pit bulls, and people who don't love them are ignoble cretins.*

Not once in Hearne's chapter, while pouring scorn on those who fear them and are disgusted by dog fighting, does Hearne adduce a *single statistic* about pit bulls' unprovoked assault records on other animals and humans that might explain the aversion to them we "ignoble" proles feel – we lesser beings who are apparently so deficient in Hearne's greatness of soul, and "spiritual responsibility" (whatever that means) and aesthetic sensitivity to the art of dog fighting that we fail to appreciate the essential aristocracy of the pit bull.

Mea culpa for not having noticed any of this the first time around with Hearne.

Ordinary people contemplating the purchase or rescue of a pit bull certainly won't be reading academic theses or books by the likes of Vicki Hearne. They read books by dog whisperer Cesar Millan (see this essay's opening quote by Millan). Or they watch dog documentaries posted on Youtube.

So I recently watched an hour-long 2007 film called *American pit bull – killer canine or family friend?* On the surface it seems objective. Many pit bull experts speak earnestly to the camera about the unique level of responsibility ownership of a pit bull requires. No one dissembles about the origins of the dog as a fighting dog. A humane society representative speaks with furrowed brow about the hugely disproportionate numbers of pit bulls that are dumped in shelters and cannot be rehomed. More than once we see distressing close-ups of a pit bull puppy that has been subjected to terrible abuse.

But the main point of the film is to show off the inherently wonderful qualities of the pit bull: his athleticism, his "gameness" (not applied in its real meaning of a willingness to fight to the death, but now modified to mean a willingness to play hard at games devised by his owner), and his loving nature. Many frames are filled with dog trainers (they're experts, so they must know, right?) smooching their pit bulls on the face after he performs well. (Dog fighting guru Richard Stratton is benignly present in the film and accorded respectful attention, but do revisit footnote 78 for a refresher on Stratton's real-life relationship with pit bulls.)

Much of the film is devoted to pit bulls in training or talent show situations, where they demonstrate absolute obedience to their handler, showing no aggression to other animals around them, and with the aggression they do show directed only where and for how long the trainer commands. None of the tricks performed are in any way unique to pit bulls (climbing obstacles, attacking and desisting on command, pulling heavy loads), but implied is a kind of triumphalism that pit bulls can be made obedient at all.

In the film we see black trainers and white trainers, but black trainers like Stratton predominate. All stress the necessity of unusual responsibility in working with pit bulls. Implied but not really emphasized is that the pit bull can be a danger in the hands of ordinary people who do not work with a trainer.

One such enthusiast, a mother of young children, shows us her arrangement for her pit bulls. Her home is crisscrossed with heavy steel gates so she can isolate them from each other and people. She laughs as she describes her arrangement, but with obvious pride in her ingenuity. Nobody asks her why she would want to have dogs that must be isolated from other dogs and people to be considered safe.

We see many black young men who are clearly besotted with the dogs, and who wax rhapsodic about their massive heads and chests. Allusion is made to the fact that the dogs are a protective accessory for black men who inhabit dangerous parts of town. The fact that the pit bull is an essential weapon in gang activities is left out, as is the fact that banning the pit bull seems to almost halve gang activity, making these fearful neighbourhoods a good bit safer for their non-gang occupants.

Also interviewed is a tattooed white biker, who proudly boasts about his biker buddies' pit bull fetish. He and his "gang" all own pit bulls and congregate with them to socialize. The real point of the interview is to show how deceiving looks can be. The biker laughingly explains that he and his (indeed!) tough-looking pals may look like bad asses, but they have hearts of gold. Implied is that their dogs also look tough, but wouldn't hurt a fly.

Allusion and footage is given over to the sad fact of the dog fighting industry and the pathetic lives of dogs who spend their lifetime either fighting or at the end of a chain, pining for the affectionate touch of a human hand. But actual footage of a real dog fight is fleeting, more like tussling than the carnage it is, and included only to emphasize the fantasy that the dogs may want to murder each other, but will never harm their human handlers.

Missing? As in the academic thesis and as in Hearne: Statistics. The only statistic adduced in the film relates to the disproportion of pit bulls in shelters. But the fact is not tied to the cause: that not only are the dogs being over-bred, but people are not being informed of the real risks of pit bull ownership, either by breeders or by rescue organizations who rehome them, which in turn leads to dumping at shelters.

Passing mention is made of the general fact that pit bulls are the worst offenders for dog bites and fatalities, but at the same time it is is firmly asserted that all human damage done by pit bulls is a case of provocation or the result of dog abuse, and no different from the case of other dogs that bite.

It is stressed that no normal pit bull would ever harm a human without cause, but the list of causes is carefully omitted. Having a cold, having a drop of food or drink on your clothing, or blood from a cut to your finger, opening a car door close to them, slipping on the ice, or trying to stop a pit bull from attacking your child or killing your dog – among hundreds of other things all of us normally do – are "causes" pit bull fans have pointed to in "explaining" past attacks.

It is reiterated several times that pit bulls were bred to fight animals, but that they were also bred not to harm humans or even to *wish* to harm them. Such a fine distinction is not genetically possible, of course, and not a single voice was raised to protest that canard, proof of which lies in the fact that pit bulls kill twice as many people each year as all 400-plus other dog breeds and types combined.

Also missing: any footage of a human victim's egregious wounds as a result of an unprovoked attack by a pit bull from a loving home – there is no shortage, and the filmmakers could easily have found them through pit bull victim groups – or any representation by individuals on the anti-pit bull side of the debate. This leaves us imagining "bites" rather than the reality of maulings, maimings, and dismemberments, the catastrophic wounds pit bulls typically inflict.

When a pit bull fancier says the pit bull was always America's favourite dog, there is no one to refute that myth. When a trainer refers to the pit bull as the "nanny dog," there is nobody to rebut her and tell that pit bulls kill a child on average every three weeks. No space is allotted to mayors of cities with pit bull bans to stand up for the success of the bans in terms of crime reduction.

After viewing this film, I daresay the average person would walk away thinking the pit bull is the quintessential American dog: spirited, feisty, a dog that protects its turf and won't walk away from a fight; but also a dog that is loyal, hardworking and fair; eager to please and especially loving. Oh, he may walk with a bit of a swagger, he may even look like the town bully sometimes, and his proud flaunting of his power gets him some negative attention by owners of wussier breeds. But honest, he's a good guy at heart, and he'll have your back against the bad guys. Yup, just like America.

All that bad publicity about these noble creatures? Bad owners, bad media rap. That film probably moved a lot of pit bull pups or rescue dogs into gullible people's homes. By now, reality having set in, a lot of those dogs are sitting in humane shelters, slated for death, to say nothing of the many maulings and deaths that could have been prevented if the film had included the facts.

But in the end...

Is there really any rational explanation that makes sense of the exponential rise in pit bull ownership and passionate advocacy over the last 30 years?

I don't mean an explanation for why society's moral trash like Lionel Asbo, gang members and sociopaths like pit bulls. They know why and we know why. Pit bulls are dangerous and they scare people. The person behind the pit bull is feared; he is accorded respect without having to earn it. Our entitlement society means there are a great many thuggish young men with no employment and enough unearned money to allow idle thoughts and inchoate grievances to drive their behaviour.[82] We get that.

But what can explain the specious category crossover of normally brilliant cultural observer Malcolm Gladwell, who defended pit bulls in a feature 2010 *New Yorker* article, later incorporated into his book, *What the Dog Saw*, arguing that profiling dogs indirectly sanctions racial profiling? It is intellectually untenable and insulting to African-Americans to conflate line-bred dogs – the *epitome* of the eugenically constructed stereotype – with naturally evolved humans.

This is the kind of morally inverse thinking that allowed German scientists and doctors to verminize Jews and justify their extirpation on the grounds of public health. In this topsy-turvy case Gladwell is exploiting a formerly dehumanized group of human beings in order to anthropomorphize a perversely-designed animal breed that deserves extirpation. One can only marvel at the misshapen hot-air filled artefact that emerges when public intellectuals, determined to amaze the public, get hold of the smoothly linear balloon of logic and begin to twist away at it.

There is probably no single explanation that explains the phenomenon. Author Martin Amis created Lionel Asbo, accompanied by his beer-chugging pit bull – as a statement about England's cultural decline, and an emblem for our culture's obsession with "fame for its own sake and terrorism," whose beginnings he traces back to 1977. I believe, as I hope I have demonstrated, that there is a good deal of truth in this assessment, and that intellectuals, far from being immune from the obsession, were instrumental in creating it.

But as a gloss on "fame for its own sake," I would add the continuing expansion of narcissism that emanates from the "therapy culture" that began to re-place replace religion's moral authority as early as the 1920s and reached full-blown mania status in the 1950s-1990s. With the death of religion amongst our *bien pensants*, and the trickledown moral relativism that began to inform our social and educational institutions, the void has been filled with belief in the self as the supreme arbiter of one's personal behaviour.

The principle of social reciprocity, implying a balance between individual self-realization and communal obligation, was traditionally fostered by com-monly-respected moral authorities speaking on behalf of established houses of worship. Nowadays this balance seems to be practiced in earnest only by Queen Elizabeth and others who adhere to their religious tenets without irony (and also without fanaticism).

But on the whole, individual and identity group entitlements are the norm to-day. One no longer feels a duty of special consideration to the organic health of one's community, or even to the comfort and well-being of one's neighbours. One no longer feels obliged to consider what used to be taken for granted as "the common good," a phrase that today, in our fragmented, grievance-col-lecting and increasingly purposeless culture, emanates more irony than aspi-ration.

The old way to become a "somebody" was through earned reward, which in-cluded building a respectable reputation in the community. Nowadays – re-member Lionel Asbo's sudden rise to prominence through a lottery win – pub-lic recognition can be achieved through luck or transgression of social norms – or a dog that gets you attention. But achieved it must be.

As Amis noted, "being famous is seen as a kind of deprivation; it's seen as a kind of a civil right." It is all too easy in a narcissistic culture to see oneself as a victim of something: capitalism, racism, sexism, colonialism. Grievance and anger are considered natural states for victims. Add speciesism to the list and it seems altogether rational that a dog who has been "excluded" or "discrimi-nated against" should act out his sense of victimhood, and that all equality-loving people should support his "protest."

When there is no sense of a common good, communities can easily implode. In recognition of this truth, social scientists James Q. Wilson's and George L. Kelling's 1982 criminological theory of "norm-setting" introduced the "broken windows" principle that underpinned the NYPD's famously effective reforms in restoring social health to their crime-ridden city.

As Brian Anderson's *City Journal* article on pit bulls, the spark that lit my journalistic fire, made clear, a neighbourhood is a fragile organism. When social reciprocity in its public spaces is menaced by narcissistic individuals and gangs intent on imposing their egos on society via the easiest legal route, canine weaponry, the health of the community can be snuffed out in short order.

Civilization is but a membrane over darker impulses mutinous psyches can displace onto animals with impunity. Our dogs are our social, psychological – and sometimes our ideological – avatars. The urge to own a pit bull is the urge to break a window. (In Amis' novel, Lionel Asbo first came to authorities' attention in toddlerhood for "a childhood interest in cruelty to animals.") Our discomfort in these dogs' presence is rational. In the end the pit bull controversy is not really about dogs at all. It is a cultural struggle, between impulses that favour social pathology and impulses that favour social health.

Therefore: Consider carefully, and reflect upon, the *manmade* nature of the dog breed that commands your devotion. As a citizen, a neighbour, a parent, a friend: You will, sooner or later, be judged accordingly. As well you should be.

Postscript: Standing your ground

I hope I have convinced you that pit bulls are a mutant breed that deserves to disappear. Even if I have, though, the question arises: What are you going to do with your newfound conviction? You may feel you want to jump into the fray when you see a news item of a pit bull mauling, or when the possibility of a pit bull ban is mooted in your municipality. What's the best way to engage?

I don't advise getting into arguments with individual pit nutters. They don't play by the rules of logic. They won't accept your sources as legitimate, even though they will earnestly tell you that you should "look into" all the terrible maulings perpetrated by retrievers and poodles that they personally know of. But when you ask them for statistics around these other marauders, you won't hear back. No matter what you say, no matter how logical or evidence-based, be prepared to be vilified as a racist or a hater of dogs or some other personal *ad hominem* that has nothing to do with the issue.

This, by the way, is one reason victims of pit bull attacks often lose heart for activism. Like rape victims who are twice-victimized by prosecutors who interrogate their credibility on the stand, victims of pit bull attacks who speak out are often subjected to PBAM harassment they are not able to endure.[83] Other reasons they do not become activists: many think – and are encouraged to think – their experience was a rare fluke; attacks are covered locally, so people have no idea how many replications of such incidents there are on a national basis. If national newspapers reported every pit bull attack, the enormity of the problem would be evident to victims.

If you are willing to join the battle for lucidity and responsible activism in the service of a safe public environment, you should go over the heads of pit bull stakeholders and talk directly to the public or to politicians, whether through letters to the editor, or through appeals to your political representatives or even to talk shows on radio. The idea is to get through to people who have open minds on the subject. If you are willing to do that do that, here is a list of useful talking points:

- This is *not primarily an animal welfare issue*, although there are animal welfare benefits to bans. Primarily it is a *public health and safety issue*;
- This is *not a civil rights issue*. There is no 'civil rights' protection of what is essentially a consumer choice. If the "product" endangers the lives of others, it has no rights at all; nor, obviously is it a human rights issue, which is why words like "discrimination" and "prejudice" should be inadmissible to the discussion;
- As a general animal welfare issue, a ban on pit bulls is good for all animals, including the pit bull; remember, very few attacks on other animals are reported, even if they include mauling, maiming, dismembering and/or killing;
- As a pit bull welfare issue: in places where pit bulls aren't banned, they represent 50 – 70% of shelter dogs. Wherever pit bulls are banned, euthanasias of pit bulls go down dramatically.

Wherever pit bulls are banned:

- It becomes almost impossible for dog fighting to take place as an underground blood sport. This too is good for pit bulls. There is no replacement breed for dog fighting;
- Gang crime is reduced, because alienated youths don't have easy access to a legal deadly weapon;
- Real estate values don't drop as they do where pit bulls are allowed and become common;
- Children of our minorities don't suffer disfiguring mauling wounds and/ or deaths at the jaws of what was originally the Ku Klux Klan dog of choice;
- Social cohesion is preserved because a small minority of bullies is prevented from intimidating and even terrorizing entire neighbourhoods;
- People don't feel the need to be armed (legally or illegally) when they go

out of their homes. [In communities where pit bulls are allowed, more and more people are carrying pepper spray, hunting knives, high voltage stun guns and/or firearms];

- There is more trust that politicians are protecting the common good rather than catering to a small minority interest group.

For information you can rely on, please consult the following websites:

http://www.animalpeoplenews.org/
http://www.dogsbite.org/
http://www.nonlineardogs.com/
http://maultalk.wordpress.com/
http://sruv-pitbulls.blogspot.ca/
http://thetruthaboutpitbulls.blogspot.ca/ (note: there are several pro-pit bull sites with similar names)
http://cravendesires.blogspot.ca/

As I wrote at the end of my memoir piece, "Acknowledgements," the essay that begins this book, in explaining what sparks my passion as a polemicist, I am motivated in my writing to make the case against the "Big Lie," wherever it rears its ugly head in our culture.

A Big Lie cannot perpetuate itself without an organized support system of true believers – or those who don the mantle of the true believer out of self-interest – and the disingenuous cooperation of those accredited professional and cultural elites who command society's respect.

PBAM is not only promoting a lie "so colossal," in Hitler's words, "that no one would believe that someone could have the impudence to distort the truth so infamously," but the promotion of this colossal socially harmful lie is enabled by those who have the knowledge and power to expose the Lie, but choose not to, by keeping silent or by active collusion in its toxic distribution through the culture.

Only the determined efforts of civically responsible people to expose the Big Lie of PBAM in the public marketplace of ideas will bring an end to the escalating multifaceted corruption in the dog industry. The extent of this cultural gangrene, wrought and nourished by PBAM's strange and disturbing obsession with fighting dogs, can be measured in the blood, invisible to the gullible masses, which flows in a steadily widening stream from the growing mass of innocent animals and people who weekly, daily, hourly fall victim to the canine terrorists in our midst.

Endnotes

1. A week after delivering this talk, a subway ticket agent in an English area of Montreal attacked a woman who challenged her on the language issue, and a paramedic refused to speak English to a father whose child was having a seizure, also in an English area of the island.

2. In the October 12 *Post*, there is a story of a theatre in Kelowna, B.C., that withdrew support for a film festival because it was going to screen a documentary film called *Donkey Love*, a film that explores the phenomenon of men in Northern Colombia with a fetish for sex with donkeys, apparently graphically in display in the film. The director tweeted, "We will not censor art to comfort the close-minded."

3. I have read many defenses of women's right to wear the niqab. Most of them posit the assumption that the niqab is a "choice" freely undertaken by the bearer. It is difficult for people raised in the West to appreciate how alien the very idea of a free choice is to women from cultures where they have been indoctrinated since birth into their roles as cogs in an honour/shame wheel. For an example of how blinkered people can be when they have no experience of the freedoms we take for granted, I offer an anecdote from the new book, *The World Until Yesterday*, by Jared Diamond. Diamond writes about the Kaulong, a tribe on an island near New Guinea, who up until 1957 practiced the custom of "widow strangulation." Diamond reports that even though the custom – not practiced by neighbouring tribes – offered neither individual nor collective benefits, it persisted. It was "just one of those things." Indeed, it was so firmly entrenched that the *widows themselves perpetuated it*, demanding to be strangled by male kinsmen, going so far as to taunt them for diminished manhood if they showed reluctance.

4. Parental Alienation Syndrome (PAS) is a disorder that arises primarily in the context of child-custody disputes. A primary manifestation is the child's campaign of denigration against a parent, a campaign that has no justification. It results from the combination of a programming (brainwashing) of a parent's indoctrinations and the child's own contributions to the vilification of the targeted parent. Source: Gardner, R.A. (1998). *The Parental Alienation Syndrome*, Second Edition, Cresskill, NJ: Creative Therapeutics, Inc.

5. Phillips, Melanie. "The jihad against Britain's Jews," *The Spectator*, [online] 6 Feb 2009. Available at: http://images.spectator.co.uk/melaniephillips/3329296/the-jihad-against-britains-jews.thtml.

6. After the 911 attacks on the USA, Michael Lerner, the editor of *Tikkun* magazine and perpetual Rabbi-Impersonator, issued a statement in the name of his *Tikkun* "progressives" suggesting that Americans deal with the attacks by "feeling the pain" of the al-Qaida terrorists who had attacked the United States because of their anguish over their grievances.

7. Berry, David. "The Fame Drain." *National Post*, [online] 4 October 2012. Available at: http://arts.nationalpost.com/2012/10/04/the-fame-drain-martin-amis-gets-joyfully-self-righteous-in-lionel-asbo/.

8. Anderson, Brian C., "Scared of Pit Bulls? You'd Better Be!" *City Journal*, [online] Spring 1999. Available at: http://www.city-journal.org/html/9_2_scared_of_pit.html

9. I have chosen to keep the first letters of the words "pit bull" in lower case, as I do for other "groups" of dogs like dachshunds and border collies; only those dogs endowed with proper names are capitalized, such as Labrador Retrievers, German Shepherds and so forth. The pit bull is known by so many other aliases – some of which have been conjured out of thin air to launder the pejorative image the words "pit bull" evoke – that it is not so much a breed as a biological class into which several breeds fall, all of whom share a now pinpointed and scientifically described, genetically determined "brain disorder" (Semyonova). Where breed associations have formed a distinctive branch of the pit bull family, I have capitalized them.

10. For example, this article about a savage mauling of a child by a "dog" appeared in February, 2012: http://www.chinovalleyreview.com/main.asp?SectionID=1&SubSectionID=1&ArticleID=54939. Another one appeared later that month that still failed to mention the type of dog that savaged the child (although no other kind of dog would try to drag a victim through a fence to maul at its leisure.) It wasn't until July of that year, when the incident came before a judge and a sentence imposed on the owner that the dog was admitted in print to be a pit bull: http://www.azcentral.com/news/articles/2012/07/25/20120725chino-valley-owner-jail-time-pit-bulls-attack-kids.html

11. Semyonova, A. 2009, *The 100 Silliest Things People Say about Dogs*. Sussex: Hastings Press.

12. Pit bull activists often try to blame pit bull behaviour on "other" breeds that merely have the same body type as pit bulls. But body type, head shape and other characteristics of the pit bull are endemic to the fighting breed model in general. By any name, the following are genetically the same as pit bulls: Irish Pit Terrior, Catch Dogs, Bear Biters, Boar Biters, Bull Biters, Mastiffs, Bull Mastiffs, Molossians, Bear Dogs, Neapolitan Mastiff, Dogue de Bordeaux, Presa Canaria, Boerbel, Olde Bulldogge, Argentinian Dogo, Tosa-inu, Colored Bull Terrier, bandogs, Hog Dogs, and Southern Hounds. For this extensive list I am indebted to Vicki Hearne, Yale academic, dog and horse trainer – and pit bull enthusiast. The list comes from her fascinating, and highly influential book, *Adam's Task: Calling animals by name* (Knopf, 1982).

13. Våge J., Bønsdorff T.B., Arnet E., Tverdal A. and Lingaas F.2010, "Differential gene expression in brain tissues of aggressive and non-aggressive dogs," BMC Veterinary Research, [research article] 1-9. Available at: www.biomedcentral.com/content/pdf/1746-6148-6-34.pdf.

14. These characteristics form the acronym SRUV, which is also the name of an

excellent blog dedicated to exposing myths about pit bulls: http://sruv-pitbulls.blogspot.ca/

15. www.animalpeoplenews.org, Clifton, Merritt, editorial in September 2012 issue, "Pit bulls and political recklessness."

16. I am indebted to Merritt Clifton, humane-movement historian and editor of Animal People News, for this information. Clifton tells me that the Mafia and the Klan were equally vile, but held sway over different territories: the Mafia went in more for urban crime, the KKK for rural areas, often in the same states, such as Florida and Illinois.

17. All children should be exposed to London's enthralling novellas, *Call of the Wild* and *White Fang*. Their plots are genetically unsound in that they turn on the myth that dogs can adapt to an atavistic wolf state and vice versa, but they are amongst the greatest dog stories ever written.

18. Semyonova, p. 102

19. Exactly the tragic problem in the 2001 Presa Canaria death-by-mauling of Diane Whipple in San Francisco: en.wikipedia.org/wiki/Diane_Whipple

20. From an abstract of the 87th meeting of the American Association of Plastic Surgeons. See also footnote 46.

21. "Medical Experts and the Injuries caused by gripping dogs," 10 July 2012, quoted in The Truth About Pit Bulls, [blog]. Available at: http://thetruthaboutpitbulls.blogspot.ca/search?q=Medical+Experts+and+the+Injuries+caused+by+gripping+dogs.

22. Semyonova, pp 102-3.

23. Van den Berg, L. 2006. Genetics of aggressive behaviour in Golden Retriever dogs. Universiteit Utrecht. Available at: http://igitur-archive.library.uu.nl/dissertations/2006-0427-200041/index.htm.

24. In an experiment over 40 years ago to make foxes human-friendly, researchers had only partial success after more than 20 generations and 45,000 foxes (Trut, L.N., 1999, "Early Canid Domestication: The Farm-Fox Experiment. *American Scientist*," Volume 87. P. 160-169.)

25. A cursory search of humane shelter advertising shows a preponderance of beguiling photographs of pit bulls in relaxed, even submissive-looking postures. Very often they are posed together with young children, even with toddlers' faces pressed up to their faces. The message is that the dogs are 100% trustworthy with children. But dog behaviourists recommend never allowing children to put their faces so close to *any* dog's mouth. Violation of this code of prudence by the very institution that is best placed to understand the reason for the caveat is a telling indication of PBAM's reach and influence.

26. You can find a partial, but very long list of such sites here: http://cravendesires.blogspot.ca/2009/12/there-is-no-such-thing-as-pit-bull.html

27. For example, one of the most-referenced websites by PBAM is the so-called National Canine Research Council (NCRC). The words make it sound like a government agency. In fact it has no official standing whatsoever. The NCRC is a pro-pit bull front operated by a Florida veterinary technician, Karen Delise. Her group is funded by the pro-pit bull Animal Farm Foundation of upstate New York, which is in turn funded by a multi-millionaire obsessed with laundering the image of pit bulls. I don't name her for fear of a libel suit.

28. "Vengeance for Johnny Justice" by Jim Gorant. [blog] 15 March, 2011. Available at: http://cravendesires.blogspot.nl/2011/03/vengeance-for-johnny-justice-by-jim.html

29. "Discrimination" is a trope that recurs again and again, as though the battle for pit bull legitimacy is just another civil rights cause. In the United Kingdom, pit bulls are banned everywhere under the Dangerous Dogs Act of 1991. One man took his case, based on his right not to be discriminated against in owning a pit bull, all the way from Magistrate's Court to the House of Lords and finally to the European Commission of Human Rights, where in January 1996, the Commission concluded: "The Commission accepts that the 1991 Act provides for a different treatment of owners of pit bull terriers and owners of other dogs who by their behaviour show themselves to be dangerous. However, the Commission finds that this difference in treatment has an objective and reasonable justification given the fact that this type of dog is bred for fighting and the experience of pit bull terriers in the United Kingdom. The Commission further finds that such difference in treatment pursues the legitimate aim of public safety and demonstrates a reasonable relationship of proportionality between the means employed and the aim sought to be realized in light, in particular, of the existence of the exemption scheme in the 1991 Order together with the relatively uncomplicated requirement to use a muzzle and lead in a public place. Having regard, in addition, to the margin of appreciation enjoyed by the Contracting States in this area, the Commission considers that this difference in treatment is not discriminatory within the meaning of Article 14 (Art. 14) of the Convention." Read more at: http://www.endangereddogs.com/EDDROtisCaseOutcome.htm

30. Clifton is the editor of the magazine *Animal People News* and his annual reports are available at www.animalpeoplenews.org.

31. Which is not to say that Clifton himself has not been reviled and denounced by "pit nutters." Invariably, when rabid pit bull activists demand my source for stats and I refer them to Clifton's ongoing reports, they reject them out of hand. But when I press them to single out the statistics they object to and invite them to offer countervailing information, they never respond. Literally never. So when I say he has never been challenged, I mean never been credibly challenged.

32. One particularly helpful source was www.dogsbite.org, an online magazine dedicated to the eradication of pit bulls through breed-specific legislation (BSL). Their annotated information comes directly from primary sources.

33. Lynn Media Group, 2007-2013. DogsBite.org. [online]. Available at: http://www.dogsbite.org/dangerous-dogs-pit-bull-myths.php.

34. Finley, D., "Pit bulls' reputation takes new hit, "[online] May 9, 2011. Available at: http://www.mysanantonio.com/default/article/Pit-bulls-reputation-takes-new-hit-1370739.php.

35. Judge for yourself. These are absolutely typical of the feedback I received from one column (with grammar and spelling as was): "People like you should not have freedom of speech! Your so heartless! The Canadian government puts innocent pit bulls to sleep just because some citizens are scared of the breed! Your a cold hearted person who obviously doesn't own any pets! Get another job because your a joke and should not be able to cause such harm as to writing an article trying to continue to kill innocent pit bulls! Go to hell."
And "How in the hell can you say pits are bred to maul? I have a pit and she is the sweetest dog you can imagine. I think they need to stop that ban on pits. You can't judge them cause of their breed. How would u feel if we killed you cause you are a bitch? Maybe they should put you down?"

36. In his most recent book, *Coming Apart: The State of White America*, 1960-2010, the brilliant cultural observer Charles Murray concludes that the top 20% of white Americans are doing very well, but the bottom 30% are leading increasingly dysfunctional lives.

37. Quoted in "More adoptions will not end shelter killing of pit bulls," *Animal People Magazine*, October 2011.

38. Slade, D., "Calgary woman fights judge's decision to euthanize her pit bulls," [online] 24 October, 2012. Available at: http://www.calgaryherald.com/news/calgary/Calgary+woman+fights+judge+decision+euthanize+bulls/7441388/story.html

39. Semyonova, pp 125-127.

40. In an interesting sidebar on this first type, Semyonova reports a new development: Islamist youth marching through the streets in The Netherlands with pit bulls, daring anyone to object. This struck her as curious, because Muslims believe dogs are ritually unclean. They are not afraid of dogs, but since touching a dog means one must change one's clothes before praying, they usually avoid contact with them. It would seem that the pleasure of intimidating people overrides religious proscriptions in this group.

41. http://www.barbarakay.ca/articles/view/661.

42. Northern Irish First Minister Peter Robinson tweeted: "Spoke to Lord Mayor about Lennox. Suggested BCC should seriously look at re-homing option. Why exercise the order if there's an alternative?" Re-homing a dog with Lennox's history would have been the equivalent of lodging a pedophile in a boarding school.

43. Crosby was also instrumental in exculpating "Memphis," a New Jersey pit bull who had been established as dangerous by the town of Bloomfield's director

of Health and Human Services, which should have been the end of the matter, but the town was bullied by an imported crowd of activists at a Board of Health meeting into calling on Crosby for his "expert" testimony. http://sruv-pitbulls. blogspot.ca/2012/09/memphis-in-bloomfield-nj.html

44. Lynn Media Group, 2007-2013. DogsBite.org. [online]. Available at: http://blog. dogsbite.org/2008/07/comment-anatomy-of-whitewash.html

45. Yes, I think it is fair to call pit bulls the canine equivalent of psychopaths. Psychopathy is largely genetically determined. Between one and four percent of the population is psychopathic, depending on whose statistics you go by. The principal characteristics of psychopaths: are lack of conscience, an easy re-course to deceit (pit bulls often wag their tails before and during unpredictable attacks); sudden inexplicable rages, and pleasure in violence. See Robert Hare's 1993 book, *Without Conscience: The Disturbing World of the Psychopaths Among Us,* and Martha Stout's 2005 book, *The Sociopath Next Door.*
As to the pit bulls' pleasure in violence, here is a description by famous U.S. writer and illustrator James Thurber's description of his dog Rex in the midst of an attack on another dog. Rex has locked onto the other dog and cannot be dislodged: "Rex's joy of battle, when battle was joined, was almost tranquil. He had a kind of pleasant expression during fights, not a vicious one, his eyes closed in what would have seemed to be sleep, had it not been for the turmoil of the struggle."

46. Following one of my columns on pit bulls, I received an e-mail from an emer-gency room physician, who wrote:
I have seen many many dog bites over the course of 5-6 weekly ER shifts for 17 years...I have seen three very severe maulings in that time, and all were commit-ted by pit bulls.
One was a man mauled by a pit bull on the loose at 4 a.m. and his face resembled hamburger. Another was a 9-year old immigrant child whose family was (incred-ibly) given a pit bull by the SPCA (or Humane Society) as a family pet; her shred-ded legs needed hours of surgery.
All the other dog bite injuries I have seen have paled in comparison to those from pit bulls; though to be fair I have seen a lot of injuries from huskies. And yes, I ask every patient with a dog bite about the breed that bit them. And yes, I remember very well all the bad ones. As well, I do not recall any pit bull bite that was in any way minor or incidental....
You may get a letter from some misguided or misinformed or willfully disagree-able (for whatever reason) ER doc saying pit bulls aren't so bad at all. I'm writing to you now to support your article, and allow you to disagree with any ridiculous support for pit bulls coming from such an ER physician.

47. What they will not tell you is that this terrible mayhem is almost always in-flicted on the dogs by their owners or someone close to them. Pit bulls are about five times as likely to be the victims of violent abuse as other dogs, and almost invariably by their owners. Michael Vick, for example, throughout his "stew-ardship" at Bad Newz Kennels, oversaw the hanging, electrocuting, downing

and savage beating of his dogs to death. He recently bought another dog for his daughter, even though such a felon should never be allowed to own any animal again in his lifetime.

48. In a five – year review of dog bites at The Children's Hospital of Philadelphia amongst 551 patients aged five months to 18 years, more than 30 different breeds were cited as the culprits. Of them 50.9% were pit bull terriers, 8.9% Rotttweilers, and 6% mixed pit bull/Rottweilers. Kaye, A.E., Belz, J.M., Kirschner, R.E., 2009. "Pediatric Dog Bite Injuries: A 5-Year Review of the Experience at The Children's Hospital of Philadelphia," *American Society of Plastic Surgeons, Plastic & Reconstructive Surgery*. Abstract only. Available at: http://journals.lww.com/plasreconsurg/Abstract/2009/08000/Pediatric_Dog_Bite_Injuries__A_5_Year_Review_of.28.aspx

49. http://www.animalpeoplenews.org/anp/2012/05/11/maryland-court-of-appeals-establishes-new-liability-rule-in-pit-bull-attack-cases/

50. *Animal People News*, October 5, 2010, reprinted in the cravendesires blog, a lively and reliable source for news of pit bull depredations: http://cravendesires.blogspot.ca/search?q=Michael+Vick

51. "The Nanny Dog Myth Revealed," 4 August, 2010. Available at: http://thetruthaboutpitbulls.blogspot.ca/2010/08/nanny-dog-myth-revealed.html

52. A pregnant woman called Darla Nepora was a pit bull activist. Her pit bull turned on her and savaged her to death. Her husband insisted on burying the beloved dog's ashes with the cremated remains of his wife and unborn child. In a 2009 Washington state case, a couple mauled by their own pit bull were too embarrassed to admit it, and told police they had been attacked by a mountain lion; the police, spotting their blood-covered dog, soon ferreted the truth out of them.

53. If ever you are at a dog run and a pit bull attacks your dog, lift him up by his hind legs and hold them high. His front legs are relatively weak, and he will not be able to maintain the attack. Hold on until the owner leashes him. If pit bulls are a serious problem in your neighbourhood, you may consider carrying a syringe of ammonia. If you squirt it into the dog's mouth as he is gripping, it will start to suffocate him and he will be forced to let go.

54. Many people have written to tell me that their own pit bulls have never been engaged in any aggressive incidents. I have no reason to disbelieve them. If every single pit bull were guaranteed to be dangerous, there would be no controversy around this subject.

55. All statistics noted in this section are taken from Merritt Clifton's October 2011 editorial in *Animal People News*.

56. Simmons, A.M., "Lancaster's dog ordinance is cited in helping to drive down gang crime," Los Angeles Times [online]. 21 January, 2010. Available at: http://latimesblogs.latimes.com/lanow/2010/01/lancasters-dog-ordinance-is-cited-in-helping-to-drive-down-gang-crime.html

57. Why kennel clubs and other commercially invested stakeholders in the pit bull industry are permitted to have a voice in the BSL debate is a mystery. Animal People president Kim Bartlett says, "People who rescue feral cats want to see an end to their breeding. People who rescue exotic animals such as parrots, lions and tigers, and potbellied pigs would like to see breed bans on these species. Why not the so-called pit bull rescuers? Allowing people with commercial interests in companion animals to have a leading voice in settling policy on dog and cat issues is in my view like allowing chicken farmers to have a leading say in whether or not the animal rights movement advocates vegetarianism. Public policy on animal welfare issues should not be set by breeders and fanciers, and certainly not by dogfighters who pose as breeders and even pretend to be rescuers."

As for veterinarian associations, I had a long and amiable conversation with a former president of the Ontario Veterinarian Medical Association, which in May 2012 came out strongly for a repeal of Ontario's pit bull ban. He readily conceded that he was neither an expert in dog genetics or behaviour. But he did subscribe to several widespread myths ("bad owners, not bad dogs," "all dogs bite," "Don't judge a book by its cover," etc), was unaware of humane shelter euthanizing stats, and expressed reflexive, not evidence-backed skepticism about statistics I adduced based on the Clifton report, which he had never consulted before I brought it to his attention. To his credit, he wishes that his clients would go in for "Heinz 57" mutts, the dogs that evolution produces. As he rightly noted, "All breeds are by definition inbred."

58. A few months ago I was interviewed about a column on pit bulls on my local radio show. They had asked a local humane society director who had written a letter to the editor criticizing my position to debate me on air. I was perfectly willing to do so, but she insisted on speaking after me. They should not have allowed that, but they did. She proceeded to parrot the usual myths that I could have shot down with ease, but which the radio host was not equipped to challenge.

59. Hernandez, C., Bagg, J., Shepard, W., "Miami-Dade Residents Vote to Keep Pit Bull Ban Tuesday," [online]. 15 August, 2011. Available at http://www.nbcmiami.com/news/local/Miami-Dade-Residents-Vote-on-Pit-Bull-Ban-Repeal-Tuesday-166056926.html.

60. http://www.barbarakay.ca/articles/view/670
The media in general has not been helpful in dispelling PBAM myths. This *Toronto Star* article is, alas, all too exemplary of the lack of journalistic rigour on this subject. Reporters and columnists often find the sentimentality-drenched blandishments of activists, suavely skilled in public relations, too compelling to resist, especially the leftist media outlets like the *Toronto Star*. For an equally inane, completely unresearched, mantra-strewn Canadian mush piece on pit bulls, see "Dog-rescue agency bullish on pit bulls," by Al Beeber in the *Winnipeg Free Press*, August 25, 2012: http://www.winnipegfreepress.com/canada/dog-rescue-agency-bullish-on-pit-bulls-167414005.html

61. Semyonova's book has information, too detailed to fit my allotted wordage, about the genetic history of dogs in general and the pit bull in particular that puts paid to any mythic nonsense pit bull advocates allege about their nature being sweet and good, and their attacks an aberration or due to "bad owners."

62. http://en.wikipedia.org/wiki/Turbot_War

63. "The myths of multicaninism": http://www.barbarakay.ca/articles/view/695

64. My ignorance isn't for want of trying to get to the bottom of this mystifying mumbo-jumbo. I contacted Mr. Weaver through his website and begged for an interview, explaining I was writing an essay on pit bulls and society, right up his alley, but alas, I had no response whatsoever.

65. Woe betide any politician who does not don the rainbow t-shirt and march with a grin in his city's Gay Pride parade, even if he disapproves of the indecency that is a featured component of them. He will feel the wrath of the intellectuals and the liberal media and be labeled a homophobe.

66. Ordinary people, unschooled in politically correct speech codes, do still find dog fighting disgusting, whoever is involved in it, and had no problem denouncing Michael Vick when he was exposed. But I am morally certain that in our ivory towers, and in Black Studies programs particularly, the issue was either massaged into sympathy for Vick or left "uninterrogated," in the academic parlance.

67. One sees the same soft bigotry at work in inner-city U.S. schools, where the failure rate for black students is astronomically high. But, concerned not to appear racist, schools are told that they must not discipline black students for showing disrespect for teachers, or even threatening them or fellow teachers. St. Paul fifth-grade teacher Aaron Benner, on being told not to suspend disruptive black students, said: "This 'let-them-clown' philosophy could have been devised by the KKK." From "Undisciplined," by Heather MacDonald, *City Journal*, Summer, 2012, p. 32.

68. Names of a famous film pit bulls and a pit bull "fighting champion" in a popular comic series, *Barrio Quien Sabe*.

69. It is annoying when academics spout such nonsense, but it is more consequential when these irrational comparisons seep into the legal profession. Here is attorney Daniel Burstein in 2004 (quoted by Allen): "In our modern culture, legislation restricting the rights of a particular ethnic group, based on some perceived stereotype, is repulsive. The analogy to breed-specific legislation is obvious. Although dogs are not people, they are sentient, intelligent individuals, capable of learning. Therefore, just as it is with humans, it is ridiculous to stereotype an entire group."

70. It is almost inconceivable that a scholar of pit bulls and society would "overlook" the single most statistics-driven researcher on this subject for the past forty years, but *mirabile dictu*, Ms. Allen's bibliography shows no reference to the decades of continually updated reports on dog-related deaths, maimings

and disfigurements according to breed that Merritt Clifton has been publishing for Animal People News. On the other hand, the thesis is chock a block with references to theorists and Marxist Critical Discourse Analysis.

71. Hearne, V., *Adam's Task: Calling animals by name*. New York City: Skyhorse Publishing Inc (2007).

72. Hearne, p. 196-7.

73. "*Ignoble*"? Whoa, we're getting into Konrad Lorenz territory here. Lorenz was the never-remorseful Nazi who is credited with starting canine behaviour science. As a specialist in birds, he knew little about dogs, but between his active racist imagination and his romancing of wolves as avatars of the Nazi hierarchy, he imposed a bogus paradigm of dog behaviour on a credulous public, suppressing real scientific opposition along the way.

74. Hearne, p. 200.

75. Hearne, p. 217. Literature is my bailiwick, but I have never heard of the character Huckleberry Finn being compared to a pit bull, nor would I consider the parallel in any way aesthetically justifiable if I did.

76. Hearne, p. 218. Normal dogs can be heroically aggressive in the line of protective duty. Heroic, because, according to dog behaviourist Semyonova, it goes against the grain of a typical domestic dog to use real aggression in anything but a life-threatening situation. The pit bull is never heroically aggressive in this way: "It just simply enjoys any excuse to unfold its genetic program." The heroism of the normal dog is a summoning of unusual courage out of social devotion; the "heroism" of a pit bull is psychopathic enjoyment of violence for its own sake. Hearne cites an incident at school (where she often brought the dog), in which an angry anti-pit bull colleague took her by the arm to emphasize his point. Hearne lavishly praises her pit bull for not attacking him even under what could be perceived as threatening circumstances.

77. Actually, that movie was eventually made, although not realistically: the 1989 film *Turner and Hooch* starred Tom Hanks as an uptight police officer who adopts a huge Dogue de Bordeaux when his owner, a friend of Hanks' character, is killed. Hooch is portrayed as a hero dog who catches his former owner's murderer, and in the end mates with the Golden Retriever belonging to Hanks' love interest, a union that produces adorable puppies. Although characterized as a household menace, Hooch is never a threat to good people and never threatens another animal. His gigantic frame and enormous strength are played entirely for laughs or admiration for his passion for justice. At the time I watched it with total credulity. I walked out of the film wishing I owned one of these gentle-to-nice-people giants myself.

78. Stratton, a dog fighting champion with a blood lust to rival Dracula's, knows about pit bulls, but his knowledge seems to be limited to dog fighting. His books are filled with what can only be described as a macho desire to prove, beyond

a shadow of a doubt, that the American Pit Bull Terrier can beat the s*** out of any other dog breed or wild animal on the planet. His "charming" stories – the ones that are meant to persuade the reader that pit bulls are great dogs – consist almost entirely of tales about dogs managing to get loose and fighting with or killing another animal. Stratton does not value dogs for their companion virtues; dogs are only worthy of his love and admiration if they are capable of winning a fight.

The photos in Stratton's books are primarily purebred fighting dogs. The captions never fail to point out fight champions. In a handful of photos, the dog is being hugged or cuddled or played with, but the vast majority of the pictures are of a dog on a heavy chain, or "stacked" in a show pose, or straining against a thick leash. The dogs are not portrayed as sweet or clever or social. They are all anonymous backyard kennel dogs churned out by dog fighters.

In an August 2005 review of Stratton's book, *The World of the American Pit Bull*, Kate Connick writes: "Stratton compares [pit bulls] fighting one another to hounds following a trail or border collies herding sheep. They are merely doing what they love and what is natural to them. The average person would consider that a potent indictment of the breed itself and a reason to extinguish it. Ironically, Stratton provides the strongest arguments against the existence of the breed (at least in its most intense, gamebred form) rather than being the advocate that he believes himself to be."

79. Hearne, p. 220.

80. Hearne, p. 223.

81. Hearne, p. 211.

82. In his 2012 book, *A Nation of Takers: America's Entitlement Epidemic*, Nicholas Eberstadt finds the U.S. government to be a geyser of entitlements: more than $7000 per individual per year. Today 27% of adult men are not part of the labour force. Indeed "labor force participation ratios for men in the prime of life are lower in America than in Europe." Which is saying a lot.

83. In the fall of 2012, anti-pit bull activists organized a "Walk for victims of pit bulls and other dangerous dogs" in Tucson, AZ. Anecdotes of PBAM harassment posted on a Facebook page I belong to that advocates for regulation of pit bulls made it clear that any victim who chooses to go public with their story needs a thick skin and considerable courage.